The
Complete
Book of
Sexual
Love

Stuart and Susan Holroyd

The
Complete
Book of
*Sexual
Love*

Bloomsbury Books
London

Editorial Coordinator : John Mason
Art Editor : Grahame Dudley
Design : Madeline Serre
Editors : Krystyna Krzyzak; Nina Shandloff
Research : Pat Vaughan

© 1979 J. G. Ferguson Publishing Company USA

This edition published 1989 by
Bloomsbury Books an imprint of
Godfrey Cave Associates Limited
42 Bloomsbury Street, London, WC1B 3QJ
Printed in Hong Kong by Regent Publishing Services Ltd.
ISBN 1 870630 33 5

Introduction

Men and women today are freer than they have
been for centuries to fulfill themselves sexually.
Probably never before have they been surrounded
with so much encouragement, whether from
so-called "experts" or from the media in general.
But this modern emphasis on sexual freedom and
sexual achievement, on new standards and goals for
sexual happiness, may all too easily leave a man or
woman with the feeling that their sex life must be
inadequate. This book aims to dispel such feelings.
The authors offer sensible, well-informed advice on
a whole range of sexual topics, from physiology to
technique, from behavior patterns to specific
problems. But, above all, they place sexual love
firmly in its true context of human relationships.
Chapters on male and female sexuality, sexual
technique, birth control, sex and marriage,
homosexuality – all these are written in a jargon-
free way supported by over 500 illustrations of all
kinds – photographs, drawings, diagrams. In a final
question-and-answer section, over 40 common
problems concerning physical and emotional aspects
of sexual love are clearly answered. The result is a
comprehensive guide to the maze of modern sexual
love, a complete guide to sexual understanding and
happiness for all.

Contents

1 The Freedom to Love   9

This first chapter puts the whole subject of sexual love into
the context of today's sexual climate of achieving complete
understanding and honesty between partners. The authors
stress that freedom – here as in other areas – carries
responsibility.

2 The Vital Ingredient   35

First emphasizing the difference between male and female
approaches to the act of sex, the chapter goes on to underline
the delicate balance between human love and sexual desire,
and the importance of the chemistry of attraction.

3 The Male Partner   65

After describing and explaining the man's sexual apparatus
and activity, the chapter clears away some common fears and
misconceptions by dealing with many of the problems and
abnormalities that men often find hard to discuss even with
their doctor.

4 The Female Partner   97

Describing first the woman's sex organs, the authors examine
changes that take place during the four stages of lovemaking,
in particular the various types of female orgasm. There is
also a frank discussion of female masturbation and fantasy.

5 Techniques of Sex   125

Variety in lovemaking is not perversion, but healthy and
rewarding. It guards against monotony, that great enemy of
a loving relationship. This chapter uses clear text and
drawings to provide a comprehensive introduction to the
whole range of methods.

6 Husbands and Wives   165

Starting from the standpoint that sexual problems are
frequently the real cause of marital breakup, the chapter
stresses the importance of companionship, communication,
and above all variety in the transition from love to loving.

7 Patterns of Relationships   193

Today's sexual climate brings wider freedom – and harder
personal choices. Society now acknowledges that sexual
partnerships are not restricted to marriage. The authors,
without disguising the danger of promiscuity, present a
balanced view of love outside marriage.

8 Birth Control – the Chance to Choose   219

Families are happiest when new babies are wanted and
planned for. Here is a detached description of the variety of
contraceptive methods now available, and an assessment of
their effectiveness, effects on health, acceptability and ease
of use.

9 When Sex Goes Wrong   247

What happens when sexual and emotional communication
breaks down? This chapter tackles such problems as frigidity
and impotence, showing how in the search for solution, a
couple may achieve a deeper understanding of each other.

10 Homosexuality   275

One half of all men and one fifth of all women have at least
one homosexual experience in their lifetime. This chapter
attempts to dispel some of the ignorance and prejudice that
still surrounds this complex subject despite our more
enlightened attitudes.

Questions and Answers   301

Index   321

Picture Credits   334

Chapter 1
The Freedom to Love

Most people would agree that a sexual revolution
has taken place in the present century, and
particularly in the last two decades. But what kind
of revolution has it been? Many are dubious as to
whether it has been a change for the better or for
the worse. The sexual revolution has had dramatic
effects on present-day attitudes which have affected
both society and the lives of individuals. Many
have been sexually liberated, but the sexual
revolution has also had its casualties. The sexual
revolution has had its protagonists, its supporters,
and its critics. Some feel that it has gone too far,
and others that it has not gone far enough. The
truth is probably that it has given people more
freedom to love but in some respects it has
diminished their chances of understanding and
experiencing what love really is.

The Sexual Revolution

The term "sexual revolution" leads to confusion. Part of the difficulty stems from the ambiguity of the word "sex." We use it to denote gender. At the same time it refers to a biological process that is itself two-fold, in that it is procreative and gives intense pleasure, and the two are not always compatible. To some people the sexual revolution implies the changed status and role of the female sex in the contemporary world. To others it means the permissive attitudes toward purely hedonistic sexual intercourse and toward overt eroticism in the media, particularly the movies and magazines. Again others think of the more open and accepting attitudes toward human sexuality that have superseded the hypocrisy, shame and guilt that blighted the sex lives of previous generations. There are yet other aspects to the sexual revolution, and it is meaningless to say that it has been a revolution for the better or for the worse without specifying which aspect is being discussed.

It is often argued that the only truly revolutionary change has been in the status and role of women in society, in the family, and in relation to men both in and out of marriage. But a change in the situation of one half of a partnership cannot take place without a complementary change in the other partner's attitude and behavior. There have been sexual revolutions in the past in the sense of abrupt changes in socially acceptable sexual manners. An example is the move from restraint and prudishness to license and outspoken behavior when Charles II was restored to the English throne after two decades of puritan rule. But these changes did not materially affect the lives of women or the prevailing order of society in which the male was incontestably the dominant sex. The fact that in our society today women are on a much more equal footing with men than ever before, and that they are not only permitted but even encouraged to recognize not only their rights but also needs and demands that serve their own satisfaction and fulfillment, is a revolution indeed.

Right : in the Middle Ages a wife was regarded as her husband's chattel. If she was disobedient, then he had a right to punish her.

Below : the Western family at the beginning of the 20th century reflected a patriarchal society. The father was the head and center of the household, legally and socially. The wife's standing was little better than that of a dutiful daughter.

Some men, and indeed some women, may feel that sexual egalitarianism has had disastrous repercussions upon society, the family, and upon rightful male privilege. The majority, particularly among the young, have found on the contrary that partnership and role exchange make life both easier and more interesting than orthodox male domin-

Above : female coke-worker during World War I.

Right : the vote was not enough ; social attitudes still discriminated against women. The Women's Liberation Movement demanded equality in employment, education, and legal status.

ance. Sexual equality gave the woman more responsibility and initiative, both as a personality and as a sexual partner.

The change in woman's status and role was the cumulative result of a number of historic and social factors. One of the most important was the recruitment of more and more women into the work force. During World Wars I and II many women took factory or agricultural jobs replacing men who had been drafted for military action. However, when the wars ended, the women were expected to give those jobs up to the men returning from action. But the great expansion in the female work force occurred with the development of light industry, which required a pool of dextrous but cheap labor. The economic necessity for many women to work – to support themselves and often their families – was as important a cause as the campaign by women to be accepted into the traditionally male dominated professions and have satisfying careers.

Women also campaigned for the right to political power – the right to represent as well as be represented. Although organized movements for female equality had been in existence for the past two centuries it was only during the beginning of the 20th century that they began to reap any success.

The life of the young woman of today is much less focused on the bearing and rearing of children than her grandmother's life was. It is no longer economically and socially advantageous to have a large family, nor is it necessarily the case that the mother will be the parent who stays at home to tend the child. Fathers are now encouraged to participate more in the child's upbringing while employers and the state are lobbied to provide child-care facilities. Many mothers devote a much smaller proportion of their time to children, both in terms of daily work and in terms of their lifespan. Consequently a woman now has more opportunity to continue and extend her

Economic independence also enabled many young women to live independently of their parents and lead their own lives.

The beginning of the 20th century witnessed a vigorous campaign for female suffrage throughout the West. In 1893 New Zealand was the first country to grant women electoral equality with men, but most Western countries resisted granting the vote to women until after World War I.

education, and develop a career.

The development of reliable methods of birth control has liberated women from unavoidable, continual childbearing. Previously the only ways of avoiding unwanted pregnancies were abstinence at the relevant periods or abortion. Relieved of anxiety about unwanted pregnancies, women were able to relax and enjoy their sexuality, and participate actively in lovemaking.

11

The Liberators

In 1918, Marie Stopes, the pioneer of birth control in Britain, brought out her book *Married Love*. Its publication, as she herself later wrote, "crashed into English society like a bombshell." Today the book and its contemporary reviews provide an invaluable social document of how appallingly ignorant people were about sex little over half a century ago.

The revolutionary theme of *Married Love* was that women were capable of enjoying and benefiting from sexual union just as much as men were. When men failed through ignorance to give their wives satisfaction they also lost out themselves, for the highest and most beautiful experience conferred by sex would elude them. Marie Stopes was a little vague about what this highest experience was, which is hardly surprising because when

she wrote her book she was unmarried and still a virgin, though in her mid-30s. She was also very vague about precisely how marriage partners could give each other this experience, although her contemporaries seemed to find her explicit enough. One critic denounced the book for "providing instruction to girls of initially dubious virtue as to how to adopt the profession of more or less open prostitution." Such reactions seem incredible today, for *Married Love* gives no specific instructions about sexual technique and its style throughout is flowery and emphasizes the mystical, spiritual satisfaction that can go hand-in-hand with sensual pleasure. Also, Marie

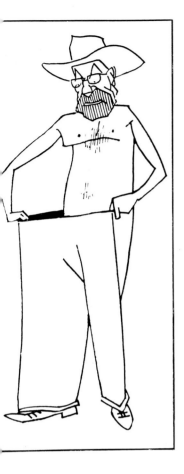

who in his *Man and Woman* (1894) and his seven-volume work *Studies in the Psychology of Sex* (completed 1910) repeatedly stressed the ills that result from women's sexual frustration and deprivation. Ellis wrote with understanding and sympathy about sexual abnormalities, and clarified the task of exploring and explaining many aspects of the vast subject of human sexuality.

While Havelock Ellis and Marie Stopes intended to liberalize attitudes to sexuality, the same cannot be said for their contemporary Sigmund Freud. Yet his ideas on sex were to have a profounder influence on culture and society. Freud's contribution was to make people realize the importance that libido, or sexual energy, plays in human life, and how it is simultaneously the cause of man's discontents and the spur to his highest achievements. The famous cartoon that shows Freud looking down his trousers neatly states that a man who sees sex in everything, as Freud seems to have done, must have had an anxiety neurosis. Furthermore, Freud's statements on the subject of women and female sexuality were often unscientific, untrue, and derogatory. And yet although his own attitudes were of the 19th century, he had a major influence on the sexual revolution because he stated the fact that sexuality must be acknowledged to be a basic drive in human beings.

Stopes was severely censorious of many sexual practices that today are considered perfectly normal. Oral and anal intercourse she considered "really disgusting and cruel . . ., acts of such gross indecency that they undoubtedly amount to cruelty mentally to any refined or sensitive woman." And masturbation, she wrote, was very harmful for young people, though "for women over 30, if they understand it is dangerous, and control the use to not more than twice a month, it is *sometimes* beneficial."

Despite her puritanical attitudes and her ignorance (she taught that the absorption of semen by the woman promotes health), Marie Stopes was a pioneer. She opened the first birth-control clinic in Britain and introduced from France the first contraceptive that women could use, the diaphragm, and she shocked her age by maintaining that sex could and should be enjoyed, and by women as well as men, or rather wives as well as husbands.

There had been other writers who had dealt with the topic of sex, but their work had been more academic and had not been addressed to a general readership. One of the most influential was Havelock Ellis,

A psychoanalyst who was to have a profound influence on sexual ideas in the 1970s was a former pupil of Freud's, Wilhelm Reich. In his works *The Sexual Revolution* and *The Function of the Orgasm* (1927) Reich sought to liberate, but he became the victim of a witchhunt and his books were burned. Reich deplored the contemporary negative attitudes to sexuality and pointed out many ways in which such attitudes did psychological and social damage. He argued that prevailing ideas of sexual morality, including the concept of lifelong monogamy, only had the effect of curtailing and stunting human development. It was alleged of Reich that he made a fetish of the orgasm, but this does scant justice to his argument, which was based on clinical experience, that when people become capable of full sexual expression they undergo a change of personality. Their compulsive attitudes disappear, they cease to be sexually promiscuous and begin to enjoy all aspects of life.

The Sexologists

After World War II the major contributions to the understanding of human sexuality were made by the sexologists. In general these were scientists or doctors who initiated the use of mass statistical surveys and questionnaires to analyze human sexual behavior. The pioneer in this field was Alfred C Kinsey, the main author of the immense volumes *Sexual Behavior in the Human Male* (1948) and *Sexual Behavior in the Human Female* (1953). Kinsey was by profession an entomologist and he undertook the study of human sexuality as a

Above : Dr Alfred C Kinsey ; his studies were the first serious attempt to quantify human sexual behavior.

Left : Dr William H Masters (right) and Virginia E Johnson. Their laboratory studies of human sexual response exploded many myths and brought dramatic new insights into human sexuality.

result of being asked by his university to teach a course on marriage. He interviewed hundreds of people, and collected and classified their sexual histories. In the course of his interviews he too was asked questions, such as "Will masturbation make me insane," which made him realize the prevalent ignorance about sex and the widespread need for scientifically based information.

Accounts of the findings of Kinsey and his associates will be found in later chapters

of this book. The importance of the Kinsey Reports (as they are often called) in their day was that they talked about sexual behavior in all its forms and varieties in a purely factual way without adopting moral attitudes. Kinsey believed that the expression of such attitudes contributed nothing to knowledge. His closest associate, Wardell Pomeroy, tells a story of how Kinsey turned down a psychologist who had applied for a job as an interviewer, telling the applicant that he did not really want to

Above : Russian housewives in the late 1940s being lectured on birth control. Active encouragement of contraception was official policy in the Soviet Union, reflecting the changing status of women in that country.

do sex research. When the psychologist insisted that he did, Kinsey said: "Well, look at your attitudes. You say masturbation is immature, premarital intercourse and extramarital intercourse harmful to marriage, homosexuality abnormal, and animal contacts ludicrous. You already know all the answers, so why waste time on research?" Kinsey never professed to know the answers, but came up with a wealth of findings about human sexuality which laid the foundations of modern sexology. Although he died in 1956, the work of the Kinsey Institute continues to this day.

Not long before he died, Kinsey had just set up a physiological laboratory where human sexual response could be observed and the accompanying physiological changes measured, but it fell to another man, and one unconnected with the Kinsey Institute, to pursue this line of research. He was Dr. William H Masters, an associate professor of obstetrics and gynecology at Washington University in St Louis. Soon after he began his research, Masters engaged an assistant, Virginia Johnson, and their coauthored books, *Human Sexual Responses* (1966), *Human Sexual Inadequacy* (1970), and *The Pleasure Bond* (1975) have greatly extended our understanding of many aspects of human sexuality.

The idea of adult human beings performing sexually under laboratory observation could never have received institutional support without the prior revolutionary change in prevailing attitudes to sex. Any

doubt about the researchers' and subjects' motivations for undertaking such studies is only expressed by those who are unaware of the clinical details and of the great help these studies have given many people. Observations of precisely what happens in the body in intercourse and sexual response have provided some answers to questions that physicians are often asked but formerly could not answer with certainty. Was it safe to have intercourse in the late stages of pregnancy? How soon could it be resumed after having a baby? Why were some couples unable to have a baby, and could anything be done about infertility? Why did unwanted pregnancies still occur when people took careful contraceptive precautions? And many more people have benefited from their findings as to the causes of sexual failure and inadequacy and the techniques they have developed to enable people to recover or develop their capacity for full sexual expression.

The psychiatrist-philosopher Rollo May writes in his book *Love and Will* that: "Whatever merits or failings the Kinsey studies and the Masters–Johnson research have in their own right, they are symptomatic of a culture in which the personal meaning of love has been progressively lost." It was in response to criticisms that they had reduced sex to mere physiology that Masters and Johnson produced *The Pleasure Bond*, a nonmedical book dealing with such subjects as love, commitment, sexual responsibility and fidelity.

15

A Song and Dance

The term "permissive society" came into currency in the 1960s. It implied a relaxation, and to some even a collapse, of moral restraints, and analogies were drawn with the decadence of the Roman Empire at the time of its decline. Fewer issues have provided the mass media with so much colorful material. Sexual issues were presented and covered in minute detail, hotly debated, and re-evaluated along with new

developments. Effective censorship of literature and films appeared to collapse. There were three interested parties: the pornographers who made money from the exploitation of sex, the various leagues to bring back morality, and the layman. It was he who worried about the effect of permissiveness and explicit sex on his children but resented being treated like a child and told what he should not read, view, or even do.

The rock culture of the young has often been accused of introducing sexual explicitness into popular music. Elvis Presley's *One Night With You* had caused a furore when he first sang it in 1958. Ten years later the Rolling Stones' disc *Let's Spend the Night Together* was banned by certain radio stations. But this was not a new phenomenon peculiar to the 60s and 70s. In 1930 a reviewer described Cole Porter's *Love for Sale* as "in the worst possible taste." The folk songs of European culture and the lyrics of the American blues with its graphic sexual imagery made these so-called permissive pop songs look very tame by comparison.

The styles of dancing that developed in

the 60s were also considered overtly sexual. But then so was the waltz in its time. When it was first introduced to Britain in the early 19th century it caused a scandal. In the 1920s the foxtrot and tango were deemed obscene. In fact since ancient times dancing has been a part of a courtship ritual as well as a social activity.

Playboy Magazine and clubs, with their emphasis on sexually liberated lifestyles, greatly influenced the mood of the affluent 60s generation. This was a period of rapid economic growth and conspicuous consumption. *Playboy* itself spawned a host of imitators that began to compete among themselves in the sexual explicitness of their photography of the female nude, and the triteness of the caption. Feminists protested that such photography degraded women, but men, as Kinsey had pointed out, delight in visual and psychological stimulation and the sales figures proved his point. The magazines were bought by the millions.

Women's fashion, too, underwent a change in the 60s, though again not as drastic as so often imagined. In fact the fashionable female figure depended not on her cleavage but rather the lack of it. The one fashion trend of the 60s that will never be forgotten was the mini-skirt. It brought legs into focus as never before and many men still hope for its return. Other fashions that could be considered sexual never caught on, and were certainly not much in evidence on the streets. Transparent blouses and topless dresses made newspaper headlines but hardly initiated a revolution in dress. And lest it be assumed that it was only the women who dressed in a way calculated to entice the opposite sex, a theory disputed in any case by most designers and women themselves, men's clothing also followed fashion. Tight jeans were not bought simply because denim was a hardwearing fabric.

And what was the result of the permissive society? For every survey published proving a marked rise in moral corruption and sexual crime, there is one that shows the opposite trend. Many welcomed the liberalizing attitudes which made contraception and sex education freely available, and no longer treated homosexuality as a crime. A minority deplored even these benefits. A number, not necessarily cynical by nature, actually got bored.

17

Sex on Screen

The Harvard sociologist Pitirim A Sorokin said some years ago: "Our sex freedom is beginning to expand beyond the limits of safety. It is beginning to degenerate into anarchy."

This was an opinion expressed by many concerned observers about trends in the motion-picture industry in the late 60s and early 70s. Their concern was not just with the overtly pornographic films, which have always been available if one was prepared to go to the trouble to look for them but also with the numerous films made by distinguished directors which were acclaimed by serious critics.

And yet were these films so revolutionary? Nudity had been introduced into motion-pictures in the 1910s, not the 60s. Sex has always been a predominant theme in cinematography. Its portrayal however reflected

problems with the censor.

During the 60s and 70s, sex on film broke new ground. Ironically many motion pictures attracted attention through their publicized battle with the censor and drew a much larger audience than any review of their artistic merit could have produced.

The Swedish director Ingmar Bergman was not actually a pioneer when in *Virgin Spring* (1960) he filmed a violent rape scene, except that he showed rape for what it was. Howard Hughes' *The Outlaw* (1943), also had a rape scene. The film was banned for three years after its completion, made Jane Russell a star, and the heroine fell in love with her former rapist. The rape scene was by no means as explicit as Bergman's, but it perpetrated that most dangerous of myths – that women secretly long for and enjoy rape. In 1963 Bergman again caused a controversy with *The Silence*, in which he conveyed a woman masturbating. In 1966 Luis Buñuel produced *Belle de Jour*, with Catherine Deneuve as the bored wife of a Paris surgeon who turned part-time prostitute in a brothel, so that she could act out her fantasies of sexual humiliation. Then in 1969 the English

Above: Alan Bates and Oliver Reed in the controversial wrestling scene in Ken Russell's film Women in Love *(1969).*

Left : Theda Bara, the first vamp. She devoured men.

Right : in Belle de Jour *(1966) Catherine Deneuve acts out her masochistic fantasies by working in a Paris brothel.*

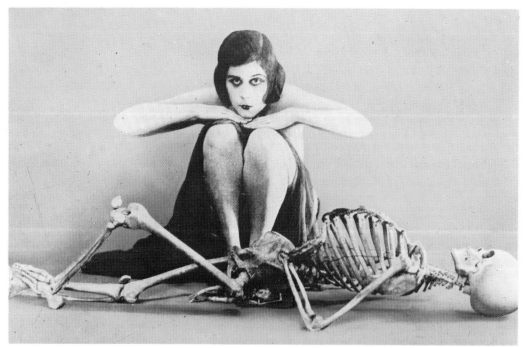

the times. Periods of economic depression and the war years were characterized by romantic films with childhood sweethearts and child stars. The vamp of the 20s and the busty sex goddess of the 50s were also products of their time. But prominent directors of each decade have experienced

director Ken Russell gave us his version of D H Lawrence's novel, *Women in Love*, which not only featured some very explicit scenes of heterosexual nude lovemaking, but also included a scene with strong homosexual overtones as the two male stars had a wrestling match in the nude.

Andy Warhol's films, in particular *Flesh* (1968) and *Trash* (1970) also contained scenes of homosexuality and lesbianism. The Yugoslavian director Dušan Makavejev's film about the work of Wilhelm Reich, *WR – Mysteries of the Organism* (1971) included a scene in which a woman masturbated a man to erection, then made a plaster cast of his phallus, which she subsequently used as a mantelpiece ornament. The film was banned in Yugoslavia, and withdrawn from the Cannes film festival, but became extremely popular in Western Europe and the United States. In *Last Tango in Paris* (1972) Marlon Brando and Maria Schneider portrayed strangers meeting by chance in an empty apartment. The film became notorious because of its controversial depictions of anal intercourse.

The film which was acclaimed as the pinnacle of artistic cinema eroticism was *Emmanuelle*, made in 1974. Billed as the film which brought taste and grace into erotic cinema, it shall be remembered for its unlikely scene of sex in an airplane lavatory, and the dozens of imitators that it spawned. While *Emmanuelle* was considered a film that anyone could see without being offended, the censorship boards did not feel the same about *Deep Throat* (1974). In Britain, for example, it was refused a certificate for public screening. The film, a story of a woman (Linda Lovelace) born with the anatomical anomaly of a clitoris located in her throat, and therefore only able to obtain sexual satisfaction through oral sex, featured her performing prolonged acts of fellatio.

Certain critics seemed more disturbed by the negative attention directed to explicit sex scenes than to films which glorified violence, both in the movies and on television. They pointed out that exposure to pornography did not appear to corrupt, or lead to an increase in the incidence of sexual crimes. In Denmark, where censorship was abolished in 1969, the number of convicted offenses of sexual crime actually decreased. Meanwhile definite correlations were being found between violent crime and violence on the screen.

It should also be remembered that sex can be beautifully portrayed. The lovemaking scene in Nicholas Roeg's *Don't Look Now* (1973) is remembered as being one of the most erotic, arousing and tender ever portrayed.

Counter-Revolution

In St Paul, Minnesota, in 1977, the Planned Parenthood headquarters and clinic was deliberately burned down. When it was rebuilt it was picketed daily, and on one occasion a nun splashed it with holy water. The director's wife was threatened several times, and all this happened, he wryly remarked, "in the name of a higher morality."

Reporting these events, *Time* magazine asked: "After an era of revolution, is a counter-revolution under way? Is it even possible that the revolution never really succeeded, that much of America watched the New Morality – voyeuristically – without abandoning the Old Morality?"

Feminist writer Barbara Seaman ob-

serves the same trend but suggests another reason for it: "The backlash is against casual sex because a lot of people were hurt. It was as if there was a train gradually carrying us away from Victorian morality,

but then suddenly in the 60s and 70s the train became a runaway, and a lot of passengers were injured. Now the brakes are starting to be repaired."

The clamping down on total sexual license has partly been the work of feminists, because many intelligent and sensitive women felt that the sexual revolution only had the effect of degrading and trivializing sex. They rightly felt that many men were quite happy to give up certain aspects of male-dominated tradition – family commitment, emotional responsibility, economic protection. But they were not willing to give up the belief that women were less than equal to men. Shere Hite, author of *The Hite Report* on female sexuality, wrote in 1975: "We haven't had a sexual revolution yet, but we need one," and she deplored the fact that the profound and personal aspects of sexual relationships were being obscured by the commercialization of sex. One cannot deny that there has been a revolution in sexual attitudes and conduct in these last two decades, but we would certainly agree that the revolution has not gone far enough or deep enough. On the other hand we do not see how a return to this so-called Old Morality is going to improve matters, particularly if it includes such activities as the burning and picketing of birth control clinics. The Old Morality's attitude to sex

Above: women demonstrating outside against the Miss World Contest, the human equivalent of the prize cattle show.

Left: some men felt threatened by the sexual revolution. Here Harry Britton, self-styled husband "liberator," parades in Washington.

61 percent. What about male nudity in movies? 59 percent were against, and 54 percent were against female nudity. As for topless waitresses in nightclubs, they were disapproved by 51 percent. And a majority of 74 percent supported the statement that "the Government should crack down more on pornography in movies, books, and nightclubs." On the other hand, 70 percent disapproved of legislation against private sexual conduct, for instance homosexual practice.

The researchers who conducted this survey stated that in different places there were between 20 percent and 40 percent of moral absolutists, people who "term everything absolutely wrong." This is a very considerable and surprising proportion of the population. Clearly, the sexual revolution has not brought as much change as some would fear. Although many of the strictures and standards of the Old Morality may be outmoded, and nobody would expect the train of Barbara Seaman's analogy to shunt us back into the Victorian age, there are

had many unpleasant aspects, including fear and repression, and the belief that it was brutish and sinful. At the same time it hypocritically supported different standards of sexual morality for men and women. We can surely do without a resurgence of such views.

To determine to what extent the Old Morality has survived the sexual revolution, *Time* magazine, in 1977, commissioned a survey of the attitudes and beliefs of a balanced sample of the American population. The interviewers asked people to make a number of moral judgements, and when the results were statistically assessed there were some surprising figures.

Is it wrong for teenagers to have sex? Yes, it is, said 63 percent of the sample. Should a woman wait for marriage before she goes to bed with a man? Yes, she should, said 42 percent, and 34 percent believed that the man also should wait until he marries. Is it wrong for a man to be unfaithful to his wife? Yes, it is, said 76 percent, and 79 percent condemned a wife's infidelity. On the question of whether it was wrong for the unmarried to live together, only a narrow majority of 52 percent expressed the opinion that it was not wrong, and 70 percent were strongly against children being born outside marriage. Was mixed nude bathing acceptable? No, said

Above left: sex shop window in Amsterdam, Holland.

Above right: a 16th-century view of sexual debauchery.

obviously a large number of people today who do not subscribe to Aleister Crowley's "Do what thou wilt" precept and who neither want nor approve of total sexual license.

Modern Morality

An American teenage girl participating in a television discussion on the subject of sexual morality volunteered the view that a lot of young people are confused about it because "There is nobody saying 'no'."

A German girl who contributed to Vance Packard's study, *The Sexual Wilderness* made the same point rather more pedantically: "Many of the conventional norms, principally those of the church under which many young people grow, produce many guilt complexes. That was my own experience. However, I feel that the greater psychological danger is in a normless society."

To be liberated from social, moral and religious rules and prohibitions is one thing, but to be obliged to make one's own rules is quite another. Some of today's young people have felt let down by a parental generation that failed to give them any guidance in matters of sexual conduct as opposed to sexual education. In tribal societies the awakening of sexuality, the transition from adolescence to maturity, and from single to married status, are stages that are accompanied by communal rites of initiation, designed to convey to a young person the meaning of the transition and the prevailing relevant rules and mores. This is not the case in modern Western societies. One reason is that historically, in Western societies, attitudes to sex go through cycles of repression and permissiveness. Consequently each generation has a tendency to overcompensate for what it sees as the mistakes of the previous one.

The majority of parents find it difficult to give effective guidance. Some apply such rigid principles that they either provoke a reaction of rebellion and rejection, or their children grow up neurotic, timid, or withdrawn. Others give up through lack of time, energy or concern. Many parents are themselves so confused about the question of sexual morality that they feel incompetent to give guidance. The psychiatrist Bruno Bettleheim, commenting on the present situation, wrote: "Whenever the older generation has lost its bearings, the younger generation is lost with it."

One consequence of the escalating birthrate in Western countries has been that simply by virtue of their numbers the young today constitute a distinct subculture. And conceivably tomorrow the subculture will be the dominant culture. As one sociologist has put it: "Society is confronted no longer with a set of individuals to be trained toward adulthood, but with distinct social systems, which offer a united front to the overtures made by adult society." Without parental guidance and control, the influence of this subculture on the young is paramount, and even when there is some parental influence the draw toward the subculture is strong. There have been signs of positive change in the values and lifestyles of today's youth, with more emphasis on love, gentleness, altruism, and spirituality, and there are optimists who foresee a much-needed change in the character and goals of Western societies emerging from the adoption of these ideals. But meanwhile there are still many young people who find themselves confused regarding sexual behavior, and who would sometimes welcome guidance (and example) from their parents.

But what are the parents to base their moral counsel on? The philosopher Immanuel Kant struggled with a similar problem two centuries ago and came to the conclusion that there is at least one "categorical imperative" that is self-validating and of universal and timeless relevance. This principle is that one should never treat another person as an object. And here is a basic principle upon which an ethic of sexual behavior can be based. Another that follows from it by implication is that there must be a reciprocal acceptance of responsibility by each partner for the other's emotional response and commitment. It cannot be denied that people engage in the sexual act with varying degrees of emotional commitment, and therefore it is unrealistic to assume that the commitment should always be profound and total. But it is not unrealistic to expect that each bears responsibility according to the other's degree of commitment, and therefore that each understands the other's feelings before they engage in a relationship. Couples have sexual relationships for many reasons. Other than profound love, these include procreation, fun, companionship, release of psychological and biological tensions, ego-boosting, affection, and admiration. Many

Right : is this a sex object or a woman with a sexual objective – an example of old immorality or new morality?

of the problems in sexual relations spring from grave misunderstandings about motivations, sometimes resulting from deliberate deception. A modern sexual morality must recognize these different motivations, and require that partners in the sexual act understand and accept each other's motivations. It would certainly not accept deception.

But such ethical guidelines, although providing a basic code of conduct, are not enough. As a girl in Packard's study of college students stated: "I'm continually struck by the lack of fulfillment that sex experiences seem to give girls here. They have no idea what context to put sex into, what to expect from it, or what to give to it." And that is the greatest failure of any parental generation – not to pass on the knowledge acquired from their own experiences – in sex as in any other aspect of life.

Sex Without Tears

"Mankind," wrote the psychologist Eric Berne, "has made a great leap by splitting off the pleasures of sex from its biological purpose, and man is the only known form of life which can deliberately arrange to have sex without reproduction and reproduction without sex." As patriotic members of the human species, Berne maintained, we should be proud of our sexuality, and "anybody who isn't should go back where he came from, which is jellyfish."

With characteristic humor, Berne expressed the fundamentally important change in attitude toward sex that did emerge from the sexual revolution: that sexual love is a natural and beautiful activity, and that it is perfectly legitimate to engage in it purely for its enjoyment. An indication of how widespread such views have become is a recent report commissioned by the Catholic Theological Society stating that any kind of sex, even homosexual or adulterous sex, was acceptable, provided that it was "self-liberating, other-enriching, honest, faithful, socially responsible, life-serving and joyous."

All revolutions have their extremists who attract a disproportionate amount of publicity. But when the excesses of the sexual revolution have been played out, we may expect to see consolidated an understanding and acceptance of human sexuality and the varieties of its expression. Many factors have contributed to the inbred negative sexual attitudes that have to be overcome. These include ignorance, fear of surrendering oneself, the influence of the puritanical belief that the pursuit of pleasure, especially sex, is sinful, and the association of sex with uncleanliness because of the proximity of the genital and excretory organs. By ridding themselves of these inhibitions people will be both happier and freer. The casualties of the sexual revolution are those whose appetites have been desensitized so that they have to seek more and more bizarre forms of sexual activity to obtain any pleasure. Its beneficiaries are those who have been freed from their inhibitions and enjoy sex fully. It is in this sense that the sexual revolution has given some people "the freedom to love."

A best-seller since it was first published in 1972 has been the self-styled "Gourmet Guide to Love Making," *The Joy of Sex*, edited by Alex Comfort and based on a text written by an anonymous couple, one of them a practicing physician. The book is aptly titled; its highly acclaimed originality in its day lay in the fact that it maintained an open and accepting attitude to all kinds of sexual practice in the context of human loving. Also it succeeded in accommodating sexual adventure and permissiveness to the concepts of sexual fidelity. The introductory chapter of *The Joy of Sex* sums up the benefits of the sexual revolution:

"The whole joy of sex-with-love is that there are no rules, so long as you enjoy, and the choice is practically unlimited. . . You can have infinite variety to taste. But one needs a steady basic diet of quiet, night-and-morning matrimonial intercourse to stand this experimentation on, simply because, contrary to popular ideas, the more regular sex a couple has the higher the deliberately contrived peaks – just as the better you cook routinely, the better and the more reliable banquets you can stage. . . This book is about love as well as sex: you don't get high-quality sex on any other basis. . ."

Below : there are no rules for a loving couple except that sex should be enjoyable and free of guilt.

The Freedom Not to Love

There is a *Time* magazine cartoon that represents a boy saying to a girl, "To tell the truth, I wish I'd been born back before sex." One could be forgiven for getting the impression that sex was invented in the 60s. Suddenly it was being presented by all aspects of the media, at every possible opportunity, and we were all exhorted to focus all our energies on our sexuality, sexual experience, sexual relationships, and sex. Little else appeared to matter.

A number of the women who contributed their views to *The Hite Report* stated that the sexual revolution had resulted in an overemphasis of the importance of sex which could be oppressive in the life of the individual.

"I'm getting sick to death of sexuality," said one woman, " – everywhere sex, sex, sex! So what? Sex is not the end all and be all of life. It's very nice but it's not everything."

Another said: "In a way I'd almost like to have back the hush-hush good old days when you just didn't talk about sex. It would not be hidden because it was dirty, but because it was a sweet, private thing."

Shere Hite remarks that the idea that sex is necessary for health has become a commercial enterprise and that the way the idea is pushed by advertisers, psychiatrists, sex counsellors, and the media makes some women feel anxious. One of her interviewees said: "If I go long without sex, my desires drop ridiculously, which worries me. I start to wonder if something is 'wrong' with me, which makes me feel obligated to have sex. I usually think, 'Wow, it's been a long time since I've had it and I guess I ought to!'" And a woman who had been involved in a very fulfilling sexual relationship confessed that the myth that frequent and fantastic sex was essential to health even affected her: "I think that sex in my life has assumed a correct proportion, that is an expression of love between us; yet, I still feel hung up about the myth sometimes – maybe having sex is less important to me than to others."

Anxieties about the quality as well as about the quantity of the sexual activity in their lives preoccupy some people. The idea has been put about that sex is not only something that human beings naturally do, but a thing that some do well and others do badly, that some have to learn and others have a particular aptitude for. There is

Below : the sports car – a symbol of sexual drive.

thought to be such a quality as sexpertise, and some people are inclined to worry that they may be sexual underarchievers. Men are particularly prone to such worries, for despite female liberation many still consider it their duty to initiate sexual activity and to pass on their experience to their partners. Anxiety runs particularly high among those men for whom a string of sexual conquests marks their most important achievement in life. Women, too, feel obliged to produce orgasms on demand, or else they will be deemed frigid.

The result of the anxiety about sexpertise is an obsession with technique, the mastery of which brings little reward unless one is going to take sex up as a profession. Many who consider themselves expert lovers leave their partners cold because they are too preoccupied with sexual performance as distinct from making love.

If sexual freedom is to have any meaning it has to include, as well as the freedom to love, the freedom not to love, without feeling guilty or inadequate on account of it. It has been said that modern man has been so preoccupied with sex because it is the last area of freedom in an industrialized society. But is it an area of freedom? There is no freedom where there is compulsion, and as Alexander Lowen has remarked "Today one can readily discern a compulsive attitude in work, play, and sex." The

Right : Titian's "Mythological Couple in Embrace." Throughout the ages artists have attempted to portray the perfect sexual experience. Many couples strive in vain for this impossible ideal and the result is usually anxiety.

compulsion is closely linked to the compulsion of consumerism, which all modern youth acquire from the pervasive influence of the media, and which very few repudiate. But, to quote Lowen again, if the sexual function is reduced to a technique, and "if this last great mystery of life is translated into a formula, man will become an automaton, completely dominated by his ego and stripped of all passion and lust." People should not feel themselves compelled to engage in or to enjoy sex in any prescribed way or with any particular frequency: that is true sexual freedom.

A Blending of Roles

One unanticipated development of the 1960s, that puzzled many, was the formulation of the concept of "unisex" and the development of appearance and lifestyles that made less distinction between the male and female roles in life, love, and sex. Boys and girls dressed uniformly, grew and styled their hair similarly, and exchanged or shared roles that were traditionally thought exclusive to one or the other sex. It was a development symptomatic of sexual liberation and egalitarianism, although it left many profoundly confused. In 1967 a psychiatrist reported that he was consulted by many females whose problem was that they did not know how to act like women, and also quite often by males who were confused about how to be men.

There has probably been more tendentious nonsense talked and written about the respective natures and roles of the two sexes than about any other subject. What is particularly surprising is the amount of material that the subject has generated considering that any scientific attempt to define masculinity and femininity is virtually impossible because all the descriptive qualities have their basis in tradition and culture. The concepts of masculinity and femininity are not the same as male and female, but are often used as if they were.

The act of the female being penetrated by the male has given rise to femaleness being equated with passiveness, maleness with activity. And because of mankind's inherent belief in the duality of nature, all passive elements have been engendered female, all active ones male. Worse still, female was also negative, dark, evil. Likewise the concepts of gender have become so deeply rooted in language that they are taken for granted in the same way that one takes it for granted that the earth is round – except that the latter statement can be verified.

There is nothing "natural" about a woman being passive and yielding – in fact childbirth, woman's "natural" function, is quite the opposite. But from infancy children have been molded into these predetermined roles. Girls were discouraged from boisterous play and taught to be "lady-like," unambitious, and marriageable. Boys on the other hand were encouraged to be as active as possible, but also to gain the strength to take on all responsibility. Any departure by either sex has been treated as deviancy.

Yet historically there is no evidence that women are naturally the weaker sex. It was a trait neither valued nor encouraged by poorer communities because it was a liability. Socially only the rich could afford a lady. And there have existed matriachies and matrilineal societies as well as patriarchies and patrilineal orders. The roles ascribed to the sexes reflected the order, so we should bear it in mind that what is so often termed "natural" – by implication unalterable, divine, and self validating – should in fact be called "cultural". We can then question its value more readily without fear of infringing laws of science.

One of the most enlightened views of

Above, just like clothing, traditional masculine and feminine roles are interchangeable.

Right : "Responsibility" by Hugh Cameron, 1869. It exemplifies the role conventionally attributed to women – that of motherhood.

modern psychology is that all human characteristics, including the traditionally ascribed masculine and feminine ones, are present in all human beings, but in different proportions in each individual. This means that the complementary sex roles need not be associated with gender, nor should the reversals and exchanges of traditional roles put a person's basic sexuality in jeopardy.

In her science fiction novel, *The Left Hand of Darkness* (1973), Ursula Le Guin imagines a distant world named Winter where the inhabitants are hermaphroditic but sexually neutral except for a few days in each month. When a sexual encounter occurs one partner becomes actively male and the other actively female, but neither knows which it will be in advance, so either may get pregnant. It is the utopia of unisex, and when the first visitor from Earth goes there he writes in his report: "A man wants his virility regarded, a woman wants her femininity appreciated, however indirect or subtle the indications of regard and appreciation. On Winter they will not exist. One is respected and judged only as a human being. It is an appalling experience." The deliberate irony recognizes the underlying truth. In human beings the fulfillment of their sex roles can become confused with the expression of their sexuality and their sense of personal identity.

29

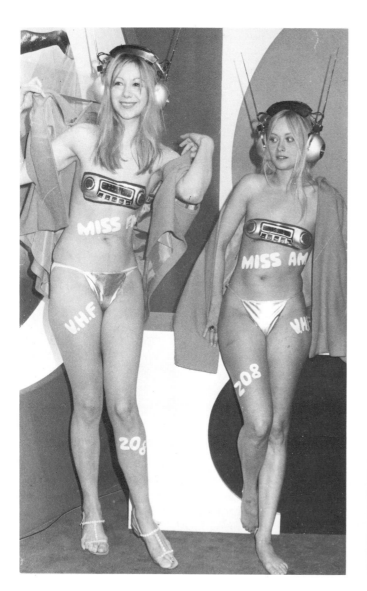

Uses and Abuses of Sex

The student in Vance Packard's study who said that her contemporaries found sex experiences unfulfilling because they had "no idea what context to put sex into, what to expect from it, or what to give to it," was a shrewd observer. For it is precisely these problems that people have to solve for themselves before they can have any expectation of sexual fulfillment.

What is sex for? An asexual alien observer of the human species could easily assume that one of the main purposes of sex is to persuade people to buy motor cars, cigars, and alcohol. A human child brought up with constant exposure to television might make the same inference, but one of the first steps toward maturity is the realization that sex involves so much more. The child soon learns that sex is for making babies, and discovers that sexual sensations are pleasurable. Then he or she may reach the conclusion that sex is for pleasure as well as procreation. Biologically, all activities essential to the survival of the species are governed by strong urges, and the gratification of these urges is a physical pleasure. In fact of the biological feelings that drive animals, the sexual urge is second only to hunger.

Many people do not progress beyond the formulation of sexual gratification, even though gratification alone detracts from human freedom and dignity by making human beings simply the tools of their natural urges. It can also produce feelings of guilt or debasement associated with the sexual act. When St Augustine prayed, "Oh

Above : sex attracts attention and publicity, and manufacturers and advertisers have long taken advantage of this to sell totally unsexual electronic and mechanical products.

Opposite page, above : on the other hand, a sexy product demands sexy promotion.

Opposite page, right : the biological purpose of sex is procreation ; psychologically, the sexual drive is toward pleasure.

The
original
French skin
boots
12½ gns.

Elliott
Knightsbridge
Bond Street and Now
KINGS ROAD
CHELSEA

tration of the basic human need to grow, develop, and mature. The growth process shall involve the whole personality, including sexuality.

In 1969 the American Psychological Association held a symposium entitled *Sexuality – Regeneration and Self-Discovery*. One of the distinguished contributors, Dr David Mace, made the point that the real sexual revolution of recent years did not consist of all the manifest changes in sexual behavior, but in "a radical change in the way we *think* about sex – a change from negative to positive, from repressive to acceptive." Another contributor, Dr Jessie Bernard, read an important paper on *Sex as a Regenerative Force*. The titles of this paper, and of the symposium signified the tremendous change that was taking place in attitudes to sex. It was a change which added the dimensions of human loving and growing to those of reproduction and pleasure.

God, make me chaste, but not yet," he expressed an ambivalence about sex that was to torment and perplex millions of people in the centuries to come, and still does today. In the past it was perhaps understandable that while sex brought pleasure, it could also bring its punishments – another pregnancy or possibly a then-incurable venereal disease. But a contemporary view of sex must go beyond its purely procreative function if it is to help human beings integrate the powerful drives of their sexuality into their lives.

Religion is often blamed for portraying sex as obscene, distasteful, and sinful. But many religions also invested the sexual act with a profound sacredness. This view of sex as one of union with the whole, of majestic transcendence, and an overcoming of man's separateness and isolation was portrayed by D H Lawrence. In his time Lawrence's novels were considered pornographic, but while they scandalized many readers, others were profoundly influenced by his writing.

In recent years yet another view of sex has arisen. It does not contest the ideas that the purpose of sex is for procreation, pleasure or communion, but accepts them all and adds moreover that sexual expression can be a means of personal growth. Today humanistic psychologists stress that many of the ills that man is prone to, both individually and collectively, result from a frus-

Sexual Expectations

What should we expect from sex, and what should we give to it? An obvious answer could be: We get as much as we put in. And while there is some truth in this, in that a person who is sexually repressed and inhibited will not experience the sexual joy and fulfillment that a sexually un-inhibited and expressive person will, it is a rather dubious answer. It encourages a cost-effective attitude to sex, considering it from the point of view of inputs and returns, or a moralistic attitude, regarding it in terms of rewards according to deserts. Yet today many people are inclined to think of sex in terms of giving and getting orgasms, thus reducing one of the most vital experiences to quantifiable economics.

There is no denying that there is good sex and bad sex, in the sense that some experiences make people feel enriched, fulfilled and vital, and others make people feel degraded, spent, and joyless. But studies in psychosexual pathology have shown that good and bad in this sense do not correlate with the moral equivalents. The most sadistic rapist may have intense and satisfying orgasms, but no personal enrichment. From the standpoint of the glorification of the orgasm, it is more correct to say that people get out of sex what they demand of it.

Obviously to demand is not so commend-able as to give, and there are a surprising number of men and women, particularly married men and women, who consider that they fulfill their sexual function by giving orgasms to their partners although they themselves remain unsatisfied. They are undemanding, and they will rationalize their conduct altruistically, even though they realize that it involves a degree of pretense and deception, which may some-times include pretending to reach orgasm. Before the sexual revolution many women took this line of conduct, being unaware of their sexual potential. But whether it is the man or the woman who acquiesces, the quality of the sexual experience for both partners will be diminished. Over a period of time it diminishes so much that either or both may seek new sexual partners, or else both may become indifferent to sex, regarding it as a youthful activity that naturally declines with increasing age.

Growing up and growing older involves planning, predicting, and often settling for compromises. But this is a dangerous and destructive attitude when applied to sex. For sex is not merely a mechanism of species reproduction which incidentally affords some pleasure, but an activity that enhances human beings' enjoyment and understanding of life. It contributes to spiritual growth and union, it is conducive to a longer, healthier, and happier life. These are the rewards to expect from sex, but not as payment for services rendered. The rewards come to the person who does not make compromises or does not accept second-best, and who demands sexual ful-fillment for self and partner. If fulfillment is missing he or she does not accept the situation but seeks the reason for the lack. These may not be characteristics generally considered as belonging to people in love, but they are characteristics of people who value remaining in love and understanding what love is, and they are not incompatible with tenderness, passion, and considerateness.

One of the problems of the sexual revolution is that many of its advocates have put more emphasis on the understanding of sexual pathology and on the cultivation of sexual techniques than upon growth and understanding. It may have given people more freedom to love, but it has not given them a profounder understanding of love, life and sex, and indeed in many ways it has confused such understanding and tended to give people an unbalanced view.

Chapter 2
The Vital Ingredient

Love, so wise men tell us, is the answer, but for many love is the problem. Just what it is, how it happens and why it disappears, whether it can endure, and how, if at all it relates to sex are questions that have preoccupied generations. In their efforts to understand love, people have distinguished many different kinds: spiritual and carnal love, romantic and rational love, *eros, agape,* and *philia,* to mention but a few. Love has been equated with compassion, sexual desire, unselfishness, loyalty, admiration, altruism, communication, pleasure, surrender, and even sickness. The list is endless but no single term nor any combination of them can pin love down convincingly. It is as difficult to define love as it is deliberately to experience it. When we experience it we know, or think we know, but still we cannot define it, only convey what we are undergoing. No subject has been written about so much, and none will oust it as the most important theme of painting, music, sculpture, and literature.

Falling in Love

We speak of "falling in love," and the phrase implies that the experience is unsought, accidental, and irresistible. The person who falls in love does not do so from choice, and probably did not expect a passionate involvement. According to ancient mythology, the act of falling in love

suspends consciousness, will, and judgement. The mischievous little god Cupid shoots his dart and the victim becomes hopelessly infatuated. The object of the person's love may be utterly inappropriate, like the donkey-headed Bottom that Titania dotes on in Shakespeare's *Midsummer Night's Dream*, for love, they say, is blind.

"Love," said Samuel Johnson, "is the wisdom of the fool and the folly of the wise." The world's literature and history bear witness that love and the pursuit of love have been major preoccupations and follies of mankind from time immemorial. The Trojan wars were fought over rivalry for a woman's love; Julius Caesar urged his armies into unpopular campaigns for Cleopatra, and Mark Antony sacrificed his career and his life for her. "The world," says the poet John Dryden, "is well lost for love." Traditions, legends, folklore, and facts of history combine to show that prudence, sense, judgement, even the basic animal instinct for survival, can be overwhelmed by the passion called love.

Most of us do not have empires, kingdoms, or fortunes to sacrifice for love, and few of us are ever called upon to give our lives for it, but many come close to giving all they possess. The man who in middle age leaves the house he has worked to buy, his children, and possibly his reputation for the freedom to go to another woman, and the person who commits suicide after being rejected by a lover, show that the legends and the literature do not exaggerate. Love is a passion that can override all other considerations, and although falling in love can be a delightful experience it can also be a most inconvenient and even a disastrous one.

The metaphor of falling is also often used for the abrupt cessation of love. For a person to fall out of love can be as bewildering and distressing an experience as falling into it, but without any compensation. Adolescents have their own terms for intense but ephemeral love; for instance they speak of "having a crush on" somebody. Often they wonder how they will be able to distinguish "true love" when it happens to them. The best that they are told is that they will know when it happens, because the emotion of true love is quite unique, while the cynic would reply that there is no such thing, that love is a snare and a delusion. The young of every generation have to find out the truths

Left : Shakespeare's Romeo and Juliet, literature's most famous lovers. They could not bear to be apart and committed suicide instead.

Above : for couples in love the world is tinted with sunlight.

Opposite page, above right : early 20th-century Italian postcard depicting lovers consumed by a flaming passion.

Opposite page, right : 16th-century metaphysical view of love as a psychic union of opposites. Taken from the "Rosarium Philosophorum," Part II, Frankfurt.

about love for themselves, and very often this proves a disillusioning process. "The joys of love," says the popular song, "are but a moment long. The pains of love last a whole life through." The fact that thousands of poems, songs, and stories convey the same melancholy message indicates how perplexed men and women are by the seeming capriciousness of the emotion that is the source of both their greatest joys and their greatest miseries.

In Plato's *Symposium*, there is a parable. Humans were once spherical creatures so clever and energetic that the gods felt threatened. So they cut each human being down the middle, making of it two halves which became male and female. Thereafter the creatures devoted all their energies to trying to become whole again, to unite male with female, and so they ceased to be a challenge to the gods.

The parable not only states that love is such a consuming passion in human beings that some impractical and metaphysical motivation must be assumed to be behind it but gives a reason for our sex and love drives being so powerful and compulsive. It suggests that through the experience of sexual love people may attain a wholeness of being and a sense of expansion and transcendence that makes them feel godlike. Could this be why some lovers often behave as they do, rejecting prudence, wealth and success in their quest of an experience that some would see as only an ephemeral and temporary joy? And this joy exacts a heavy price: at best prolonged servitude and at worst distress and even death. And yet the same patterns repeat themselves generation after generation, and the reason must be deeper than a congenital deficiency in the makeup of man.

Romantic Love

Just as the artists over the years have tried to describe love, so certain scientists have tried to evaluate and quantify it. The idea may sound unlikely and some consider it objectionable and sinister, because love is thought to be a sacred mystery. But so were lightning and gravity once. It is hardly to be expected that such a major preoccupation of the human race, one that has inspired so much effort both for good and ill, should escape scientific inquiry. It is unlikely that these sorts of inquiries would destroy love by demystifying it, and there are certainly aspects of love that cannot be scientifically investigated. But considering the perplexities and the distress that it causes human beings when it goes wrong, any understandings that scientific investigation can contribute should be welcome.

Scientific investigation is a process of putting questions to nature and devising means of obtaining unequivocal answers.

Below : despite the popular belief that women are the romantic sex, they have generally been more reluctant than men to marry into a lower social class.

Opposite page, center : some women choose the direct approach in preference to romantic courtship.

Opposite page, right : a single-stemmed red rose, one of the most popular tokens of romantic love.

People who deplore science probing into love themselves make categorical statements on the subject, and many of these statements can be turned into questions and subjected to scrutiny.

Does like attract like or do opposites attract each other?

Are women generally more romantic in their attitude to love than men?

Is a sexual partner who presents a challenge more highly appreciated and valued than one who submits immediately?

The proposition that like attracts like cannot be put to the test without specifying the nature of the likeness, for example in looks and degree of physical attractiveness. One psychologist conceived the idea of taking a batch of wedding photographs, cutting them in two in order to separate the couples, mixing up all the pictures, then giving them to a group of judges to assess the individuals' relative degrees of attractiveness. He found that according to the judges' assessments, the people had chosen partners of a similar degree of attractiveness to themselves. Tests to ascertain whether like attracting like applies to personality have produced more ambiguous results. They have however tended to go against the theory of complementariness – that opposites attract. Interestingly enough, one of the most quoted examples of complementariness, that dominant people tend to partner submissive people, has been proven untrue.

To the question whether women are more romantic than men, most people would unhesitantingly answer that they are. But some research findings suggest that men may be more romantic than women in the sense that they are more inclined to put love before more practical and material considerations. For instance, more men than women marry below their own socioeconomic level. Also, after the age of 20 young men report an increasing number of romantic experiences whereas young women report a decreasing number, which suggests that the women are either exercising more rational control, or become disillusioned by the romantic aspect of sexual love earlier in life. Most revealingly, when a large mixed sample, aged 18 to 24, were asked whether they would marry someone they were not in love with if that person had all the other desirable qualities, two-thirds of the men said "no," but less than one-third of the women said they would not. These facts and figures suggest that the conventional view of women as the more romantic sex may be incorrect.

What about the effectiveness of "playing hard to get"? In one experiment to test the hypothesis, men who applied to a computer dating service were put in contact with a girl who eagerly and gratefully accepted

dates from half of them but told the other half that she was already very busy and did not really want to get involved with anyone else but would agree to meet them for coffee. When the men's impressions of a girl were later assessed, they did not support the hypothesis that playing hard to get increases a person's desirability. But when the experiment was varied so that one girl always acted available, another was always booked up, and a third made it clear that she was generally very popular and busy but was willing to date that particular subject, the latter was the one the men considered the most desirable. Other experiments extending the research beyond first contact have shown that more passion is generated in a man by a woman who at first is resistant and critical but then eventually becomes interested in him than by one whose attitude is either consistently positive or negative from the beginning.

To our knowledge no experiments with women as the subjects have been done, which probably reflects psychologists' bias as to which sex should be the pursuer and which the pursued.

Types of Love

Psychologists at the University of British Columbia devised an ingenious experiment which involved male subjects being required to walk across either a hazardous suspension bridge with a low hand-rail which swayed over a 230-foot drop, or an ordinary bridge which nobody would be apprehensive about crossing. Before the subjects made the crossing they were interviewed by an attractive woman who asked them to complete questionnaires and gave them her phone number saying they could contact her if they wanted more information about the experiment. The finding was that the men who had to cross the suspension bridge put more sexual innuendo into their answers to the questionnaires. Also more of them contacted the girl after the experiment than those who had to cross the ordinary bridge. The experimenters concluded that people who are apprehensive or fearful are particularly susceptible to sexual attraction and to the formation of emotional attachments.

Many experiments have clearly demonstrated that emotional arousal of any kind is conducive to attraction and love. People who share exciting, highly enjoyable, dangerous, or frightening experiences are likely to find themselves, sometimes to their surprise, attracted to or in love with one another. During wartime, and also on vacation, people are prone to form romantic and passionate relationships. But many such relationships soon disintegrate, and the reason for this may be explained by what is known as the attribution theory of love. The theory holds that experiencing a particular emotion involves two types of arousal: a physiological response and a mental attribution of that arousal to, for instance, fear, anger, or love. Incorrect attributions can be made in the best of faith, and probably everyone at some time manifests symptoms of physiological arousal at the sight of or in the presence of a member of the opposite sex and mistakenly labels his or her feelings "love."

A group of college students were shown a series of pictures of nude women from *Playboy* and simultaneously given feedback about their heart rate which apparently indicated which pictures excited them most. The feedback, however, was false, but when the men were later shown the same pictures they picked out as the most attractive the ones they had been led to believe had aroused them before. Women often complain that men are fickle in their emotions, but such experiments suggest that men do not know what their emotions are, or rather have difficulty in differentiating them. They deceive themselves as

Below: the many emotional attachments and marriages that took place during the World Wars, often between comparative strangers, were precipitated by the imminence of danger and death.

40

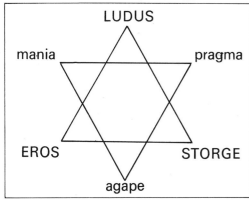

LUDUS

mania   pragma

EROS   STORGE

agape

Above left : the arrival of an absent lover is a poignant and intense moment.

Above right : holiday affairs in romantic settings are exciting but usually short-lived.

Left : the three primary and three secondary types of love.

much as women do. Both sexes are, in fact, prone to the same mistakes and confusions of feelings.

To help ease the confusion, psychologist John Lee of the University of Toronto produced a classification of the types of love. Basing his formulation on an analysis of replies to a long and detailed question-

naire about people's feelings and relationships, Lee proposed that there are three primary, different kinds of love. He calls them *eros, ludus,* and *storge.* Erotic lovers are sensual, self-confident, concerned with physical beauty and physical rapport with their partners. Ludic lovers are inclined to be playful, pleasure-seeking, and loath to take on commitments. Storgic lovers are affectionate, make good companions, and lack passion. These primaries blend to create three further categories of love, *mania, pragma,* and *agape. Mania* is obsessive love which is very vulnerable to jealousy, *pragma* is realistic, practical love which seeks compatibility, while *agape* is altuistic, selfless, and dutiful love. The six types, Lee proposes, can be represented diagrammatically as the six angles of two intersecting triangles, and this diagram can be used to calculate the compatibility of two people and the probability of their relationship enduring by determining which category predominates in their attitudes to love. It is acknowledged that most people have a mixture of attitudes, different ones predominating in different circumstances. But even when allowance is made for this it is generally possible to determine a person's bias. If the distance between the bias of two potential partners is great, for example if one is storgic and the other ludic or manic, their chances of having an enduring and mutually satisfying relationship are slim.

When two people meet socially their initial attraction to one another will be visual. Conversation is used to strengthen this bond. It also necessitates closer bodily contact.

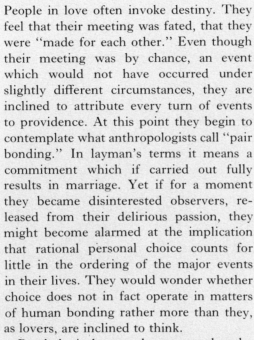

Points of Attraction

People in love often invoke destiny. They feel that their meeting was fated, that they were "made for each other." Even though their meeting was by chance, an event which would not have occurred under slightly different circumstances, they are inclined to attribute every turn of events to providence. At this point they begin to contemplate what anthropologists call "pair bonding." In layman's terms it means a commitment which if carried out fully results in marriage. Yet if for a moment they became disinterested observers, released from their delirious passion, they might become alarmed at the implication that rational personal choice counts for little in the ordering of the major events in their lives. They would wonder whether choice does not in fact operate in matters of human bonding rather more than they, as lovers, are inclined to think.

Psychological research suggests that the fatalistic hypothesis is false and that at a subconscious level people make a series of judgements, assessments, and computations when they choose a mate, although the only subjective state they may be aware of is one of joy, thankfulness, and euphoria.

We have already mentioned some of the research demonstrating that people tend to be attracted to those whose physical attractiveness is comparable to their own. The point has also been demonstrated by Ellen Berscheid at the University of Minnesota. In her simple experiments, people were shown a series of pictures of members of the opposite sex and asked to choose which they would like to meet. People themselves not endowed with good looks very rarely chose the more conspicuously attractive of the people in the pictures, presumably because they were apprehensive of rejection or failure if they did, and felt they would be more comfortable with someone on the same level of attractiveness as themselves. In other words, their choice was determined by rational, practical considerations.

It is often said that women are less concerned with physical appearance than men are, and are more likely to choose their partners for such characteristics as warmth, sincerity, and sense of humor. The general principle is supported by much research evidence, though there is some ambiguity as to the characteristics that women tend to rate most highly. In a study conducted among students at the University of California at Los Angeles, the four attributes that men found most desirable in women were physical attractiveness, eroticism, affectionateness, and sociability, in that order. Women listed achievement, leadership, and occupational and economic success as the most desirable qualities in male partners. We can assume a bias in the sample as the subjects were all young and of a high educational level, and we would expect that older and more secure women would put more emphasis on character than on success. But the priorities listed still bear out the belief that women tend to take more qualities into account and be less influenced by looks when choosing a partner than men are.

Of course, this type of research is open to the criticism that it has not been conducted with people in love and therefore does not apply to them. Mythology and literature promote the view that love repudiates calculation and prudence, and maintains that people are irresistibly attracted to each other despite apparent incompatibilities and great obstacles. Psychologists would say that this romantic "love conquers all" belief owes it appeal to the fact that it represents a situation that many would acknowledge to be wonderful and even ideal, but only vicariously. When love comes into their own lives they may be inspired by the great lovers of legend, literature, and history. They may feel themselves carried away by an overwhelming passion. But when it comes to choosing a long-term partner the assessment is done on a material, practical basis, albeit obscured.

"The Heart has its Reasons"

A marriage counsellor, Ethel M Nash, reported how a young couple, aged 19 and 20, put an advertisement in her local paper which read: "Painting done, with love, husband-wife team." She contacted them and they called on her to discuss work. They explained that they were so much in love that they could not bear to be apart for a moment, and they had set up as house-painters because this was work they could do together. Ms Nash engaged them, and observed that while they worked they were continually touching each other or expressing their love by gesture. They even stood on either side of the same stepladder so that they could kiss as they painted. Here was a couple manifestly in love, who cared nothing for anything or anybody outside their love bond, but whose love was really very vulnerable and fragile. What would happen to them, she wondered, if they eventually had to come to terms with the world? How would they deal with inevitable disagreements? What would happen when one or the other began to tire of "the need for perpetual togetherness?" And what if the girl became pregnant and they were forced by circumstances to accept a degree of separation?

Ethel Nash was asking whether they would be able to make the transition from being in love to loving? For the fact is that being "in love" is a short stage and unless there is a basis for loving, the relationship will crumble. If the couple's love really was blind, if they had idealized each other and not seen each other as human beings with certain faults and shortcomings, their chances of establishing an enduring, fulfilling relationship will be slim. For loving is an emotion of maturity.

"The heart has its reasons," said Pascal, "that reason does not know." We talk about the heart as the seat of emotion, and the center of emotional love. The heart is the symbol of lovers, pierced by Cupid, broken by infidelity. Language abounds with metaphors such as "affairs of the heart," "lonely hearts," "broken hearts." It is true that the heart is an indicator of physical arousal, and we are very aware of how our heartbeat and blood pressure rises in emotionally charged situations. But the heart is not the center or instigator of these feelings, simply an organ responding to hormonal changes. In fact if we take quotations in which the heart metaphor is used and substitute the term "the subconscious," we find that they make much better sense. Pascal's statement, often used by those romantic about love, simply means that while a person is only aware of his or her consuming passion, at their subconscious level they are busily assessing the relative merits of their partner. Perhaps it needs to be said that these assessments are not necessarily of material things, but involve such factors as mutual development and personal growth.

Ethel Nash remarked about the loving house-painters: "This pair revel in the close bond that is filling some of the void left by unmet needs in infancy and childhood." In other words, the context of their loving was not the adult world of demands, challenges, work, change, responsibility and others' scrutiny, but the cushioned world of the nursery. Couples in love tend to inhabit an exclusive world of their own making. Loving couples have to confront reality; their relationship involves other people, particularly children, and the transition from being in love to loving can only be accomplished successfully by those who bring intelligence and maturity into their relationship. There is truth in the dictum of the Roman dramatist, Seneca, that "Only a wise man knows how to love."

Rituals of Courtship

Amid the scientific analyses, sociological surveys, and psychoanalytic studies, not to mention the exhortations for individual independence and rational behavior, romance disappeared. Or rather, when sex became a respectable topic, the trappings and prelude to it did not seem to merit much attention. It is often alleged that modern attitudes to love and sex have killed romance, an allegation not borne out by the current content of songs, literature, movies, poetry, and drama.

The meaning of the word "romance" is very much a personal one, not unconnected with nostalgia. When people

human activities. They invest an act with significance, provide a framework to ease "social behavior," and create an atmosphere or state of consciousness appropriate to the situation. Many of them are pleasant in themselves. Unfortunately rituals tend to become mere formalities, particularly when people acquire them from their culture instead of creating them for themselves, and then they no longer serve to enhance experience but on the contrary inhibit it, obscure it, or serve as a substitute.

The Western notion of romance had its origins in such a peculiar cultural aberration that it is surprising that it survived as long as it did. In the Middle Ages when life was rough and brutal, and sexual license was a matter of brute force, the European nobility invented a civilizing ritual. A knight would select for his attention and adoration the wife of another man, and proceed to "pay court" to her. He sent her flowers, wrote poems to her, composed and

Left: "St George and the Dragon" by the 15th-century painter Paolo Uccello. The ritual of courtly love in the Middle Ages demanded that a man risk his life for his lady. He was her champion and her protector.

regret its passing they generally think of the formalities of chivalry, and a gradual escalation of eroticism in the relationship before sexuality is permitted to make its appearance, if it ever is. It is in effect a series of rituals that traditionally involved the man courting and winning over the woman.

Rituals have an important role in many

played music, and would wear her colors in tournaments. Ardent and elaborate declarations of passion were permitted in this ritual, but never would the knight attempt to make love to his lady physically. She was on a pedestal, a creature too godlike to profane with brute sex. Romantic tradition and ritual produced a wealth of passionate and inspired literature, culminating in

Dante's adoration of Beatrice (whom he had never become acquainted with) in the *Divine Comedy*. The literary tradition of love continued up to the last century, inspired by Goethe's aphorism, "The eternal feminine leads us ever onward and upward."

Elaborate courtesy on the part of the male toward the female remained the rule in social intercourse until very recently, and indeed still survives in some quarters and classes, but to many people nowadays it seems an anachronism. As one young woman bluntly put it: "I think my generation has lost the ability – or need – to delude itself with romantic bunk."

What this woman possibly meant is elaborated by the highly articulate Kate Millet, in her book *Sexual Politics*. "Romantic love obscures the realities of female status and the burden of economic dependence," she writes. "While a palliative to the injustice of woman's social position, chivalry is also a technique for disguising it. One must acknowledge that the chivalrous stance is a game the master group plays in elevating its subject to pedestal level . . . Both the courtly and the romantic versions of love are 'grants' which the male concedes out of his total powers. Both have had the effect of obscuring the patriarchal character of Western culture, and in their general tendency to attribute impossible virtues to women, have ended by confining them in a narrow and often remarkably conscribing sphere of behavior."

It is true that an elaborate meal, a ring, and a bouquet of flowers are a small price to pay for obtaining in effect unpaid domestic labor. The pleasanter aspects of romance should not become either objects in themselves or means to an end, but a means of enhancing the occasional situation. They should be presents, given with thought, not the reenactment of a supposed behavior pattern.

Left: "Minuetto in Villa" by Giovanni Domenico Tiepolo. In 18th-century Europe a gentleman wooed his lady with protestations of love and tokens of his affection. She did not succumb immediately but remained aloof until sufficiently impressed.

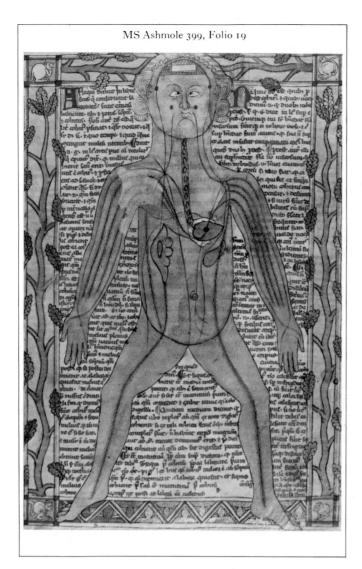

MS Ashmole 399, Folio 19

The Chemistry of Love

Lovers who sense changes in their bodies when they touch each other often say, "It's chemistry." And by way of explanation as to why an affair did not work out a person might say, "The chemistry wasn't right." Although this reaction between two people is analogous to a chemical reaction, the expression is not entirely metaphorical. The arousal of sexual feelings produces very marked biochemical changes.

Hormones are chemical substances produced in the body which travel through the bloodstream and affect a person's physical response and readiness for sexual activity. Similar to hormones are phero-mones, chemical substances emitted by the body for the purpose of stimulating or attracting a member of the opposite sex. The production of both hormones and pheromones increases when a person is sexually aroused or in love.

The three main sex hormones are the androgens (the primary male hormone), estrogens and progestogens (main female hormones). All three are present in both sexes, but in differing amounts. In both sexes the intensity of libido depends on the levels of the main androgen – testosterone. These levels go up and down throughout the woman's menstrual cycle, and likewise oscillate to an extent in the male. However, in a human being with normal sexual arousal potential, production is quickly stepped up when a stimulus is experienced. Pheromones do not play so large a part in human sexuality as in that of other species. In fact many people go to great lengths to cover them up with perfumes, and deodor-

Above left : long before hormones were discovered it was recognized that sexual attraction and drive cause changes in the body. Early medical thought ascribed this to the coursing of various "spirits" through the blood.

Above : the personal perfume that comes from the hair, arm-pits, skin, and genital area is a more potent fragrance than any artificial scent.

Right : alcohol in moderation releases tension and inhibitions, and makes a good prelude to lovemaking. Too much and the effects can be highly undesirable.

ants. The French have the term *Cassolette* for the sexual smell of a person, which they recognize can be highly individual. Alex Comfort writes in *The Joy of Sex* that: "The woman's *Cassolette* is her secret weapon to an extent that women in America don't seem to realize – French women know better. Some men respond violently to it without realizing the fact ... but at the same time a skillful man can read it, if he is an olfactory type, and if he knows her, to tell when she is excited." They further suggest that a discreet touch of genital secretion behind the ear can often arouse a man more effectively than any perfume.

People today speak of being "turned on" by something or somebody, and the expression acknowledges that stimuli produce physiological responses, and that some are more effective than others in increasing the flow of sex hormones. Human beings have long searched for aphrodisiacs, and many substances have been reputed to achieve this desired effect, from champagne and oysters to the velvet that grows on the antlers of deer. The *Kama Sutra*, for example, recommends that a man carry a hyena bone covered in gold to increase his attractiveness. In fact no chemical substance has been found that has a general aphrodisiac effect. Even supplements of testosterone will not increase a normal healthy male's sex drive, although they are effective for people whose sex drive has greatly diminished, for instance with age. Champagne and oysters make a good overture to lovemaking not because they affect the sexual physiology but because the champagne may have the effect of supressing inhibitions and therefore releasing libido, and the oysters contain quickly assimilable protein.

The phenomenon that zoologists call "imprinting" undoubtedly plays a part in human sexuality. This was demonstrated by the ethnologist Konrad Lorenz, whose ducklings took him for their mother because he was the first moving thing they saw immediately after they hatched. Imprinting occurs when a response becomes fixated on a particular stimulus. In human beings lasting fixations do not normally occur, except in fetishists whose first experience of orgasm was associated with a particular object or part of the body. But most people are aroused by a particular stimulus because the response was imprinted by a past experience that was exceptionally exciting.

It may be a perfume, a fabric, an article of clothing or footwear, a particular kind of food or drink, a piece of music, in fact anything that has acquired an erotic significance through association. The imprinting mechanism can have the effect of cementing a relationship, and most couples who have been together long enough get to know which are the effective and most potent stimuli. Unfortunately it can also have the effect of triggering sexual responses out of context or inappropriately, as for example when a man feels attracted to one woman because she is wearing a perfume he associates with another.

What Attracts You?

Popular newspapers and magazines often run features about what arouses women or men, which are presumably read by members of the one sex for tips they may pick up as to how to enhance their own attractiveness, and by members of the other for curiosity, to see if their own sexual tastes are the general rule or exceptional. Psychologists have also tried to examine the general rules of sexual attraction, and have come up with the fairly obvious finding that while there are many idiosyncracies of

taste there is also a broad consensus among the members of each sex as to what constitutes attractiveness in the other.

The reported research has concentrated on physical attributes, although researchers generally acknowledge that personality characteristics also play an important part, particularly as regards the male's attractiveness to the female.

From very early life, males in our culture are conditioned to be turned on by particular female characteristics. These, quite naturally, are the characteristics that most conspicuously distinguish the female from the male of our species: the breasts, the narrow waist and wide hips, the softness and hairlessness of the skin. Formerly the woman's hair was a major sexual stimulant, but is less so nowadays with fashions in hairstyles overlapping so strongly.

Men sometimes ask each other whether they are more stimulated by breasts, or buttocks in a woman. A survey by the psychology department at the University of Illinois established that men not only tend to have distinct preferences for one or another of these anatomical features, and for the favored feature to be particularly large or small, but also that their preferences correlate with certain male personality characteristics. For example, large-breasted women tend to appeal to males who are extrovert, masculine in their tastes, sporty, smokers and frequent daters, while small breasts are on the whole preferred by men who drink little, are religious, and are inclined to be depressive and submissive. A tenet of Freudian psychology, that "oral" personalities, that is males with a strong element of dependency, are attracted to females with large breasts, has been proved wrong by this and other research; in fact it has been shown that dependent males tend to prefer small breasts.

The generally attractive facial features of the female are again those that distinguish her from the male: fuller lips, softer complexion, hairlessness and narrow eyebrows; and of course the cosmetics industry deals in products designed to enable women to emphasize these features. Large eyes are also an asset. In one interesting test, men were confronted with two photographs of the same girl and asked to choose which they preferred. Few actually spotted that the only difference between the photographs was that in one the pupils of the girl's eyes had been touched up to appear larger, but the majority chose the touched-up picture. Enlargement of the pupils occurs, of course, when a person is interested in or somehow aroused by what he or she is looking at.

Expressions in the eyes are also a stimulant for women, but not necessarily or always expressions that signify arousal. In fact, the expression in a man's eyes is a far

Right : the various parts of the human body attract different people in differing ways.

Left : an expression of personality is as important a feature in attractiveness as the shape of the body.

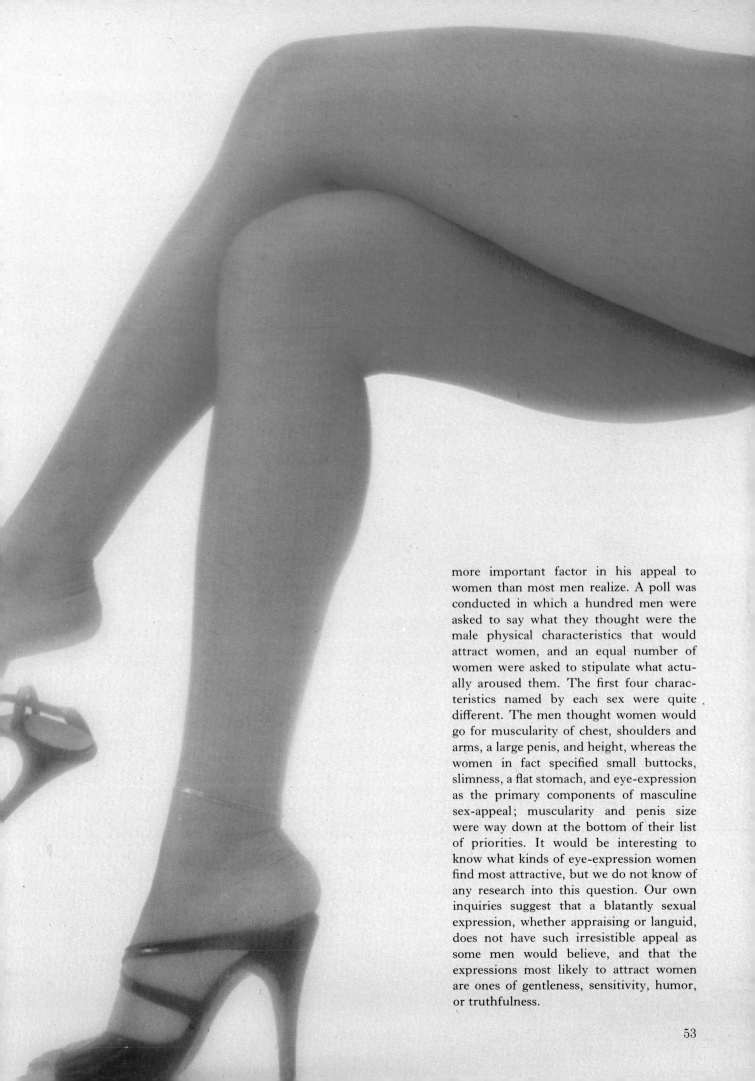

more important factor in his appeal to women than most men realize. A poll was conducted in which a hundred men were asked to say what they thought were the male physical characteristics that would attract women, and an equal number of women were asked to stipulate what actually aroused them. The first four characteristics named by each sex were quite different. The men thought women would go for muscularity of chest, shoulders and arms, a large penis, and height, whereas the women in fact specified small buttocks, slimness, a flat stomach, and eye-expression as the primary components of masculine sex-appeal; muscularity and penis size were way down at the bottom of their list of priorities. It would be interesting to know what kinds of eye-expression women find most attractive, but we do not know of any research into this question. Our own inquiries suggest that a blatantly sexual expression, whether appraising or languid, does not have such irresistible appeal as some men would believe, and that the expressions most likely to attract women are ones of gentleness, sensitivity, humor, or truthfulness.

Sex Without Love

People have sex *drives* but love *needs*, and it is generally believed that the former predominate in men and the latter in women. Indeed they might appear to, although it is not clear whether the difference is biological or attributable to sociosexual conditions in our culture. The recent liberation of female sexuality and the movement toward more women being capable of living independent lives, has to some extent equalized the situation. More women express their sex drives and more men admit their need for love. The failure to integrate sex and love still causes many people personal problems, as do the inability or refusal to recognize that the two are different.

In Roger Vadim's science fiction fantasy movie *Barbarella* (1968), we witnessed Jane Fonda writhing in orgasm induced by a "pleasure machine" that she was strapped to. Since the discovery of the pleasure centers in the brain that can be electrically stimulated, the idea is not so far-fetched; whether it will replace sexual intercourse is doubtful, in the foreseeable future at least.

It does, however, illustrate that sex can be totally divorced from love. The conduct of the rapist and the fantasies of the man in the street about sex with a stranger also illustrate the fact. Loveless sex used to be thought brutal, demeaning or sinful, but today many people see nothing wrong with the practice provided that it is understood

Above : the typewriter-like "pleasure machine" featured in the science-fiction movie Barbarella *(1968).*

Below : "The Orgy," William Hogarth's view of 18th-century indiscriminate sexual pairing.

to be mutual. As the psychiatrist Albert Ellis writes in his book *Love Without Guilt*: "Sex without love is hardly a heinous crime, and appears to be quite delightful and to add immeasurably to the lives of literally millions of individuals."

Love may also be divorced from sex. There are couples who cease to have sexual intercourse after some years of marriage but still find fulfillment in their relationship, and sometimes such couples even have an arrangement whereby one or both of them have their sex needs catered to outside marriage. Love for them is companionship, sharing interests, enjoying family life, caring for each other. These aspects of a relationship may bind them more closely than others whose relationship is based mainly on sex.

Yet it can be argued that the most fulfilling relationships are those in which love and sex are united, just as the most enjoyable acts of sexual intercourse are with a loved one. According to one Greek

Above: "La Resistance Inutile" (vain resistance) by Jean-Honoré Fragonard. In rape the sexual act is an expression of many powerful emotions: fear, passion, desire for conquest, and even hate. But love is never present.

myth, Eros, the God of Love, alarmed his mother Aphrodite when he did not grow up as her other children did, but remained a small, rosy, chubby child. When she consulted Themis about the problem, the latter told her: "Love cannot grow without Passion." The answer puzzled Aphrodite, but later she gave birth to Anteros, the god of passion. Then, according to the myth, "when with his brother, Eros grew and flourished, until he became a handsome slender youth; but when separated from him, he invariably resumed his childish form and mischievous habits."

Eros separated from Anteros is sex divorced from love, and he is childish, mischievous and silly. In another development of the myth, Aphrodite searches for Eros to urge him to get on with his task of spreading love in the world, and she finds him gambling and cheating at cards: which expresses an even more striking insight, namely, that *eros* eventually even loses interest in sex.

The Meaning of Love

It may be unromantic to respond to the declaration, "I love you," with the question, "What precisely do you mean by 'love'?" It is a question often in the mind, though not so frequently expressed. Yet it is impossible to give a single answer to a question which has so many meanings and connotations.

Relationships between lovers are often discussed in terms of giving and taking. It is almost a cliché in that there has to be give and take in every relationship, because each party has to take into account the other's wishes and needs, and make certain allowances, concessions and compromises. But give and take in a loving relationship goes much deeper than this. It is the entire self that is given and taken in mature and fulfilling sexual love, and nothing less.

The feminist writer Kate Millett rightly deplores the use of military metaphors in descriptions of sexual acts and relationships, but one that is surely apt is that of "surrender." When lovers make love they surrender themselves to each other and to the experience. It is not a matter of one yielding to the other's desire after initial resistance; the military metaphor really does mislead in this respect. Self-surrender can only occur when a person has complete trust in the other, and has no unresolved fears of losing rights or of being manipulated. Any negative attitude to the other will inhibit surrender, causing a person to hold back something of himself or herself. This refusal to give oneself entirely in the sexual act results in inhibition, and very often the failure to experience orgasm.

There is a paradox about surrender in that only through it can freedom be attained. As Wilhelm Reich convincingly demonstrated, in the process of growing up every human being develops "character armor" which affords protection from the hostile, the alien, and the unknown. To shed this armor, to release oneself totally in relation to another person, becomes very difficult, although it is what everybody wants to do because only then can they become truly themselves. The paradoxes multiply. We only attain freedom through surrender, only become truly ourselves when we unite with another, we cannot receive unless we can give. But paradoxical though the statements are, lovers will recognize truth in them. A person who gives without taking diminishes and dominates the other; and one who takes without giving finds that what he has taken has no substance or

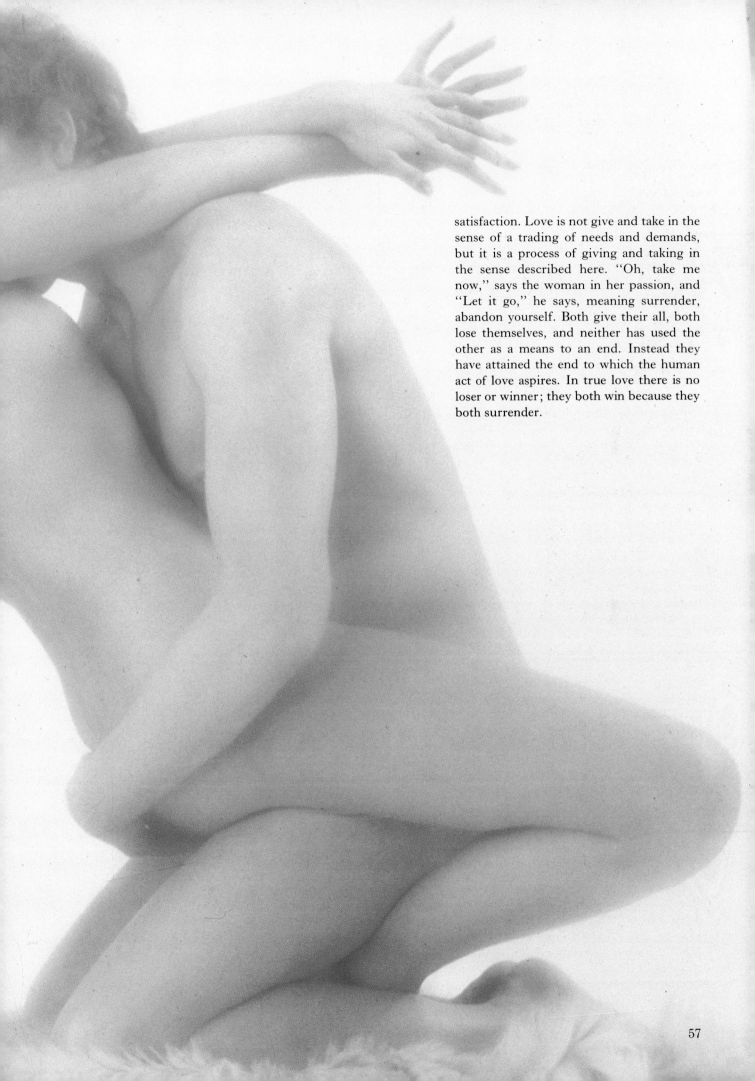

satisfaction. Love is not give and take in the sense of a trading of needs and demands, but it is a process of giving and taking in the sense described here. "Oh, take me now," says the woman in her passion, and "Let it go," he says, meaning surrender, abandon yourself. Both give their all, both lose themselves, and neither has used the other as a means to an end. Instead they have attained the end to which the human act of love aspires. In true love there is no loser or winner; they both win because they both surrender.

Accepting and Possessing

Accepting, respecting, admiring, adoring: these are some of the important aspects of loving.

"Home," said one man who was interviewed in a study of successful marriages, "means you can expose your weaknesses without shame, can brag a little without fear of misunderstanding, and can make mistakes without being ridiculed." In other words, in his home and in his marital relationship he had the satisfaction of being accepted for what he was.

Accepting a person for what he or she is means having no reservations. It certainly does not mean being blind to shortcomings, but on the contrary means being aware of them and accepting them too. It is in the love relationship that people remove their "character armor," but do not do so unless they are sure that without it they are unreservedly accepted by their partner. To want to fashion the other person into a particular mold is not love but possessiveness. Love is fully accepting one's partner without reservation despite the fact that they are not the same as one's ideal. When couples make love for the first time they often expose their nakedness to each other with some trepidation, both afraid that they will fall short of the other's ideal of physical beauty. Yet to accept the naked body, with all its imperfections, is truly to love. People who are casual about sex do not, of course, appreciate or experience the significance of nakedness, for they do not sense the identity of the body and its vulnerability, and they are inclined to be, as Rollo May has written, "more wary of . . . psychological and spiritual nakedness than they are of the physical nakedness in sexual intimacy."

The philosopher Ortega y Gasset went so far as to say that love is "intense affirmation of another being, irrespective of his attitude to us." This is romantic or religious love, the love of the chivalric knight for his lady though she ignores him, or of man for

God who may send him only suffering and woe. It is adoration, and in the context of human loving it is not generally an aspect of love that endures, for contrary to the romantic myth unrequited love soon palls for the majority of people. But if we disregard the second part of Ortega's definition, and say that love is "intense affirmation of another being," we have a statement of more general relevance. Not only to accept the other, but to affirm him, is a mark of love. And affirmation can be of two kinds. We all have within us, particularly when we are young, a feeling of alienation, and it is gratifying and important for another person to affirm that our existence is real and relevant. Then there is the affirmation of one's personality; of *what* we are as well as of the fact *that* we are. This kind of affirmation manifests as respect and admiration, the discrimination of qualities and characteristics that are valuable to others as well as to the lover.

To love, then, is to see the loved one as a unique being, and to see him steady and whole without his protective armor. But then there arises the sense of possessing. Although possessiveness is generally a deplorable characteristic, people intensely in love do feel that they belong to each other and the sexual act becomes an act of taking possession. "You are mine," lovers constantly tell each other, and they feel that for a third party to have a sexual experience of the other would be an intolerable violation of their property rights.

Possessiveness invariably brings jealousy. No human being can regard another as property, yet many, while intellectually agreeing with this, cannot deny that they have experienced at some time in their lives that destructive feeling. Jealousy is an emotion not generally susceptible to reason, but reasoning is the only remedy. It is pointless to fret about being unable to do what it is not in one's power to do; for nobody has the power to coerce love.

Right : nakedness is private and an expression of sexual intimacy. The first exposure, whether provocative or coy, is a sensual yet tense moment.

The Commitments of Love

There is a distinction between a feeling and an emotion. A feeling need not have an object but an emotion must have one. We can feel pain or melancholy alone but anger, hate or love are emotions that are directed toward another person, who incidentally may be an aspect of oneself.

The confusion about feeling and emotion is found in articles about sex and love today. When love is presented as mutual indulgence in pleasure, and sex as the release of tension or gratification of desire, it is feelings that are being discussed. Being internal, feelings do not involve any commitment to another person. Love that is mutually undemanding and involves no commitment, only pure joy, can be very convincing; but there is no emotion involved in such loving. We can control our feelings better than we can our emotions. Emotions are more enduring than feelings; they can last a lifetime, and they can be obsessive and consuming. That is why the arousal of the emotion of love in a person involves a commitment.

True lovers do not resent their commitments, they embrace them because they afford a means of expressing their love. They marry because they want to declare to the world their commitment to each other. It is a commitment strengthened by every act of love, for in each act both engage their emotions, and the effect of emotions shared is to bind people. The more intense the emotion and the more frequently it is experienced, the stronger the bond becomes. Masters and Johnson speak of *The Pleasure Bond*, and write that "mutual pleasure sets a seal on emotional commitment." The idea is right but the metaphor may be misleading because to set a seal on something is to finalize it, and in a relationship of love the emotional commitment needs to be regularly expressed and thereby renewed.

This is where many relationships go wrong. In fact, the very word "commitment" is partly responsible because to many it implies that when they marry they "take on" commitments, for instance a mortgage payment or a house to maintain or children. These secondary and incidental commitments tend to become primary, particularly where children are concerned. Parents of young children often ask themselves why and how they got into their situation. They think that life has burdened them with commitments they would rather be without, and what in fact has happened to them is that they have neglected their emotional commitments to each other as two separate beings and have come to regard their life together as a commitment to share a number of tasks. Too many people sadly find, when all the tasks have been done and the commitments met, when the children have grown up and left home and the mortgage has been paid, that they are living with a stranger.

Commitment must be, first and always, to the partner, and to his or her emotional being. He or she alone is capable of experiencing satisfactions and joys that make the mundane, inevitable aspects of life worthwhile.

Loving is caring, both caring about and caring for. It is also communicating, and it is wanting to be together and do things together, not just the daily tasks but play and relaxation as well.

The psychologist Abraham Maslow proposed that human beings have a hierarchy of needs: physiological needs, safety needs, love needs, esteem needs, and self-fulfillment needs, in that order, and that each need becomes pressing only when the ones before it have been satisfied, which normally happens in this sequence in the first two decades of life. Sex needs may become urgent before love needs because they may be purely physiological. But when the love needs appear they tend to encompass the sex needs and the love needs show themselves as both a need to receive and a need to give love.

And, Maslow further proposed, love that began as needing love should develop in the course of time into unneeding love. He distinguished deficiency love (or D-love) from being love (or B-love). D-love is the love that needs the partner to fill an emptiness or to heal a wound, and its motivation is basically selfish. B-love on the other hand is "love for the Being of another person, unneeding love, unselfish love." D-love can be gratified and sated, but B-love cannot be.

Right : "Ennui" (boredom) by Walter Richard Sickert. Relationships frequently stagnate because domestic responsibilities take priority over emotional growth and development.

It is the B-lover who really cares about and cares for the loved one. And an important aspect of this caring is wanting the other to develop and grow as a person. The conservatism of the lover who wants nothing ever to change is an irrational if understandable reaction to the experience of being ecstatically happy. But change and growth is essential to love; without them love stagnates and atrophies. "B-love,"

writes Maslow, "creates the partner. It gives him a self-image, it gives him self-acceptance, a feeling of love-worthiness, all of which permit him to grow. It is a real question whether the full development of the human being is possible without it." And B-lovers, really mature lovers secure in each other's love, "are more independent of each other, more autonomous, less jealous or threatened, less needful, more individual, more disinterested, but also simultaneously more eager to help the other toward self-actualization, more proud of his triumphs, more altruistic, generous and fostering," than D-lovers. Also they see each other more clearly, truly and penetratingly than D-lovers see each other. "Far from accepting the common platitude that love makes people blind," Maslow writes, "I become more and more inclined to think of the *opposite* as true, namely that non-love makes us blind."

These are the perceptive insights of a psychologist who made it his task to study not the causes of psychopathy but the conditions of psychological health, the optimum conditions under which human beings function and are able to fulfill their potential. Another of Maslow's concepts that is highly relevant to the subject of human love and sex is that of the "peak experience." Peak experiences may occur in many different circumstances. A mother may have one nursing her baby, as can an athlete breaking a record, a philosopher

hitting upon a new idea, a music-lover listening to a favorite performance, or a lover in the moment of sexual orgasm. Peak experiences bring feelings of goodness, unification, wholeness, and integration. The feeling makes a person energetic, ready for action. People feel grateful for the experience, and "often this feeling of gratitude is expressed as or leads to an all-embracing love for everybody and everything, to a perception of the world as beautiful and good, often to an impulse to do something good for the world, an eagerness to repay, even a sense of obligation."

The slogan "Make love, not war," was thought by some to advocate a retreat from the harsh realities of life into a cult of sensuality, but it should be understood to mean rather that a peak experience of sexual love so strongly affirms life that the issues over which men make war seem absurd and irrelevant. The world's scriptures and religious leaders have always taught this, though their devotees have often thought that the love they spoke of was a spiritual concept distinct from physical love. What psychologists such as Abraham Maslow and Wilhelm Reich have shown us is that true physical love is an experience that gives human beings their sense of fulfillment and wholeness. It makes them selfless, creative, outgoing and giving, non-striving, disposed to celebrate, to worship, to praise, and to affirm. In fact, it is akin to the experience of religion.

Chapter 3
The Male Partner

An alien visitor to our world looking at our entertainments and advertising industries, and our literature and art, would probably assume that the human male is a highly sexed animal. On the other hand, he might on the basis of the same evidence assume that man is an animal highly perplexed and anxious about his sexuality. A commonly held idea is that men are more interested in sex than women, and possibly more confused by it. Also, men are at least as vulnerable as women to criticism of their sexual competence, for masculinity is socially and psychologically more closely identified with sexuality. But the social attributes that are considered to constitute masculinity, such as toughness, aggression, strong will, and intransigence, do not necessarily make for good sex. Nor, probably, are they attributes that are going to be as important in the future. Consequently many men need to have a deeper and more realistic understanding of their true sexuality.

The Phallic Obsession

There is a novel by Alberto Moravia titled *The Two of Us* (1972) in which the hero, Federico, is continually in conflict with and forced into embarrassing situations by his gigantic and demanding phallus, which he calls "Federico Rex." The novel's title is apt. Many men sometimes feel that their phallus has a will and a way of its own, and like Federico they can glorify it one minute and be ashamed of it the next.

Moravia's novel not only expresses some basic truths about male sexuality, but has also contributed to the propagation of one of its commonest myths: that penis size correlates with virility, and that the bigger the phallus the more demanding it is and the more able to satisfy a female. This is simply not true. It is men, not women, that are concerned about the size of the male member; and that Moravia should have chosen to write a novel in which one of the

central characters is a phallus of extraordinary dimensions is itself an indication of the male's concern about the matter.

In this book we are using the word penis for the male organ in its unaroused state and phallus for it in its aroused, erect state. One important fact which many men are unaware of is that there is little variation in phallic size, whereas there are considerable variations in penis size. That is to say, the smaller penis extends itself more in erection than the larger one does.

Masters and Johnson, in one of their studies, measured the penises of 300 men. They found that the largest one measured 5.5 inches, and the smallest was 2.25 inches. Furthermore, the former belonged to a slim and fairly short man and the latter to a heavily built and quite tall man. It is another curious fact about the penis that its size relative to general body size is less constant than that of any other organ.

Of course, there are average dimensions. Most penises are about 3.75 inches long, while the average phallus is about 6 inches. The measurements are taken from the root of the organ on the side nearest the stomach. An organ of abnormal dimensions should not be a cause either of anxiety or of pride. As a woman's sensitive sexual organs are not located deep inside her body a small phallus can satisfy her quite as much as a large one, and as her vaginal passage is capable of expanding sufficiently for a baby to pass through it is obviously able to accommodate the largest phallus. The only thing that the man with an exceptionally large phallus should bear in mind is that the vaginal passage expands gradually as a woman becomes sexually aroused, so he should not introduce his phallus prematurely or too roughly.

In most animals the penis retracts into the body when not in use, and in many its

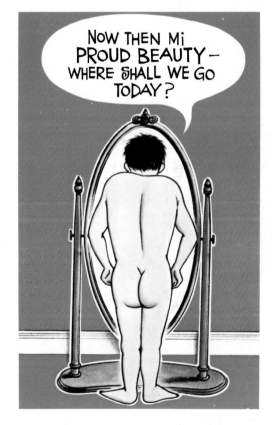

NOW THEN MI PROUD BEAUTY – WHERE SHALL WE GO TODAY?

structure includes a penile bone. This is not so in either case in man. Instead of a bone to ensure firmness, man has a spongy network of blood vessels. When sexual arousal occurs the blood vessels become distended and the muscles around the veins contract preventing the blood from leaving. It is this congestion of the tissue with blood that causes the penis to become erect.

What Makes a Man?

The skin of the penis is hairless, thin, elastic and very sensitive, particularly so on the upper- and undersides. In uncircumcized men it fits loosely over the shaft and slips back and forth during sexual activity. When it is pulled back it reveals the glans or tip of the penis, which is generally cone-shaped, at the base of which there is a ridge known as the corona. The glans is the most sensitive part of the phallus, richly endowed with nerve-endings, and it is highly responsive to stimulation during sexual foreplay.

At birth the glans of the penis is covered by a foreskin, which in some societies is routinely removed by circumcision. Some people believe that circumcision enhances sexual pleasure, but in fact there is no evidence that there is a difference in sensitivity between the circumcized and the uncircumcized penis. The only possible disadvantage of noncircumcision might be that as the foreskin traps dirt, uncircumcized men should be particularly scrupulous about their genital hygiene. They should regularly push the foreskin back and wash the glans and corona with warm water.

After the penis, the testicles are the main focus of male anxiety and misplaced pride. The testicles are extremely vulnerable and sensitive, in fact too much so to be organs of pleasure. The author of *The Sensuous Woman* (1971) urges her readers to give their men a wonderful thrill by gently taking a testicle into the mouth like an egg. This is not a practice ve would recommend, for any thrill conferred by the novelty of the experience would be cancelled out by the reflex anxiety it induced.

The testicles are sex glands whose function is to manufacture sperm. They vary in size, but any exceptionally large one usually has more fluid. Testicle size is not related to the number of sperm produced. It is normal for one testicle to be a little smaller than the other, and it is also normal for one (usually the left) to hang lower than the other, two common factors that still cause anxiety. Men are sometimes alarmed, too, to find that they appear to have only one testicle, when in fact what has happened

Right : the male sex organs.

is that one has retreated into the canal that leads to the abdomen. This canal serves as a kind of refuge for the very vulnerable glands. They get drawn up toward it, for example, when a man wades into cold water, or when any kind of danger threatens, and also during sexual arousal. A very small number of males have an undescended testicle, one that has not descended to the scrotum but remained in the abdominal canal. This condition can be corrected surgically, preferably at an early age.

The reason why the testicles are outside the body is that they need to be a little below body temperature in order to produce sperm efficiently. This is also why the sac that encloses them, the scrotum, is made of deeply wrinkled skin. When the temperature is too high, the wrinkles smooth out in order to lose heat, and if it gets too cold

KEY
1 glans
2 prepuce
3 penis
4 urethra
5 testicle
6 scrotum
7 epididymis
8 vas deferens
9 bladder
10 seminal vesicles
11 prostate
12 bulbo-urethral glands
13 rectum

they close up. This is why the scrota become tight and shrivelled if one plunges into cold water.

When sperm cells have been manufactured in the testes they pass up two long narrow canals known as the *vas deferens* to the prostate gland, where the seminal fluid is produced. Seminal fluid forms the greater part of the substance ejaculated by the male at the climax of sexual intercourse, and its purpose is to preserve and nourish the sperm, and provide a fluid medium in which they can move. The prostate lies just behind the bladder, and ducts lead from both these points into the urethra, or urinary passage. Although this passage is used for passing urine as well as semen, the two functions are never confused because a man cannot urinate when he has an erection.

In the forward part of the urethra there are some small glands known as Cowper's glands which secrete a thick slippery substance during sexual arousal. This substance has the dual purpose of counteracting the acidity of any residue of urine present in the urethra since this could be injurious to sperm, and at the same time providing a lubricant to facilitate sexual intercourse. Many men who notice its appearance on the glans of the penis during sexual arousal mistake it for a premature seepage of semen. Interestingly, this secretion occurs as a result of psychic as opposed to mechanical sexual stimulation. It may not occur at all during an act of masturbation, but a male who is psychically aroused, may find that his Cowper's glands have been busily secreting even though his penis has only just begun to stiffen.

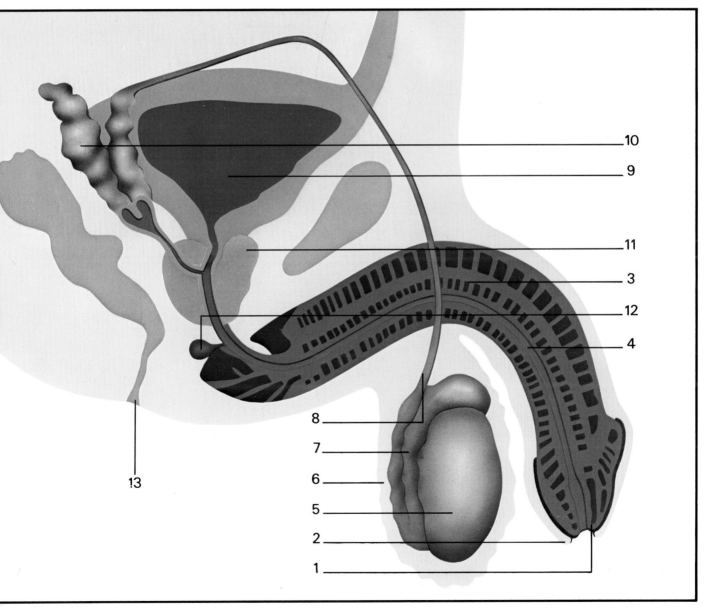

Masturbation

The practice of masturbation, which most human beings and many animals engage in at some time in their lives, has probably been the subject of more misunderstanding and moralizing than any other sexual practice. An 18th-century Papal medical adviser, who published a widely read and influential treatise on the subject, declared that masturbation resulted in melancholia, fits, blindness, catalepsy, impotence, indigestion, and idiocy. The idea that the practice is dangerous to health is still prevalent, even in modern times. Another 18th-century writer recommended masturbation as a remedy against the dangerous attractions of woman, an idea which might now be seen as a recommendation of the right action for the wrong reason.

Modern sexologists do strongly recommend masturbation. Masters and Johnson had some of their experimental subjects employ it as a means of achieving orgasm, and they recommend its use for therapeutic training in sexual response. Modern sex manuals such as *The Joy of Sex* enthusiastically urge its use as a component of normal sexual practice, both solo and heterosexual. It can be highly exciting to watch one's partner bring him- or herself to orgasm. In fact, some of the modern literature on the subject suggests that it may even be the non-masturbators who are abnormal.

We do consider, however, that the case for masturbation may have been overstated and that the emphasis on pleasuring and on mechanical sexual stimulation tends to obscure the fact that the ultimate sexual joy is a total bodily response of two individuals to each other. Purely genital sex, and particularly autogenital sex, is distinctly less fulfilling, and although there is no harm in the activity, it is unfortunate if a person's capacity for sexual response becomes fixated upon autoerotic stimulation. That it can do this is attested by a female correspondent to *Forum* magazine, who wrote with regard to her new husband: "He has masturbated excessively in the past, having previously been married to a woman who did not want much of a sexual relationship. Most of the time he cannot climax inside of me and has to masturbate, which upsets him, as he wants to complete the act of love naturally."

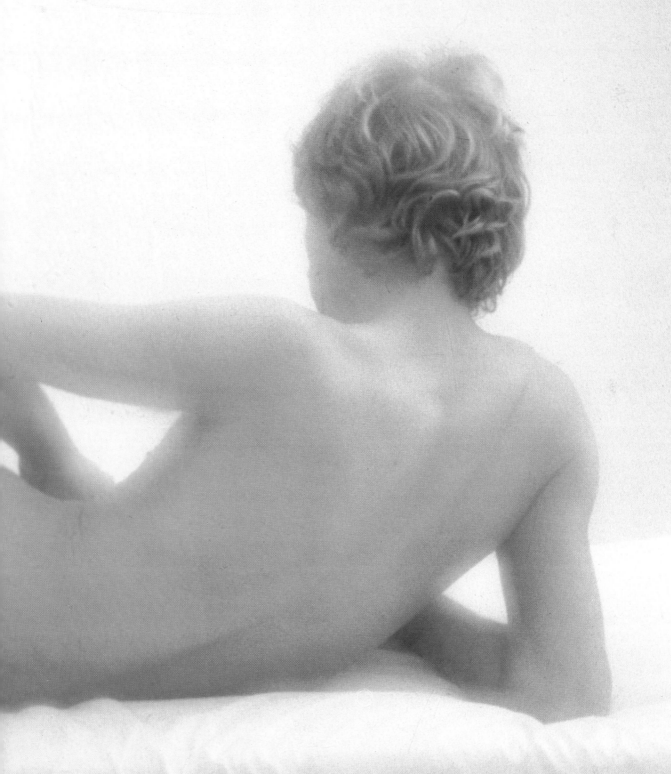

We are not suggesting that masturbatory fixation is common in adult males, but we think that the point that it can happen needs to be made. So does the point that masturbation is essentially a secondary mode of sexual satisfaction, one which provides sexual release but not sexual fulfillment. The revolution in attitude was certainly needed. The unhealthy attitude of the 19th century is well illustrated by the fact that a book titled *Spermatorrhea* sold out 12 editions in the 1880s. Among its recommendations were the use of special cages with spikes for boys to wear over their genitals at night, and even a device which caused a bell to ring in the parents' room if a boy had an erection. The practice of making boys sleep with tied hands was considered to be quite common, and even some adults supposedly adopted it voluntarily. It is hardly surprising, in such circumstances, that masturbation often resulted in feelings of guilt and shame. Modern sex studies and attitudes have changed that to some extent, and by establishing the fact that self-stimulation is a normal practice have made it unnecessary for anyone to feel ashamed or guilty about it.

Masters and Johnson found, however, that most of the men who participated in their research were of the opinion that what they called "excessive masturbation" was harmful. Their ideas of what was excessive varied greatly, but for each man it tended to mean a little more frequently than his own practice. The sexologists attributed the idea to a residual taboo which was groundless but needed to be treated tactfully, although perhaps it is possible that some men feel deep down that there is a point beyond which indulgence in masturbation becomes a fleeing from the woman, and, therefore, a denial of life. There may also be the fear that too much masturbation will spoil their chances of obtaining complete fulfillment with their partner. Masturbation certainly should not be associated with sexual immaturity or impropriety, but on the other hand, it should not be regarded as an alternative to sexual love. It should be recognized for what it is: a perfectly harmless secondary mode of sexual satisfaction available to everybody. There may be times when it is the only form of release possible, for example during a period of separation. It is a practice that can provide sexual release, but cannot give sexual fulfillment.

Male Fantasies

Right : watching a professional striptease artist is, for many men, the most acceptable way of fulfilling visual sex fantasies.

One pronounced difference between male and female sexuality is the male's greater dependence on psychological arousal. One way that this dependence manifests is in the male's tendency to fantasize about sex. Kinsey found that 90 percent of men, as compared with 50 percent of women, entertained erotic fantasies while they masturbated. He also found that male fantasies were quite frequently about unfulfilled or repressed desires, whereas the fantasies of women as a rule tended to be about experiences that they had enjoyed. The profusion of magazines on the market of literary and pictorial material that expresses and stimulates male sexual fantasies, and the lesser

amount of corresponding material catering to women, seems to indicate the differences between the sexes in this respect.

At the time when Kinsey and his fellow researchers were conducting their investigations the availability of material specifically designed for the stimulation of male sexual fantasies was very much more limited than it is today. Nevertheless, his findings are still relevant. Among his sample, 62 percent of men who had seen striptease shows had been sexually aroused, whereas only 14 percent of women admitted

Perhaps one of the strongest and most common male fantasies is to be made love to by several women simultaneously. It features prominently in dreams and erotic literature.

to such arousal. 77 percent of men admitted to having been aroused by graphic portrayals of sexual action, whereas only 32 percent of females had been, and many said that they were offended by such portrayals. Of the men who had had opportunities to observe other persons in sexual activity, a majority admitted that they had been aroused, but most women who had not been positively offended by the sight said that they had felt unmoved and indifferent. However, more women than men (48 percent as compared with 36 percent) said that they had been sexually aroused by scenes in commercial movies, but in the 1940s and early 50s, of course, sex tended to be implied rather than portrayed, and the commercial pornographic movie was unknown. Less than 50 percent of women said that they had been aroused by observing male genitalia, and many of the rest expressed surprise that any woman

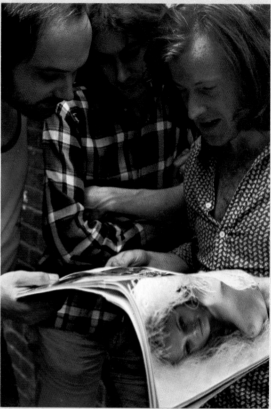

Above : magazines of nudes provide an inexpensive way of sexual arousal with no personal involvement.

Left : the sexually precocious schoolgirl is a fantasy of youth and innocence ready to be corrupted.

Above: "The Death of Sardanapalus" by Eugène Delacroix, 1827. The classical style of painting used historical and mythological events as an excuse to depict passionate, erotic and exotic fantasies.

could be so aroused, whereas the percentage of men who were aroused by observing female genitalia was well in the 90s.

Apart from illustrating the male's dependence on psychological stimuli, these findings showed that men are generally susceptible to sexual arousal by thinking about or looking at women with whom they are in no way acquainted, or even women in general, or by witnessing or contemplating depersonalized sexual activity. This may simply be a fact of male sexuality, and certain problems that sexual partners can have may be avoided if the woman can acknowledge and accept the fact.

Various explanations of the difference have been suggested: for instance, that the male sex drive is stronger than the female one, that women have stronger innate moral capacities, that the difference is attributable to the roles the sexes play in reproduction, or that the difference is due to physiological makeup. But there is no agreement about the matter. Sexologists all acknowledge that males are much more prone to general sexual fantasizing than females, but they differ in their opinions as to why this is so, and many of them frankly confess that they do not know. It is important to both sexes to accept the fact; to men so that they should not have feelings of guilt or thoughts that their love for their partner may be inadequate because they entertain erotic fantasies, and to women so that they will not feel repelled or betrayed if they discover that their partners enjoy erotic fantasies. Kinsey mentions cases of wives who had instituted divorce proceedings when they discovered that their husbands possessed pornographic pictures, and he considers such cases to be instances of how ignorance of basic facts about human sexuality can have tragic consequences.

The Four Phases

The normal male response in the sexual act is a series of phases. The four phases specified by Masters and Johnson, the arousal, the plateau, the orgasm, and the resolution phase, although they merge into each other imperceptibly, have quite distinct physiological and emotional aspects.

The first obvious sign of sexual arousal in a man is tumescence, the swelling and erection of the penis, although the lubricating secretion from the Cowper's glands may precede erection. Erection can occur quite quickly – the fastest recorded is three seconds – and it can even be triggered by thoughts or sights that leave no chance of full orgasmic release, sometimes in circumstances embarrassing for the man concerned. Few fully erect phalluses are completely upwardly vertical (about 8 or 10 percent according to Kinsey). The average position is just above the horizontal, and in about 15 to 20 percent of cases the angle of erection is about 45° above the horizontal. The degree of the angle tends to decline with age.

During the arousal phase muscular contractions draw the testicles up closer to the body. Another change, of which people are not generally aware, was observed in three-fifths of the men who participated in the Masters and Johnson research: the erection of the nipples. Also both voluntary and involuntary muscles throughout the body tense up, the pulse rate quickens and blood pressure rises, and in the case of one man in four a "sex flush" may spread over the body as it does with a majority of women.

This condition of arousal can last for a long time. Kinsey noted that with continued sexual stimulation "many a teenage male will maintain a continuous erection for several hours," although the average period for a man in his sexual prime is about one hour, and when a man reaches his late 60s it is only about seven minutes. C Hurana and W Lu, the authors of *The Ying-Yang* (1971), a book on sexual life in China, say that busy men would often spend hours each day with concubines and that "there

are many instances in both novels and court records, of papers being signed without the male member being withdrawn, and of urgent matters being discussed with callers to the accompaniment of occasional movements to insure that the erection was not lost." This suggests that the decline, with advancing years, in the capacity for maintaining arousal may not necessarily be as dramatic as Kinsey said. Certainly it would have to be low-keyed arousal, but even in normal lovemaking if the couple want to prolong their pleasure they may allow their excitement to escalate and decline several

The plateau phase of the man's sexual response is short relative to that of the woman. Shortly afterward he is ready for the thrusts of climax.

times before entering into the second phase, which Masters and Johnson called the "plateau."

The plateau is the immediate preliminary to orgasm, and of short duration. Once in the plateau phase, a man soon knows that there are only seconds left before he ejaculates. Changes that normally occur during the plateau phase are the full elevation of the testicles, their increasing in size by about 50 percent over their unaroused state, a further slight swelling of the ridge of the corona at the base of the glans of the penis, and in some cases a

deepening of the reddish-purple color of the glans. Breathing, blood pressure, and pulse rate all increase, and there is further tightening of muscles throughout the body, including in many cases involuntary contortions of the face muscles. The muscles of the rectum and buttocks contract particularly hard and some people deliberately tighten them in order to increase the tension. At this stage in the act of sexual intercourse, with the man's phallus located in his partner's vagina, his pelvic movements will become increasingly vigorous as he delivers his final thrusts before orgasm.

Male Orgasm

The sexual response of the man is much faster than that of a woman. Achieving mutual orgasm requires skillful manipulation by the woman as much as restraint on the part of the man.

The physiology of the male orgasm is complex. During the plateau phase of sexual activity semen accumulates in the tiny sacs known as the seminal vesicles, and when orgasm begins these sacs contract in order to discharge the semen into the urethral passage. The prostate gland also contracts and expels its fluids. In the urethra, there is a bulb just at the base of the penis which doubles or triples in size at this stage in order to receive these fluids. These internal contractions and expansions are experienced by the man as the onset of ejaculation and give him the delightful sensations of the first stage of orgasm.

He may feel that he would like to prolong this stage and his enjoyment of these sensations, but voluntary control is no longer possible and he reaches the peak of the orgasm, a series of rhythmic contractions of the urethral bulb and of the muscles of the penis itself which force the semen along the urethra and project it from the tip of the glans. These contractions are experienced as the very climax of the orgasm, and in a fully developed orgasm there may be from five to eight of them at intervals of four-fifths of a second. This is precisely the timing of the female's vaginal contractions in orgasm, so that when a man and a woman climax together his ejaculation is assisted by her contractions to project the semen as powerfully as possible toward its goal; a phenomenon which the psychiatrist Eric Berne has called "one of the wonders of evolution."

Unassisted by vaginal contractions, the semen may be propelled a considerable distance. Kinsey states that distances of 5 or 6 feet have been known, although in three-quarters of males the semen just exudes from the tip of the penis or travels a very short distance.

Ejaculation and orgasm are two quite distinct processes, and one may occur without the other. Preadolescent boys, whose glands are not yet producing seminal fluids, can experience orgasm; so can men who are no longer capable of ejaculation because they have had their prostate glands removed. A man who has several orgasms with short intervals between will not ejaculate in the later ones because he will have exhausted his supply of semen. In some men ejaculation occurs some seconds after orgasm, and in others it occurs without orgasm and they experience the release of their pent-up sexual tensions but not the culminating spasms and well-defined peak of sensation that constitute a full orgasm.

An Italian psychiatrist, Sandor Ferenczi, has proposed that the reason why men and women seek the experience of orgasm so obsessively is that it is a symbolic return to the womb. And when the French refer to orgasm as *le petit mort*, the little death, they imply the same desire. In the experience of orgasm, consciousness of self is obliterated. A man might have a sense of floating. The image of a vast and swelling ocean is often used by film makers to suggest the sense of the orgasmic experience. Ferenczi suggests that the womb itself represents the primordial sea, from which life originally emerged.

Wilhelm Reich took the theme of ego-obliteration further and said that in orgasm man finds his identification with cosmic processes. Alexander Lowen agrees, but also makes the point that although orgasm may at first be a "little death" it is also a rebirth: "Man is reborn through orgasm. If this is speaking figuratively, let us not forget that orgasm is often experienced as a re-birth. One feels renewed and refreshed through orgasm. The whole act of sex can be viewed for the man as a symbolic return to the womb and rebirth."

These ideas of the symbolic and transcendental significance of orgasm are attempts to express the meaning of the mystery and to explain why the experience is so sought-after and so satisfying. But its great satisfaction lies primarily in the way it confers a feeling of complete union with another who is profoundly loved.

Resolution

It has been said that the only time when human beings are completely sane is in the 10 minutes following orgasm. And the sense of fulfillment, of release of all tensions, of warmth, love and well-being that follows the complete orgasm, might well be described as constituting a state of higher sanity. When Shakespeare wrote in one of his sonnets that orgasm was "a joy perceived; enjoyed a very woe," and when the 2nd century Greek physician, Galen, penned his dictum, *post coitum tristitia* (after coitus, sadness), they may have been referring to failed or partial orgasms. As Kinsey has written: "There is neither regret nor conflict nor any tinge of sadness for most persons who have experienced orgasm. There is, on the contrary, a quiescence, a calm, a peace, a satisfaction with the world which, in the minds of many persons, is the most notable aspect of any kind of sexual activity."

The postcoital state is called by Masters and Johnson the "resolution" phase of sexual response. Its most obvious feature in a man is the rapid deflation of the penis. Generally, a man loses his erection quite soon after ejaculation. His organ does not immediately return to its completely unstimulated condition, however; it remains for some time slightly tumescent, but not stiff. If he leaves it inside his partner and they remain still it will eventually slip out.

Muscular contractions throughout the body are utterly relaxed in the resolution phase. Blood pressure, and pulse and breathing rate quickly return to normal, and all the physiological processes that took place in the arousal phase are reversed. The testicles descend again and the scrota relax. In some people sweating, particularly of the palms of the hands and the soles of the feet, occurs. In most, sensory perceptions are quite quickly reoriented. The outer world that was obliterated from consciousness moments before is suddenly present again. The sound of a telephone bell that was ringing but unheard throughout the plateau and orgasm phases may suddenly penetrate a person's awareness. Also, an awareness of subjective states often returns and many people feel hungry, thirsty or in need of a cigarette after orgasm. In others the sense of fulfillment and contentment soon leads into sleep.

A feature of the resolution phase which Masters and Johnson found only in the male was what they called the "refractory period." In this period a man is unable, at least for a time, to be sexually aroused again, and he may find continued sexual activity with his partner, even if she has not yet achieved orgasm, difficult.

The length of the refractory period varies greatly and is not a constant with individuals. On one occasion a man may be quite incapable of being aroused again for hours or even days, and on another he may be ready to start the whole process again after 5 or 10 minutes. His general state of health, the time of day, and his feelings for his partner, are some of many factors that could affect a man's ability to achieve orgasm again. In some cases the woman can arouse her man for a second encounter after a fairly short interval, and in other circumstances a man will find his penis becoming erect again and urging him on to further sexual activity without any prompting from his partner.

The question of how many orgasms a man can have in succession is often raised, and men given to sexual boasting often make remarkable claims, but facts are hard to ascertain. One young man in the Masters and Johnson study achieved three orgasms in 10 minutes. Out of a sample of 182 preadolescent boys studied by Kinsey 12 were able to achieve more than 10 orgasms in succession, though, of course, without ejaculation. As the diagram based on Kinsey's studies shows, a man's ability to reach orgasm more than once in a single session rapidly declines after his teens. But to equate this fact with a decline in sexuality is a mistake, just as in many areas it is a mistake to identify quality with quantity. A sense of total fulfillment can be achieved whether or not the encounter leads to sequential orgasms.

Impotence

Most men have experienced the failure to achieve erection. It is the reverse of the problem that Moravia's hero had with his "Federico Rex." In the previous pages we have described the phases of male sexual response under ideal conditions, but it does not always work like that and indeed sometimes it does not work at all. Sometimes a man may ardently desire a woman, only to find to their mutual chagrin at the crucial moment that his penis does not respond. He may even have had an erection and have passed through the arousal phase only to have his organ become flaccid again. This can be a very embarrassing experience, and even a traumatic one which may make a man think he is becoming impotent.

Sometimes the problem of the loss or lack of erection can be traced to the man's motivation, or a repressed inhibitory feeling of guilt. It may occur if he is more interested in making a conquest than in making love, if he has lied to get the woman to go to bed with him, if he is using her for his pleasure but basically has no regard for her, if he suddenly gets scared of the consequences of what he is doing, or feels guilty because he is cheating his wife or regular sexual partner.

There are many factors that can affect sexual performance and either suddenly turn a man off or make it impossible for him to get aroused however much he may think that he wants sex at the time. A man in that situation will often try fantasizing or get his partner to try to stimulate his organ in some way, but unfortunately such stratagems very rarely work.

The man who suddenly finds that he cannot perform may think that he is becoming impotent, particularly if he is unaware of the reason for his failure. The

actual anxiety about this may even make him impotent. Men ought to be aware that occasional failure, even when there is no obvious reason for it, is a common experience and should be accepted and not worried about too much.

There are two kinds of true impotence – an inability to achieve an erection and an inability to have an orgasm. There can be physical causes of erective impotence, such as hormonal disorders, genital diseases, surgery affecting the spinal cord or prostate gland, continual heavy indulgence in alcohol or drugs, or a long debilitating illness or a heart attack, although in some of these cases impotence is probably more psychological than physical. The man fears that the exertion may cause a relapse or has

resigned himself to the fact that he is well past his peak. But in 90 percent of cases impotence has no physical cause; it is entirely psychological. Masters and Johnson have distinguished four common psychological causes as a result of their studies of impotent males: the experience of sexual overtures from the mother in adolescence, religious restrictions and the sense of sin, homosexuality, and an experience of initial sexual failure, which in many cases occurred in an encounter with a prostitute which made the man feel that sex was a degrading activity.

Of the 32 men whom Masters and Johnson treated at the time, 19 suffered from impotence from one of these causes and the other 13 suffered for a variety of other psychological reasons. Orgastic as distinct from erective impotence may proceed from the same causes, or from other causes which we shall consider in Chapter 9.

Many people are confused about the difference between impotence, infertility, and sterility. Briefly, impotence is sexual inability, infertility is temporary inability to procreate, and sterility is permanent inability to procreate. An infertile or sterile man need not be affected sexually by his condition; it does not prevent him having an erection, ejaculating, or orgasm. Indeed, some men who choose to be sterile, and undergo a vasectomy, find their sex lives enhanced afterward. Infertility is generally due to failure to produce and ejaculate sperm in sufficient numbers, and may take the form of low sperm concentration in the semen, abnormal formation of the sperm that are produced, or inability of the sperm produced to keep moving for long enough to reach the ovum. The cause of infertility may be excessive heat around the testicles, general low health and vitality, prolonged sexual abstinence, exposure to radiation, or some illness, for instance mumps if it occurs in adulthood.

Fetishism

Consider the following description of a build-up to orgasm: "A mysterious change came over my feelings. I entered a plane of being where nothing mattered save the infusion of joy brewed within my body. What had begun as a delicious distension of my innermost roots became a glowing tingle which *now* had reached that state of absolute security, confidence, and reliance not found elsewhere in conscious life. With the deep hot sweetness thus established and well on its way to the ultimate convulsion, I felt I could slow down in order to prolong the glow."

Most readers, we imagine, will find nothing objectionable in that, and many would probably agree that it is a good description of what the initial stage of orgasm feels like. But now, examine your reaction when we disclose that the quotation is from Vladimir Nabokov's novel *Lolita* (1959) and describes the sensations of a middle-aged man, Humbert Humbert, as he cautiously masturbates by rubbing his phallus against the young girl Lolita. Probably most people consider pedophilia, or the use of children for sexual purposes, to be a perverted, disgusting and heinous practice. But does that make Nabokov's description obscene whereas it would not be so in the context of a heterosexual sex act with an adult? The point that Nabokov's novel makes is that it is not Humbert's sexual pleasure that is abnormal, but his means of securing it.

We cannot write about male sexuality without tackling the question of abnormal, deviant, or perverted sexuality. The word one chooses to call it is indicative of one's attitude to it. The enlightened modern attitude is that nothing is perverted if it is engaged in by consenting adults and does not injure anyone physically or psychologically. The law does not always take this attitude and in some places even oral or anal sex between husband and wife is a crime. This latter fact points up the difficulty of establishing any criteria of normality or perversion, for oral sex is enthusiastically recommended by most modern sex coun-

selors as a part of normal loveplay. Most people, however, would consider a person sexually aberrant if he required some kind of ritual, or special conditions before he could achieve orgasm, or if his sexuality could only be triggered by an inappropriate object.

Many sexologists feel that sexual deviation is a predominantly male phenomenon. Several reasons why this should be so have been suggested, and there is probably some truth in all of them in so far as they apply to different deviations. Kinsey associates the phenomenon with the male's dependence on psychological stimuli, his tendency to fantasize about sex and about women in general, and the fact that compared with the female he is "more easily conditioned by his sexual experience and by objects that were associated with those experiences." Havelock Ellis tried to explain some devia-

Above : commercialism caters for many of the common fetishes, such as uniforms, leather, bondage straps, nuns, and boots.

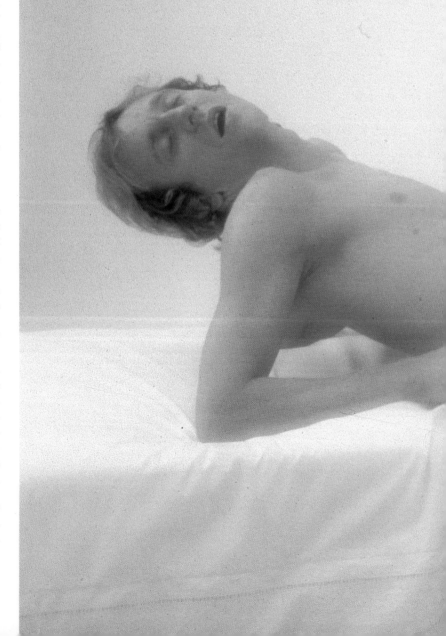

86

Below : whereas oral sex used to be viewed as a gross perversion or fetish, and still is in some quarters, many couples regard it simply as an expression of sexual love.

tions by pointing out that assertion of male power and dominance over the female was a feature of the primitive courtship of man the hunter and therefore deeply ingrained in male sexuality. The English author, Colin Wilson, in his *Origins of the Sexual Impulse*, has argued that there is a "need for more intense consciousness that dominates all human activity" and which is a generally ignored aspect of the sex drive, and has made an important distinction between two elements in abnormal sexuality, the "element of vitality striving to cut its own channel, and the element of degeneration making a last feeble effort to achieve 'alienness' through a new sensation."

There is a very thin dividing line between what is actually abnormal, in that it is a prerequisite of sexual satisfaction, and what may be termed unusual, but is not an essential component. This is particularly true of sadism and masochism, respectively the infliction and suffering of pain as a means of achieving sexual satisfaction. There is often an element of minor violence

and the enjoyment of it in basic human sexuality. Biting, scratching, and slapping are common components of healthy sex, and do not constitute true sado-masochistic behavior. Neither does bondage when used, as recommended by Alex Comfort, to heighten sexual tension. "Tying up your partners," writes Gillian Freeman in *The Undergrowth of Literature*, "and pretending to rape or tease them is a venerable and effective human sexual trick, and one of the few symbolic aggressions which women favor as much as men." The true sadist is not concerned with the sexual satisfaction of his partner, and therefore the partner does not necessarily need to be willing or a masochist. It is just that a masochist will put up with being physically or mentally abused more readily. Likewise masochists do not need sadists, and may inflict the pain themselves.

Sexual abnormality is a difficult thing to define, especially as it varies with time and place. Nabokov's Humbert Humbert would have been considered perfectly normal in those societies where young girls are married off before they reach puberty. As we have mentioned before, masturbation was once considered a perversion, and in some of the United States a request for sex in a position other than the missionary (man on top) constituted grounds for divorce.

Sexual Deviation

A 14-year-old boy was attracted by the 20-year-old daughter of a family that he was staying with. One evening he was lying on the floor in front of the fire when the girl wanted to get something from the mantelpiece and jokingly said she would have to stand on him to reach it. She raised her skirt a little and stretched out her foot over him. Excited by her teasing, the boy took her foot and put it on his penis. The girl then stepped on him with all her weight and he had an orgasm. Thereafter this became a game that they often played, and as the girl showed the symptoms of flushed cheeks, bright eyes and trembling lips, it appears that she also derived sexual pleasure from the practice. But when the boy grew up he had become so conditioned to obtaining his sexual satisfaction by being trodden on by a woman that he could not achieve orgasm in any other way.

This case, recounted by Magnus Hirschfeld in *Sexual Anomalies and Perversions* (1966), is typical of the numerous incidents in which male sexuality has become fixated on a particular mode of satisfaction by a first intense experience, usually in adolescence. This fixation often takes the form of a fetish, the focusing of erotic interest on an inanimate object or a part of the body that is not generally considered erotic. The young boy could have become a shoe fetishist or a foot fetishist, in which case in adulthood he might only have been able to achieve orgasm by holding or caressing a shoe or a foot while masturbating or having sexual intercourse.

It was a French psychologist, Alfred Binnet, who first studied fetishism. Considering the question why virtually every man does not become some kind of fetishist, since for all men the first orgasmic sexual experience must have certain strong associations, Binnet proposed that the experience only became traumatic in psychologically unstable individuals. Other psychologists have argued that it is a matter of degree, and that males are generally inclined to form powerful associations with factors they identify with a particularly

intense sexual experience, seeking these on future occasions in the hope of recapturing the intensity. A fetish only becomes aberrant when orgasm is impossible without it. Kinsey says that his data suggest that fetishists "are not rare in the population," and the correspondence columns of *Forum* magazine seem to confirm the fact. This means that many women must have to cope with the problem of having a sexual partner who has a fetish. Unless the fetish is repulsive or dangerous, a woman might try to be understanding and help her partner. Curing a man of his fetish is not often possible. Fetishes are very tenacious, but at least they are usually not physically harmful to the fetishist's partner.

Transvestism, says Kinsey, is the most striking illustration of the fact that males are more liable to be conditioned by psychological stimuli than females. The compulsive need of male transvestites to dress up in women's clothes sometimes develops out of a fetishistic attachment to certain items of clothing, or it may be that the man so dislikes other males and is so attracted to females that he wants to be identified with the latter. In some cases the cause is a result of the man's childhood: his mother wanted a girl and dressed him up in girls' clothing.

Whatever its cause, transvestism can create great distress both for the man and his partner. It is not generally understood that transvestites are not necessarily homosexuals. Nor do they cross-dress only for sex or depend on cross-dressing for orgasmic experience. Many married transvestites try to keep their habits a secret from their wives, but an eventual discovery will often wreck the marriage. Obviously the transvestite should inform his partner and try to get her to understand his condition before he marries her. It is a difficult condition to understand and make allowances for, however, and one can sympathize with the transvestite in love who does not want to risk ruining his relationship and hopes he will be able to keep his secret. On the other hand, some wives of transvestites see their husband's behavior as quite harmless, and even help him choose his female clothes.

Voyeurism is generally considered a sexual deviation but as the majority of men would respond to an opportunity to observe a naked female or sexual activity, and a considerable number would actively seek such opportunities it is doubtful whether

Above: black stockings and suspenders are a visual turn-on for many men. They become a fetish when their presence is a prerequisite for climax.

it can be called abnormal. It is, of course, a matter of degree. The "Peeping Tom" whose only mode of sexual satisfaction is masturbation while observing naked women or sexual activity is suffering from a general personality deficiency which prevents him from achieving any direct relationship with

Above : the voyeur obtains sexual satisfaction as a spectator because he is unable to have a direct relationship with a woman.

a woman. The same can be said for the male exhibitionist, who derives his tortured satisfaction from the shock created by exposing his genitals to women or children. The majority of exhibitionists are harmless, in that they are themselves terrified of direct sexual contact.

Medical Problems

Left : Akhenaton, king of Egypt from 1379 to 1362 BC, suffered from an endocrine deficiency. His statues show a very unmanly body with heavy hips, breasts, and a pronounced stoop. Surprisingly, he was not infertile, and fathered six daughters.

There are a number of congenital sexual defects, although fortunately they are very rare. Some people are born with genitals that are neither distinctly male nor distinctly female but intermediate between the two. When they reach puberty, hormonal activity might stimulate development of predominently male or female characteristics, and in some cases the sexuality of the person does not match his or her sexual anatomy. Surgery, combined with hormonal treatment, can sometimes establish unambiguous sexual characteristics and genital formation.

Another congenital defect is displaced outlet: the urethral outlet is not at the tip of the penis but on its upper or underside. The sufferer has problems with his aim when urinating, and in intercourse he may be unable to project his semen in the right direction to cause conception. The condition can, however, be corrected by surgery. The condition of undescended testicles, in which one or both testicles fail to descend from the abdominal canal into the scrotum, can also be surgically corrected.

There are other disorders that show themselves not at birth, but at puberty. Some people have genetic anomalies, or an abnormal number of sex chromosomes. The usual result is that their genitals fail to develop or they show anomalous sexual characteristics, such as the development of breasts in men. Other disorders that can appear at puberty are connected with failure of the glands to secrete the hormones that are responsible for normal sexual development.

There are conditions that can occur at any age which affect the scrotum or the penis. Varicocele is the development of varicose veins on the scrotum. As a result the testicles get too hot to produce sperm efficiently. They can also become too hot as a result of the excess accumulation of fluid in the scrotum, which can manifest as enlarged testicles; this condition can be treated by draining off the fluid.

Left : priapism takes it's name from Priapus, the Roman god of Gardens, and son of Dionysus and Aphrodite. He had an enlarged, deformed penis.

A condition which can be very distressing, particularly as it is inclined to evoke hilarity rather than sympathy in insensitive people, is known as priapism, after the Roman god Priapus. It is the nonsexual and prolonged erection of the penis. It may occur as a result of spinal injury or clotting of the prostate veins, or as a side-effect in epilepsy, leukemia, or drug abuse. A minor, but common form of priapism is the occurrence of a painfully hard erection during sleep; the pain can be sufficiently painful to wake the man. The condition is not accompanied by any sexual feelings, and neither intercourse nor masturbation can relieve it. Such experiences can be so recurrent as to cause severe loss of sleep, and they can be a cause of great anxiety, but generally the condition disappears after a time.

Below : a true hermaphrodite has external features of both sexes. Only one set is functional, however.

Skin disorders, such as ulcers or cold sores sometimes affect the penis. Warts may also form under the foreskin. These respond readily to medical treatment. There is also a condition known as phimosis, in which the foreskin is long, but its opening is small, so that it cannot be pulled back over the glans and corona. The condition may not be painful, but it should be corrected by circumcision because such a foreskin is prone to infection.

Some men have a penis which is bent, arched, or curved when erect. Sometimes the condition is congenital, due to the ligaments on one side being shorter. In later life it may develop as a result of the formation of inelastic tissue in the penis. Again this is a problem that can be surgically corrected.

The sex gland known as the prostate can be another source of trouble. In middle age, for some unknown reason, it can begin to enlarge and in some cases can get so big as to interfere with the flow of urine. When this happens, surgery is essential, otherwise death from urine poisoning can occur. It is important to stress that not all enlargements of the prostate are cancerous, although prostatic cancer kills more European and American males than any other cancer. The frequency of its occurrence, and the fact that it can easily be detected and treated in its early stages, are strong reasons for men having regular medical check-ups as they get older.

Prostitis, or inflammation of the prostate, can occur at any age. The cause is often a virus, but it can also be the result of excessive sexual stimulation without outlet, for instance if a man frequently masturbates and stops short of orgasm or practices Karezza, a form of prolonged intercourse which does not culminate in orgasm.

Venereal Disease

It cannot be denied that one of the most unpleasant consequences of the sexual revolution has been the tremendous increase of sexually transmitted diseases. In some parts of the world these have reached epidemic proportions.

The most common of the venereal diseases is infection by lice. The lice are generally known as "crabs," though the French have a more romantic name for them: *papillons d'amour*, or butterflies of love. They clasp onto the hair with their claws and pierce the skin to feed on blood. The symptoms are severe itching in the pubic area, and the lice are visible on close inspection. They are generally transmitted through sexual contact. Fortunately lice can be eliminated easily and quickly with a prescribed medicated ointment.

The incidence of the disease known as gonorrhea, or "clap", is said to be second only to that of the common cold. It is caused by bacteria which thrive in the warmth of the vagina, the rectum, or the urethra, and is invariably transmitted through sexual contact. A reason why it is so common may be that it is possible for a woman to have the disease for some time without being aware of the fact. In men the symptoms of gonorrhea generally appear two to seven days after infection. The first sign is a yellow-greenish discharge from the penis, which becomes thicker as the condition deteriorates. There is also a burning sensation in the urethra when the man urinates, and eventually the glans of the penis becomes red and swollen. The condition can be treated with antibiotics, though many strains are developing resistance to treatment. It is essential that the sufferer informs all his recent sexual contacts, and also abstains from sex until declared clear. If it goes untreated it can spread to the testicles, causing severe swelling, and to the prostate and the seminal vesicles. The reproductive organs can be

Below: historically, syphilis was supposed to have been introduced to Europe by Christopher Columbus' crew on their return from the New World.

Opposite page, below: before the introduction of suitable drug therapy in the early 20th century, mercury was the most effective substance available for the treatment of syphilis. It was, however, unpleasant, and in itself toxic. Syphilis was sometimes referred to as the Naples disease.

permanently damaged, and gonorrhea can also infect the joints.

A disease with symptoms very similar to those of gonorrhea is nonspecific urethritis, generally known as NSU. It is not known for certain whether it is caused by a bacterium. Some doctors believe that its cause may simply be a reaction of the penis to the biochemical environment of the vagina, and that some male and female organs may unfortunately be biochemically incompatible.

Sufferers of gonorrhea and NSU normally seek treatment in the early stages of the disease because of considerable pain incurred. This is not the case with the most serious of the venereal diseases, syphilis, sometimes referred to as the "pox." Syphilis is caused by a microorganism called a spirochaete. In its early stages syphilis is susceptible to simple treatment, but if undetected the disease later invades the entire body, resulting eventually in insanity, paralysis, or death.

In the primary stage, the first symptom can occur between nine days and three months after contact with an infected per-

son; the average period is three weeks. A chancre, a hard sore or spot, appears at the point of contact, which in the male is generally on the penis, but in homosexuals may also occur internally, in the rectum. A chancre may also appear in the mouth transmitted through oral sex. The sore may

Above : direct genital contact is not the only source of syphilis infection. If the primary sore is on the mouth the disease can be transmitted by kissing.

L'ESPAIGNOL AFFLIGÉ DV MAL DE NAPLES.

ooze a little colorless fluid, but it is not painful, and eventually disappears. A few weeks later the secondary stage appears, by which time the microorganism will have spread through the body. Headaches, sickness, fever, loss of appetite, mouth ulcers and other body sores, hair loss, and a dark red rash on various parts of the body, particularly the arms and legs, are some of the possible symptoms. This stage, too, can pass without treatment after anything between three weeks and nine months, and then the syphilis enters what is known as the latent phase, which can last for many years. When the disease eventually erupts again it is virulent and can attack the heart, causing swelling and death. It can also attack the nervous system, causing meningitis, brain tumors, cerebral haemorrhage, blindness, deafness, paralysis, and insanity.

Although a genital sore is the first symptom of syphilis, not all such sores are syphilitic. The venereal disease known as soft chancre can appear up to two weeks

Above : the French artist Henri Toulouse-Lautrec (left) contracted syphilis in 1888 from a Montmartre prostitute called Rosa la Rouge.

Right : Ivan IV (1530–1584), the Russian Tsar who became known as Ivan the Terrible. He ruled wisely (by contemporary standards) in the first years of his reign, but by 1564 was showing signs of cerebral syphilis. Because of an imagined conspiracy he initiated mass executions and torture, and the terror lasted for the rest of his reign. He killed his heir in a fit of rage, and his surviving son showed signs of congenital syphilis.

after intercourse in the form of a red lump on the penis which, unlike the syphilitic chancre, exudes pus after a few days and then becomes a painful ulcer. Another disease is *granuloma inguinale*, which produces red sores around the genitals that are painless at first, but then turn ulcerous. The disease known as *lymphogranuloma venereum* is more serious. It appears in the form of a

Left : Paul Ehrlich, the German scientist who in 1910 developed Salvarsan 606, the first drug effective against syphilis.

Below : free VD clinic testing at the Venereal Diseases Exhibition, Museum of the City of New York.

genital blister which soon bursts and disappears, leaving a scar, but this is only the primary stage of a disease which left untreated can lead to gross swelling of the penis and scrotum, and in some cases can result in death.

If everyone sought treatment as soon as they noticed the slightest sign of genital infection, venereal disease could probably be completely eradicated. Early treatment is simple, cheap and effective, and it is tragic that ignorance, shame, guilt, and perhaps in some cases the superstition that the disease is a just punishment for sexual misconduct, have enabled sexually transmitted diseases to become so widespread in the world today.

Chapter 4
The Female Partner

Men have always fantasized about the sexually
uninhibited woman. She was a rare find in a society
which permitted a woman to have sex only in the
context of her biological role – that of bearing
children. But the concept of female sexuality, and
the ideas that women actually enjoy sex and derive
fulfillment from it, have only comparatively
recently been accepted in our culture. Incredible
as it may seem, the days when a mother's advice to
her daughter on her wedding night might have
been to "close her eyes and do her duty" are not
all that long past, though hopefully they are gone
for good. Gone too are the days when the wedding
night was supposed to be a woman's night of
initiation into the mysteries of sex. The majority
of today's women happily acknowledge the fact
that they have sexual feelings and desires, but not
all of them understand that their sexuality is
different from the man's, a misunderstanding
shared by many men. The resulting conflict can
be easily avoided if a few basic facts are appreciated

The Changing Role of Women

It is undeniable that there has been a sexual revolution in modern times and today's woman is freer than her mother or grandmother were to express her sexuality. However, many women have reached the conclusion that the so-called sexual revolution is a sham because they have found

Below: Venus of Willendorf, earth mother and bringer of life. This paleolithic figurine is one of the earliest known representations of a human being.

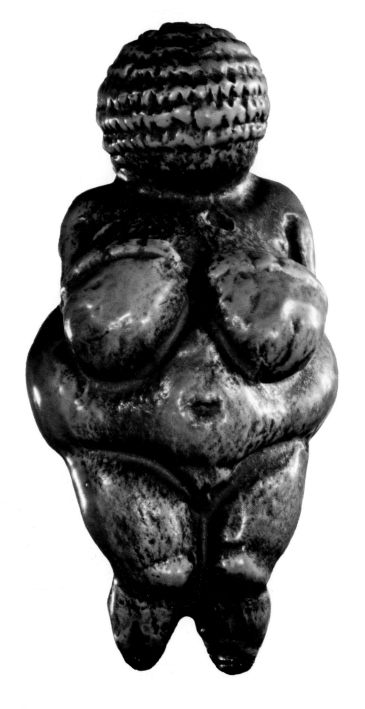

that their freedom is not supposed to extend to being able to choose *not* to express their sexuality. As one of the contributors to *The Hite Report* on female sexuality put it, the sexual revolution "was about *male* liberation, women being shared property instead of private property," and it "liberated a vast amount of masculine bestiality and hostility and exploitiveness."

Sexual freedom for women required independence, and freedom of choice, and so in the wake of the sexual revolution came the women's liberation movement, which was basically a campaign for liberation from male sexual dominance and from the role of sexual object imposed upon women by culture, convention, and society. Women were saying that they would express their sexuality however and whenever they liked, and not at all if they chose not to, and that no man, not even a husband, had a right to cast them in a sexual role.

Unfortunately, like all campaigning movements, it was sometimes misrepresented by the media. Tritely described as "women's lib," it became synonymous to many with such newsworthy items as bra-burning and man-haters, women who des-

pised men and claimed that women could get along very well without them, even in their sex lives. The vaginal orgasm, these women said, was a myth that served the cause of male dominance: the only real female orgasm came from clitoral stimulation, for which no male member was necessary. Not that any men were available, for according to this publicity, they were all suffering from an epidemic of impotence and exhaustion, brought on by the awakened sexual voracity of their partners.

Exposed to these presentations and to the social pressures of the sexual revolution, especially the need to be seen actively participating, it is not surprising that many young women are confused about their sexuality. Also, the sex education they received at school or from their parents would probably have given them an understanding of their sexual anatomy and physiology to prepare them for menstruation and childbirth. It would not have dealt with sexuality itself, the emotional and psychological changes that accompany the process of sexual maturation, or the feelings involved in sexual experience. Furthermore, the contradictory views of sexual pleasure for its

Above: the Women's Liberation Movement united women of all nations, creed and color in a common struggle.

Right: Women's Liberation march, Trafalgar Square, London, 1971. The objects carried – tailor's dummy, aprons, shopping bags – symbolized the enslaving nature of the woman's traditional role.

own sake and sex as part of a loving experience only make the confusion worse.

"Man's love," wrote Byron, "is of man's life, a thing apart; 'tis woman's whole existence." Many women dispute that idea.

99

The American journalist Marion Meade, for instance, in her book titled *Bitching*, quotes Byron and comments "They finally came up with a full-time occupation for us: loving. Not just loving any old body but loving one of them, clearly an example of the most blatant self-interest." Probably for many women there is some truth in Byron's words. It is not only that a woman's roles as a mother and wife demand a continual giving of love, but also that many women cannot easily separate sex from love. Sex for them is not a detached activity but requires total emotional involvement. Of course, the same is true for many men. But in a culture which still equates emotion with weakness, many would not admit it, even to themselves.

Generally speaking, the woman reaches her sexual peak in her late 20s, whereas the man reaches his in his teens, and this difference, of course, can cause some problems. Statistical studies show that the average age at which girls in Western societies have intercourse for the first time has significantly diminished in the last two decades. However, this does not necessarily imply that the age of reaching sexual maturity has done likewise. It is probably broadly true to say that girls toy with sex before they understand it because they want love, whereas boys profess love before they understand it because they want sex. As the American sociologist Jessie Bernard

Above : as the idea of education for women became more acceptable, so many were able to obtain power and influence, initially by working behind the scenes. Learned women in the 17th and 18th centuries held salons to further art and culture.

Center : Golda Meir, Prime Minister of Israel from 1969 to 1974, showed that political ability is not confined to the male sex.

has written: "Most young women in their teens, although suffused with sexuality, are not driven by strong genital urges. If they had their way, most would not feel compelled to seek genital sex relations. . . They want caresses, tenderness, sexual appreciation; they want the interested attention of men; the relationships they want are playful, meaningful, but biologically superficial."

Many a young girl who has suffered from being called a "prick teaser" or accused of being frigid or having unhealthy inhibitions about sex would surely be relieved to read such words. The sexual revolution has changed many prevailing attitudes to sex, but it is doubtful that it has brought about a change in female sexuality itself. If her grandmother had problems with repressing her urges, today's young woman sometimes has the problem of being expected to manifest urges that she does not feel, or to adopt so-called sexually liberated attitudes that she finds in conflict with her natural feelings. But at least these are problems that she can find help with today, for one of the benefits to emerge from the sexual revolution is that information on the formerly taboo subject of female sexuality, as distinct from the process of reproduction, is now readily accessible. There are also in existence many groups which have been formed for women of all ages to discuss their problems and obtain advice and support.

Breasts

In female babies the vagina is located in the same frontal position as the penis in the male. When a girl reaches puberty her pelvis enlarges and tilts backward, which results in a shift of the vagina to a position between her thighs. This is one of the changes in her body which prepares her for sex and reproduction.

Right : the classic pinup breast, accentuated by folding the arms.

Left : the model in this early 1920s pinup appears, by comparison, flat-chested.

The most conspicuous change is in the development of her breasts. Despite the fact that it is physiologically just an organ for feeding babies, the female breast is made a subject of such obsession in our culture that in many girls breast development causes embarrassment or anxiety. A girl who develops late, or who develops only small breasts, may have feelings of inferiority or inadequacy compared with her more busty contemporaries, and the well-endowed girl in her early teens may find that her breasts draw unwanted atten-

Above : corsetry, illustrated here in a fashion drawing, 1909, was most effective in altering the body's shape.

tion from boys and men. Because breasts are composed mainly of fatty tissue, dieting can often reduce their size. In extreme cases a surgical operation called mammoplasty can be performed. Plastic surgery can likewise increase the size of the breasts. Bust-enlarging creams and other proprietary treatments, on the other hand, should be avoided. Not only are their claims generally unsubstantiated, but they can also be dangerous. In any case breast size has nothing to do with a woman's sexuality, or with her capacity to function as a woman, and has only little to do with her initial attractiveness to the opposite sex.

Breasts come in quite a variety of shapes and sizes, and although the firm outstanding type with its upward-curved undercarriage is popular with the advertising media, it is not that common. Nor should it be seen as the desired norm. The gamine figure with fairly small breasts is far more typical in young women. Also the shapes and sizes of breasts are often more apparent than real, and are produced by clothing, especially the brassiere, in response to fashion. In the 1920s, when boyish figures were in fashion, more substantially endowed women wore clothes that flattened their breasts. In the 1950s fashion dictated that breasts were supposed to be conical.

Nipples and areolae also vary considerably. The areola is the pigmented area around the nipple, its shade and size differing greatly between women. It is often surrounded by fine hairs. Nipples may be protuberant or short, or in some cases retracted into the areola. However, their prominence can be affected by a number of factors, by cold for example, and especially by the attentions of a lover.

What Makes a Woman?

As there are normal variations in breast size and shape, so there are differences in the vulva. This is the anatomical term for woman's external genital organs. The internal organs – the uterus or womb, the ovaries and Fallopian tubes – are there strictly for procreative purposes as distinct from sexual pleasure.

There is more ignorance about the structure of the vulva than about the corresponding male organs. Yet it is through stimulation of her external genitalia that the woman primarily experiences sexual desire and arousal.

Viewed sideways on, the vulva looks rather like a mouth. It has two sets of lips, an outer one (labia majora) and an inner set (labia minora) which closes on the opening of the vagina. Above the vagina is the opening of the urinary tract and above this is a small and extremely sensitive organ, the clitoris. The head of the clitoris is particularly sensitive and responsive to stimulation during sexual intercourse or masturbation.

In young girls and virgins the outer lips touch, protecting the parts between them. The outer lips end in a triangular bone, poetically called the mons veneris or mount of Venus, which becomes covered with hair during puberty.

The inner lips are small and narrow and

The female sex organs.

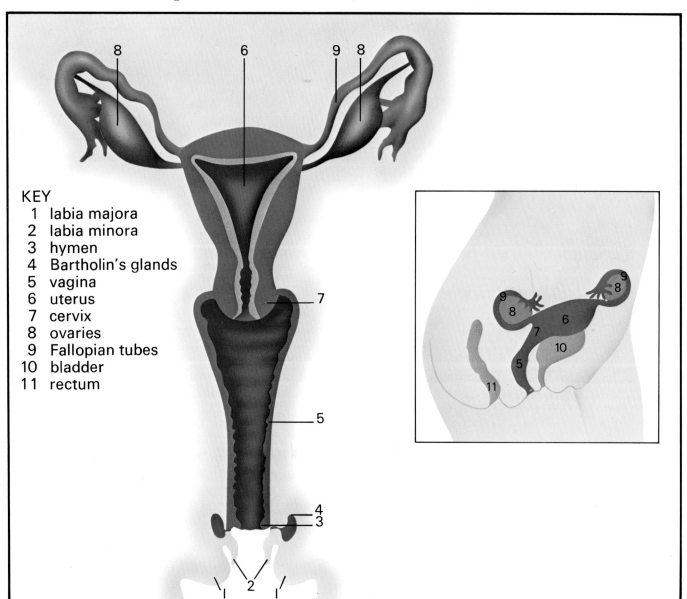

KEY
1 labia majora
2 labia minora
3 hymen
4 Bartholin's glands
5 vagina
6 uterus
7 cervix
8 ovaries
9 Fallopian tubes
10 bladder
11 rectum

form a ridge just below the clitoris. They are rich in highly sensitive nerve endings, and their stimulation can produce intense sexual feelings.

Connecting the internal and external organs is a passage known as the vagina. The word comes from the Latin for "sheath," which aptly describes its important function. Although the average vagina is about 3 inches long, it has a great capacity for expansion and when required can accept a phallus of any length and width. The walls are lined with soft corrugated tissue. The lower part of the womb projects down into the upper end of the vagina and can be felt as a little hard knob of tissue. This is known as the cervix, the neck of the womb, and although there is some doubt as to whether or not it is sensitive, it plays an important function during intercourse in stimulating the tip of the penis.

Just inside the vagina is the hymen, sometimes known as the maidenhead or virgin's veil. In young girls this thin, half-moon-shaped membrane partially closes the vaginal canal. There is a great deal of misunderstanding about the hymen. It is not, for example, an impenetrable barrier, but porous to allow menstrual blood to flow through. It used to be regarded as proof of virginity, and in many cultures still is, but this is not necessarily true. Occasionally, during strenuous exercise or sports such as horseback-riding or cycling, it can be torn. Usually it is ruptured during a woman's first sexual experience. There are cases of extremely tough hymens impossible to penetrate during intercourse, but these can be removed by a minor surgical operation.

The position of intercourse determines which areas of the vulva are stimulated.

1 Male superior positions

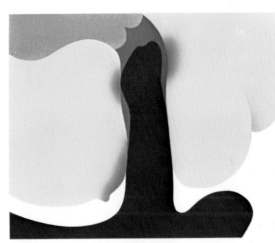

2 Female superior positions

3 The X position

4 Rear entry positions

Sexual Response

The American sex researchers Masters and Johnson have distinguished four phases of sexual response, changes which affect the woman emotionally and physically. These are arousal or excitement, the plateau phase, orgasm, and resolution.

The first physical sign of sexual response in a woman is that the vagina secretes a lubricating fluid. This secretion can occur involuntarily and without any particular emotional stimulus, and like a man's inopportune tumescence it can be embarrassing. Generally it is a sign that she is physiologically ready for sex and if she is emotionally willing to continue, it marks the start of a series of physical changes.

During arousal an important change also occurs in the clitoris – it becomes erect and swollen. Masters and Johnson observed that direct touching of the clitoris is not necessary to stimulate it. Like the penis, the clitoris is responsive to psychological stimuli, even to an erotic train of thought. It can also be excited by kissing or caressing the breasts, back, or neck. The breasts themselves enlarge, the muscles tighten, and the nipples become erect.

Toward the end of the excitement phase the outer lips of the vagina open up and are displaced upward toward the clitoris; the inner lips also swell during this phase.

In the vagina the blood vessels become engorged and the walls swell, while more lubricating fluid is secreted. But it is not just the sexual organs that respond – the whole body of the woman takes part in the gradual process of sexual stimulation. The muscles become tense, the pulse speeds up, and blood pressure rises. Often a "sex flush" spreads up over the abdomen to the breasts.

In what Masters and Johnson call the "plateau" phase – the brief period before actual climax, breathing and pulse rate become faster, the blood pressure rises even more and the vaginal walls fill with blood and swell so that the outer part of the passage closes tightly on the penis. At this stage the clitoris becomes hypersensitive and further stimulation is not desirable; in fact it can cause pain or discomfort. The vaginal lips change color, becoming scarlet or wine-red. The woman's senses tend to blank out so that she may be unaware of noise or pain, as her physical and mental tensions crescendo and she enters the third stage of sexual response – the orgasm.

The Four Phases

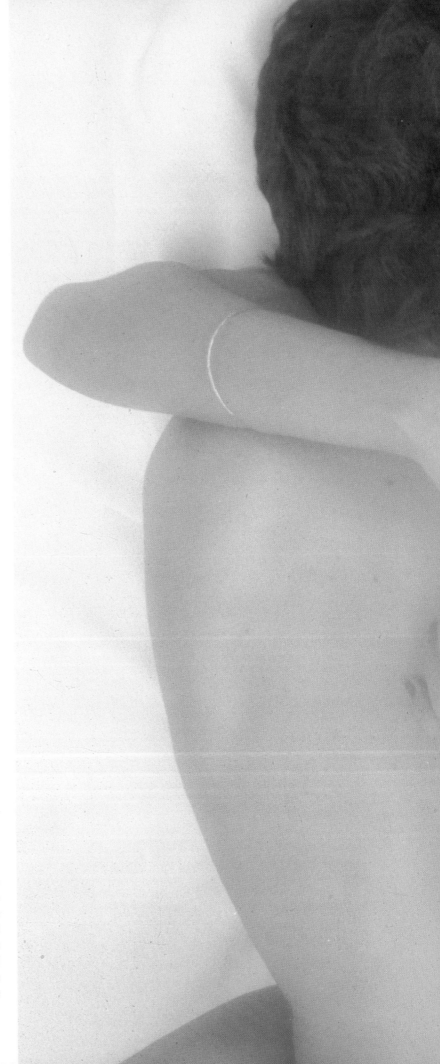

In their laboratory studies Masters and Johnson noted that the most important feature in the orgasmic pattern is a series of muscular contractions of the orgasmic "platform" – the engorged tissues surrounding the outer part of the vagina.

The first contractions occur at intervals of four-fifths of a second. They then become longer and their intensity gradually begins to fade. In a mild orgasm only three to five contractions occur, whereas if the orgasm is intense there may be between eight and 12 contractions. In a particularly intense orgasm 25 contractions were recorded over 43 seconds.

The beginning of orgasm occurs at the same time as an initial spasm of the "platform," followed by a rythmical series of contractions over a period of a few seconds. Together with these contractions, the womb also contracts rhythmically, the spasms beginning at the upper end and moving in waves down to the cervix. These contractions are similar, but not as strong as those which take place during childbirth, and the more intense the orgasm, the more severe they are.

Other muscles, such as those around the anus, may also contract. Powerful contractions can also take place in arms, thighs, back, and pelvis. The hands and feet often clench. Women are generally unaware of these muscular contractions during orgasm and afterward may experience the types of aches and pains that follow vigorous exercise.

Orgasm is the shortest of the four phases. The "resolution" phase follows immediately, starting with the relaxation of muscle tension throughout the body, and the release of blood from the engorged vessels. First the swollen areolae surrounding the nipples return to normal size. The sexual flush disappears and instead the woman may perspire. Within 5 to 10 seconds the clitoris returns to its normal position above the pubic bone, but it takes about 10 minutes for it to return to normal size. The orgasmic "platform" relaxes. The "ballooning" of the vagina decreases, the

uterus begins to shrink, and the cervix returns to its normal position. Pulse and breathing rates slow down and blood pressure drops to normal. This series of changes can take up to half an hour before a woman is completely restored to an un-stimulated condition.

The release of tension brings a feeling of peace and contentment if the lover continues to be tender, instead of just turning over and going to sleep, or getting up briskly and attending to other matters.

However, there is no rule which decrees that lovemaking must be terminated at this stage. If the woman is willing, she can be re-excited to further orgasms.

The Female Orgasm

The acknowledgement of the female orgasm is one of the most important aspects of the sexual revolution. It used to be widely believed that the majority of women accepted sex as a necessary evil in their roles of dutiful wives and mothers. Only a certain number were thought to have actually enjoyed it – those who made a living out of it or had dubious reputations. The changes in attitude affected both sexes. Women were freed to make love without feeling guilty or sinful. Many went further and demanded orgasm as a right – the natural consequence of an event in which they had participated on equal terms. For men the emphasis in sexual intercourse shifted. They were expected to provide sexual fulfillment as well as obtain it for themselves. They were also relieved of the guilt of imposing a supposedly unpleasant task on their loved one. Many discovered that the giving of pleasure gratifies the provider as well as the receiver.

Orgasm in males is of course essential to procreation, as climax brings about the release of sperm. In women this is not so. Her ovaries are not involved in the climactic response and achieving an orgasm has no effect on her fertility at the point of union. It was once believed that during orgasm the vagina sucked up the sperm, and increased the chances of conception but this has since been disproved.

In all studies and reports of the findings of sexologists, the majority of women say that there are different kinds of orgasm, and that orgasms can vary both in intensity and duration from a superficial pleasurable spasm lasting a few seconds to a deep intense series of spasms leading to a peak of the ultimate pleasure that the human body is capable of. These variations may depend on many factors such as time, place, and atmosphere. There are also powerful emotional and psychological influences.

A woman can achieve orgasm in a number of ways.

1. If she is in a state of aroused desire a passionate kiss from her lover can produce an orgasm.

2. Some women are said to be able to achieve orgasm by fantasizing alone. Kinsey found that 2 percent of his subjects reported this, but Masters and Johnson did not record one single case.

3. Kinsey also found that about 8 percent of his subjects has experienced nocturnal dream orgasms.

4. Breast stimulation can produce orgasm.

5. A woman can orgasm by touching her sexual organs, especially the clitoris, or

having someone else touch them.

6. She can achieve orgasm through sexual intercourse with a man's penis inside her vagina.

But unless the love element is present and an intense physical experience is combined with the satisfaction of emotional fulfillment, it would appear (according to Masters' and Johnson's findings) that women are able to have much more pronounced orgasms by masturbating alone.

Kinsey found that only 37 percent of women, as compared with 68 percent of men, had experienced their first orgasm through masturbation. The other main

Above : "The Ecstasy of St Theresa" by Gianlorenzo Bernini. Orgasm is similar to religious ecstasy in that both produce a heightened state in the body and psyche. Some even see religious ecstasy as a manifestation of repressed sexuality.

sources were nocturnal dreams (5 percent; in males 13 percent), petting (18 percent; in males 5 percent), and intercourse (30 percent; in males 11 percent). The higher percentage of females who experienced their first orgasm through intercourse is a factor that correlates with the fact that females are generally older than males when they have their first orgasm. Kinsey found that in the early adolescent years, when 95 percent of boys were having two or three orgasms a weeks, only 22 percent of girls had experienced orgasm. In the late teens, 99 percent of males but only

Below : for many women masturbation is the only means by which they can achieve an orgasm.

53 percent of females were having orgasms. And whereas all the men in the Kinsey study had experienced orgasm by the time they married, there were some 36 percent of women who had not. Nine percent of the Kinsey sample had not experienced orgasm by the age of 35, and probably would never do so, although many of these experienced erotic arousal. Some of the unfortunate 9 percent were married women who had had intercourse regularly. Among other married women success in achieving orgasm in marital sex correlated with their premarital experience: those who had had premarital experience, whether through masturbation, petting, or intercourse, were more success-ful in reaching orgasm with their husbands. And the longer a woman was married, the better her chances became of experiencing orgasm. In the first year of marriage, Kinsey found, 63 percent of intercourse resulted in orgasm, whereas by the 20th year 85 percent did.

These are some of the statistics that sexology has established about the female orgasm. Let us now consider the facts in the controversial debate about the clitoral orgasm versus the vaginal orgasm.

The Myth of the Vaginal Orgasm

It was Freud who first drew the distinction between the clitoral and the vaginal orgasm. He maintained that the clitoris was the organ of female sexual pleasure in the years of immaturity, and that maturity in woman consisted in a shift in primary sexuality from the clitoris to the vagina. Clitoral satisfaction was regarded by Freud and his followers as basically masculine sexuality, the clitoris being considered a substitute penis. They maintained that it was only through the experience of vaginal orgasm that a female reached peak satisfaction.

The trouble with these views was that they deprecated a type of sexual experience that the majority of women enjoyed, and also caused anxiety for many women. Kinsey wrote that his research team knew of thousands of women who had "been much disturbed by their failure to accomplish the biologic impossibility" of transforming "clitoral responses" into "vaginal responses." He pointed out that most of a woman's body is involved in the experience of orgasm, and that many women have extensive spasms or convulsions throughout their bodies, including intense vaginal contractions, in orgasm. "No question of 'maturity' seems to be involved," he wrote, "and there is no evidence that the vagina responds in orgasm as a separate organ and apart from the total body."

From the findings of both Masters and Johnson and *The Hite Report* it would seem that the majority of women who experience orgasm speak of clitoral stimulation. In *The Hite Report* 87 percent of the women who said they like vaginal penetrations almost always gave the reason that it was a marvelous way to express love and create a feeling of intimacy and closeness with their loved one.

It would appear that only a minority of women experience vaginal orgasm. In fact in Kinsey's report, of the women tested in a gynecological study, less than 14 percent felt any sensation in the vagina. The reason for this is physiological. In most females the walls of the vagina are devoid of nerve endings, and only in a few were such sensitive patches found in the vaginal walls.

The women who were able to experience both a clitoral and a vaginal orgasm said that there is little comparison between the two and that the clitoral orgasm alone is not a fully satisfactory experience. In his book *Love and Orgasm* (1976), the Reichian psychoanalyst Alexander Lowen quotes remarks made by several patients who were able to describe the difference. Here are two examples:

"The clitoral orgasm is felt on the surface of the vagina like a trickle of sweet pleasure. There is no satisfying release. The vaginal orgasm is like the opening of a dam which floods my body with pleasure and leaves me with a feeling of deep release and satisfaction. There is no comparison. The next day after a clitoral orgasm, I am hot, disturbed. After the other, I wake up in one piece, relaxed."

"The vaginal orgasm I experience, limited as it may be, fills me with a sense of completeness, of satisfaction. I have a feeling of being full – filled up. The clitoral orgasm is more high level in excitement but leaves me with no after-effect of completion. I feel I could have one clitoral orgasm right after another."

These testimonials support the theory that there is a distinct difference between the clitoral and vaginal orgasm. The clitoris may be the more sensitive area, but to claim that the clitoral orgasm is the only type of sexual satisfaction of which a woman is capable is to take a rather mechanical view of sex. It implies that orgasm proceeds from tactile stimulation, and ignores the fact that the sexual act is fundamentally an expression of feelings and emotions. We consider that Lowen came nearest to stating the truth about this controversial matter when he wrote: "The vaginal orgasm differs from the clitoral orgasm in that it is a total body response of love. It is, therefore, relatively independent of any single part of the body, either the clitoris or the vagina, but it is dependent on the total bodily feeling of contact, intimacy, and fusion with another person."

Multiple Orgasm

The whole idea of women being able to achieve multiple orgasms has become, as one of Shere Hite's interviewees put it, a "competitive" matter, a kind of "Orgasmic Olympics." As a result many women have begun to see themselves as sexual underachievers. The question whether a woman can, during one session of lovemaking, achieve multiple orgasms, has over the years been almost as contentious as the debate about the clitoral versus the vaginal orgasm. Kinsey found that 14 percent of the women in his study reported having multiple orgasms. Other writers have expressed uncertainty as to the truth of the reports of female subjects who claim to have multiple orgasms. Instead, they have suggested that their experiences were, as one sexologist put it, "nonterminative" minor climaxes rather than complete orgasms.

Masters and Johnson, however, established beyond doubt that many women are capable of the experience and they actually observed multiple orgasms, and measured the accompanying physiological spasms and contractions. They wrote: "If a female who is capable of having orgasm regularly is properly stimulated within a short period after her first climax, she will in most instances be capable of having a second, third, fourth and even fifth or sixth orgasm before she is fully satiated. In contrast with the male's usual inability to have more than one orgasm in a short period, many females, especially when clitorally stimulated, can regularly have five or six full orgasms within a matter of a few minutes."

Masters and Johnson also found that the orgasms did not diminish in intensity – on the contrary many of the reports proved that the orgasms after the first or second often increased in intensity.

But many women are not aware that they have this potential. Among those who do, there are also some women who are reticent and reluctant to seek more than one orgasm, even if they need it, after their partner has had his. According to Shere Hite: "There often seemed to be an unconscious rejection of the possibility of having more than one orgasm." The following quotations from *The Hite Report* illustrate this point:

"It's hard for me to indicate that I want more than one orgasm . . . ."

"I've never felt that I couldn't come again with pleasure, but am hesitant to pursue it."

"I think I could have several if he used his tongue, but I don't like to make him stay down there that long."

". . . On the rare occasions in the past when I came with my partner, two or three was 'enough': i.e. I couldn't admit to the man I wanted more. . ."

"With men I never have more than one. I have the feeling . . . they aren't really interested in your capacity for many orgasms."

Some women are confused about what exactly constitutes multiple orgasms:

"I'm not sure whether I have one long orgasm or several shorter ones."

". . . My orgasms are usually so prolonged that I wonder if they may represent 'multiple orgasm.' I don't know how many I'm capable of."

Hite makes a distinction between the multiple orgasm and the sequential orgasm, and writes: "Multiple orgasms, which are much rarer, are several orgasms with no break in-between. Sequential orgasms can be continued indefinitely . . . but *you must wait a few minutes after each orgasm, until you feel* the return of the focus of sensation."

The differences between the types of orgasm different women experience seems to account for the statements made by some women that after the first orgasm they can have as many as five or six following. But others said they could not have more than one orgasm as their clitoral area became too sensitive to touch. Or again that one deep orgasm was satisfying enough.

So from all the facts we must conclude that although many women are *physiologically* capable of multiple orgasm, and some clearly enjoy the experience, many find that emotionally and psychologically one is enough, and others that the sensitivity of the clitoris after one prevents them being stimulated into having further orgasms.

The Importance of Orgasm

How important is it for a woman to experience orgasm? Kinsey states that "it cannot be emphasized too often that orgasm cannot be taken as the sole criterion for determining the degree of satisfaction which a female may derive from sexual activity." He points out that although many married women never responded to the point of orgasm, their marriages had remained happy because of the wife's satisfaction in not only being able to give pleasure to her husband but also in the social and emotional security of family life.

But this is only part of the truth. As Kinsey goes on to point out, clinical data confirm that the persistent failure of a woman to reach orgasm can seriously damage her relationship. The woman becomes disappointed because of her inability to achieve what she believes she should. This disappointment develops into a feeling of inadequacy or inferiority which reflects on all other aspect of her relationship with the man, and indeed with men in general where there is any sexual element implied.

The failure of his lover to achieve orgasm is naturally a disappointment to a sensitive and emotional man. It can lead to his also developing a feeling of inferiority which will result in friction and discord.

So, even if orgasm is not the sole criterion of satisfaction for a woman, it is very important, both for her personally and for her relationship. To illustrate this point, here are some descriptions culled from *The Hite Report*:

"Orgasm feels great! Like a combination of intense pleasurable sensations plus an ecstatic frenzy of love, energy and emotion all mixed together."

"Orgasms are a renewal of all my senses — an awakening of life, spring, refreshing, sparkling, exciting, and the complete relief of everyday boredom."

"They make me feel incredibly happy, everything on the way to orgasm is heavenly. An orgasm cancels out all rage and longing for at least 48 hours, and the day an orgasm bores me, I think I'll commit suicide."

"A marvelous happiness, comparable to no other."

"Orgasm. The most fantastic sensation I've ever experienced."

"At best, an organ-moving cataclysm: my ovaries, uterus, breasts, and brain become one singing dark pulsating sea of the most exquisite feeling."

One woman said: "Whoever said that orgasm wasn't important for a woman was undoubtedly a man."

But it appears that the pressures of the sexual revolution have had some unfortunate repercussions. A lot of women feel that if they do not always have or demand full sexual satisfaction, they are somehow failures.

"Yes, I must have orgasm. Otherwise I feel I'm not a real person. . ."

"I would enjoy sex with no orgasm at times, if I felt other people weren't so uptight about it and if the reasons were my own. . ."

"I'm afraid that new partners will think I'm weird and not as sexy as other women if I don't have orgasms. . ."

"I wish orgasms didn't exist. Then maybe sex would be fun."

"I don't think orgasms are that important; the literature has given women another burden. But I'm ashamed to admit, because of the myth, I feel 'good' having an orgasm — like I'm a *real woman*! Arrgh. . ."

On the other hand, not having an orgasm with a man is frustrating to a lot of women who feel cheated knowing he has had one.

". . .Without orgasm I feel robbed."

Left : sex should not be gauged in terms of productivity output. There are no norms to fulfill.

Right : the most satisfactory sexual relationships occur when there is trust and emotional security. Often it is a lack of mutual trust that prevents a woman from relaxing and "losing control."

"Having sex without an orgasm makes me feel I was along for the ride, but why? (except when I'm really emotionally involved)."

This last statement in parenthesis brings us to what is surely the most important point of all – emotional involvement. "*So what about love?*" was the title of a delicate and sensitive play by English playwright Leonard Webb. And so what about it? As Alexander Lowen writes in *Love and Orgasm*: "The great importance of the sexual function for human happiness requires that it be studied in terms of its emotional significance and not as a mechanical or physiological act of release or discharge."

Many modern writers on sex give the impression that the orgasm is a treasure that lovers should earnestly seek, a kind of trophy they can win, or a gift they can confer. And yet perhaps it should be regarded rather as something that happens in the context of human loving, and to be enjoyed when it does happen. If it does not always happen, or does not always happen for both partners simultaneously, it is not a problem.

Masturbation

When Kinsey conducted his survey he found that 62 percent of women admitted to having masturbated at some time in their lives. When Shere Hite conducted her research 25 years later 82 percent said they had done so. The difference may be indicative of the differences in social attitudes toward female sexuality and of the fact that more women today consider the self-induced orgasm as just one means of normal sexual outlet available to them. Shere Hite says that society has now accepted that females enjoy sex when it consists of giving pleasure to men, but does not yet acknowledge a woman's right to enjoy her own body in any way she wishes, and she argues that masturbation is "a cause for celebration, because it is such an easy source of orgasms for most women." The journalist Marion Meade goes further. She quotes with approval a woman who said, "Who wants men? I could do a better job than most men I know," and she quips: "When a woman masturbates, she's guaranteed to be in bed with a person she likes."

We have discussed masturbation in the previous chapter on male sexuality, and what we said about the practice of male masturbation applies equally to the female. It is a mode of sexual release but not of sexual fulfillment, and it *is* normal and is *not* reprehensible. Nor is it, as the Freudians maintain, a sign of immaturity, that is, unless it is the only sexual outlet sought by an adult in circumstances when others would be available.

Kinsey found that quite a few females in his sample not only had not practiced masturbation but did not even realize that it was possible for a woman, although they knew that men did it. Kinsey also found that women tended to start masturbation at a later age. A greater proportion of women than men had discovered it in their 20s and 30s, and in some cases even later in life, which indicated both a lesser dependence on the practice and also that women were not prepared to discuss their sexual experiences as openly as men. Among these women who had masturbated, there was also a smaller proportion (relative to the male sample) who did so regularly throughout their lives or for long periods. Kinsey found that with women there tended to be long discontinuities in the practice, and he estimated that in any one year only about 20 percent of women were masturbating as compared with 75 percent of single men and 30 percent of married men. The frequency of the practice with women also showed a greater variation than with males, ranging from once or twice a year to quite regular sessions producing multiple orgasms. Another interesting fact that emerged from the Kinsey studies was that among adolescent girls there was a striking correlation between educational level and the use of masturbation as a sexual outlet. Only 52 percent of the lower educated masturbated, whereas 90 percent of the

higher educated did, and the lower group often considered it physically harmful, morally wrong, or both. Members of the higher educated group, on the other hand, were less often in conflict over the physical outcome or moral aspects of their masturbation.

As far as the actual technique is concerned, Kinsey wrote, "females may choose from a longer list of techniques than men ordinarily utilize. He distinguished six different methods, combinations of which were normally used by women in their masturbatory practices. Stimulation of the clitoris and the inner vaginal lips, with rhythmic strokes of one or two fingers, was by far the most popular method. Rubbing the outer lips and the entire genital area was another. Crossing the legs and exerting regular and rhythmic thigh pressure was a third. Lying down on the back or stomach and developing muscular and nervous tensions throughout the body by stimulating coital movements was another. A fifth was stimulating the nipples, and the sixth was vaginal penetration with the fingers or with some object. Only 20 percent of the females had ever practiced vaginal penetration, and of these the majority had only made an insertion into the vestibule of the vagina and not along its length. Men tended to think that deep vaginal penetration must be the main way that females obtained satisfaction in masturbation, but Kinsey said that this was a misconception based "upon their conceit as to the importance of the male genitalia in coitus."

Kinsey's data also suggested that premarital masturbation contributed to a wo-man's capacity to respond sexually in her marriage. Many young married women did not experience orgasms, and this often caused problems in the marriage. Of those who had this difficulty three out of four had not learned how to masturbate to the point of orgasm.

Several of Shere Hite's interviewees also made this point: that masturbation was a learning experience that had a beneficial effect on their heterosexual sex lives. "How can you love or satisfy someone else if you can't satisfy youself?" one of them asked. On the other hand, the 1975 study showed that very many women, even though they masturbate, are not entirely happy that they do so. Some even despised themselves for the practice, others still had guilt feelings about it, and many made a distinction between enjoying it physically but not psychologically. "There is a feeling of foolishness attached to the act," one said; and another, "I always feel cheap and dirty afterwards." Some had overcome feelings of guilt about masturbating and learned to enjoy it, while others regarded it simply as an uncomplicated way to experience pure joy.

Female Fantasies

One of the great works of modern literature, James Joyce's *Ulysses*, was banned as an obscene book for many years, largely because of its superb final chapter in which Molly Bloom lies in bed fantasizing about sex. The modern revolution in attitudes to sex had hardly begun when *Ulysses* was published (1922) and to suggest that women entertained and enjoyed sexual fantasies was considered by many to be an infamous slur upon the "gentle sex."

Nowadays we know better, and we are able to appreciate James Joyce's marvelous artistic insight. Not only did he show that women do fantasize but he also demonstrated that they do so differently from men. Their fantasies tend to be based more on their actual experience than on repressed or unfulfilled desires. Molly Bloom does drift into contemplations of what it would be like to give herself to anonymous sailors on the docks, but most of her fantasies are re-enactments of scenes from her past sexual life with her husband Leopold, or

her lover Blazes Boylan.

This would appear to confirm Kinsey's finding that female masturbatory fantasies "were usually in accord with the overt experience of the individual." Kinsey does make the point, however, that men are much more dependent on fantasy and psychological stimuli for their sexual arousal than women, and his statistics seem to confirm the fact, as does the commercial success of selling male sexual fantasies in the form of movies and "girlie" magazines. "We have nearly no cases of females utilizing erotic books or pictures as sources of stimulation during masturbation," Kinsey wrote. But some women would disagree about their susceptibility to such forms of arousal. To quote one example: "I know that they say women aren't turned on by visual stimuli; I think it's untrue. *It's another unexplored area where women are*

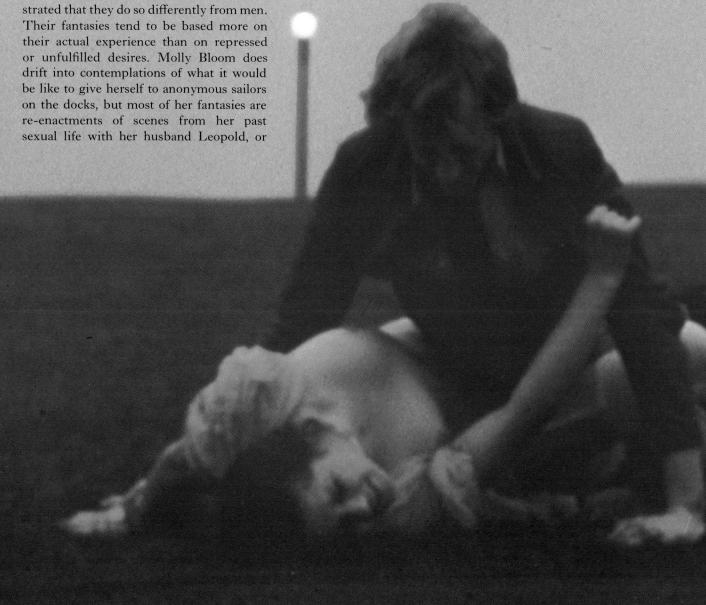

silent or ashamed. I am very aroused by hard-core pornography. If I see a picture, for instance, of a black man and a white woman, I'm ready for sex almost immediately."

The sentence we have italicized raises the important question of whether women have always been entirely frank with sexologists about the sensitive subject of their private fantasies. Have the statistics been falsified by women's inhibitions and secretiveness? Kinsey found that there were 2 or 3 percent of females in his sample "who were psychologically stimulated by a greater variety of factors, and more intensely stimulated than any of the males in the sample," and who could actually reach orgasm by fantasy alone without any physical stimulation. The question is, is that 2 or 3 percent too low an estimate?

When the American journalist and writer Nancy Friday advertised in British and American newspapers requesting material for a study of women's sexual fantasies, she had a flood of replies. She followed up more than 400 of them with interviews, and in 1975 published *My Secret Garden: Women's Sexual Fantasies*. The book is an eyeopener, for some of the fantasies are as elaborate and remote from normal experience as any male's.

Nancy Friday identifies a number of principal themes that are recurrent in female sexual fantasies, and gives some examples of each.

Anonymity. Linda fantasized that at a hair salon she was in a reclining chair with a facial mask on. There was a silk curtain from ceiling to floor which fell across her and the other women lined up in the salon so that the lower parts of their bodies were on the other side of it, where a group of strapping young men were employed to perform acts of cunnilingus on them.

The Audience. Celeste fantasized that she was lying naked on a gynecologist's stirrup table with her legs spread out, and that the table was on a revolving platform in a huge stadium filled with men who were clamoring with desire for her. Then she was wheeled by uniformed ushers into a room where her husband Charlie was waiting with an immense phallus upon which, silently and apparently emotionlessly he impaled her.

Rape. Dinah fantasized that she went into a chemist's shop to buy a tube of contraceptive cream, and a number of men present locked the shop door and said she should try the cream out. They stripped her and squeezed the cream into her vagina and anus and then raped her, at one time three of them having their penises simultaneously in her vagina, anus, and mouth.

Below : the most powerful element in the female rape fantasy is that the woman is so desired by the man that he is prepared to go to any lengths to make love to her. The crucial difference between the fantasy and the reality is that in the former the woman desires the man and she ultimately wants to be taken while in the latter she most certainly does not.

Other Women. Christine fantasized that she was in a steam bath where the steam was so thick that she could scarcely see. She reclined on one of the tiled seats, closed her eyes and began fondling her genitals. But she became aware that there was another woman present, and in shame lay back and pulled her towel up over her face. She felt the woman's hand stroke her thighs and gently part them. Gently, slowly, and expertly, the woman began to work with her mouth on Christine's genitals until she reached an intense orgasm.

The Thrill of the Forbidden. Emma fantasized that she was at a party where they played a game of sardines. She found an empty room at the top of the house and hid under a bed, and soon a man in the group she hardly knew joined her. In the dark they began to make love wildly and without inhibition. People kept calling her name, and she heard the voice of her boyfriend Larry the sound of which excited her to do "incredible things" to the stranger. Her build-up to orgasm was paced by the sound of Larry's approaching footsteps, and her orgasm came just before he discovered them.

These, then, are some of the female fantasies from Nancy Friday's book. Some of the other principal themes she illustrates are: pain and masochism, domination, the sexuality of terror, transformamation (imagining oneself as a different woman), incest, animal contacts, black men, young boys, and prostitution. The study certainly illustrates that some women do fantasize vividly. But as the data were obtained through advertisements and not through the statistical study of a random sample of the female population we still do not know whether such fantasies are typical of more than the 2 or 3 percent of women who are greater and more responsive fantasists than the men of Kinsey's sample.

The Deviant Woman

When we discussed deviant sexuality in the previous chapter, we said that it was a predominantly male phenomenon. This is particularly true of the deviations described there, sadism, fetishism, and transvestism. It is generally true that a far greater proportion of men than of women have "special tastes" or are dependent on unusual circumstances for orgasmic experience, but there are some abnormal sexual practices that a sufficient number of females engage in to warrant a mention in a discussion of female sexuality.

Obviously, when a deviant man's taste requires a woman's cooperation, that woman has to be something out of the ordinary. Most women would consider the prostitute who offers chastisement to be sexually abnormal, but on the other hand there is an acknowledged rule of fidelity among such professional females and their mates according to which no services rendered to a client constitute an infidelity provided the female does not have an orgasm. Professional services have to exist for the sadomasochist, presumably because there are not enough women of complementary tastes and inclinations but there undoubtedly are some females who are truly masochistic in the sense that they need chastisement in order to achieve orgasm. For instance, one woman wrote to the Hegelers, the Swedish sex counsellors, as follows: "When I got married, my husband soon found out the best way to make me satisfied. I get a thorough spanking from him at regular intervals, and now and again I have a

violent orgasm right in the middle of it." The correspondent attributed her preference to the frequent beatings her father had given her when she was a child, and the Hegelers found that when the subject was brought up a surprising number of other females wrote confessing to similar experience and tastes.

Males and females alike have an element of exhibitionism in their sexual make-up, so it is difficult to determine a precise point where exhibitionism becomes abnormal. Many females deliberately dress in a manner with which to arouse males and obviously enjoy displaying their sexuality in their mode of dress, but we know of no female equivalent to the male exhibitionist who exposes his genitals to strangers. However, women who do have similar tendencies might be able to manifest them in other ways.

One of Nancy Friday's correspondents, an actress, recounts how she got a part in a stage production that required her to be nearly nude on stage and very realistically to simulate making love with a man. She was very nervous at first, but said after playing the part a few times: "I found I was looking forward to it. My nipples would become tight and erect. It was a surprisingly seductive feeling, one I enjoyed. I began wearing tighter and tighter blouses, filmier ones, more see-through, so that the audience could see the excitement I felt right down – or up – to my nipples."

The interesting point about this is that the actress had no idea that she would have these feelings before she got the stage part. It makes one wonder what proportion of women would find they had the same feelings once they had overcome their inhibitions.

Probably the most surprising, and for many people shocking, of the disclosures in Kinsey's report was that it was not as uncommon as they would have thought for people to have had sexual contacts with animals. His data indicated that 8 percent of the male population and 3.6 percent of the female population of the United States had had such contacts. Among the women, three-quarters of the contacts had been with domestic dogs, and had mostly taken the form of manipulating the animal's genitals; 21 percent had induced the dog to lick their genitals and a considerable proportion of these had thus attained orgasm, and in a few cases the women had actually had coitus with the animal.

However, there are no reliable statistics on bestiality in private circumstances, especially as in many countries it is considered a criminal offense. Adolescent girls have occasionally been reported to derive erotic excitement from masturbating horses, and one *Forum* correspondent reported how the pleasure she had experienced as an adolescent from frequently manipulating a stallion's phallus had made her subsequently consider a man's organ as a puny thing incapable of giving her any satisfaction. She preferred to think of horses and masturbate.

The only exclusively female sexual abnormality that language recognizes is nymphomania. The compulsive pursuit of sex with a succession of males more or less indiscriminately chosen is still seen as abnormal in many societies, but it is not deviant in the sense of being the nymphomaniac's only satisfying way of achieving orgasm. In fact the true nymphomaniac's problem is precisely that she is nonorgasmic, and so she copulates with one man after another in the vain hope of finding the one who can give her an orgasm.

The highly sexed woman who enjoys orgasms and does not much mind who gives them to her can be described as promiscuous, but should not be confused with the true nymphomaniac.

Exhibitionism plays an important part in the performance of a striptease. The sexual satisfaction derived by the performer stems from the arousing effect she has on the audience.

Medical Problems

Above: reception desk at VD clinic. Any suspicion of VD should be checked out and treated immediately. The procedure is not embarrassing as VD clinics treat patients in privacy and strict confidence.

Disorders and infections of the sexual organs cause more anxiety and tension than almost any other kind of illness or malfunction. Quite apart from the natural shyness and embarrassment most people experience in consulting a doctor about such disorders, the stigma of being considered "unclean" prevents many sufferers from seeking treatment. Unfortunately, most of these diseases do not go away; worse still, in the case of infections, they can be passed on to other sexual partners. So treatment should be sought at the first sign of trouble – and any contacts notified.

In women one of the first signs of trouble is an abnormal vaginal discharge. Most discharges are normal vaginal secretions. They include menstrual blood and a thin, clear mucus from the cervix, which increases during the middle of the menstrual cycle. There is also a colorless fluid which "sweats" through the vaginal walls, and which is usually unnoticeable except in pregnancy and sexual excitement. During intense sexual arousal there is a slight secretion from the Bartholin glands at the opening of the vagina. This is often milky, and has only a very slight odor if any; it is slippery to touch and keeps the vagina moist and clean. Dead tissue sloughed off from the vaginal walls also forms part of normal vaginal secretion.

Abnormal discharges, on the other hand, involve irritation, an unusual color, or unpleasant smell. The irritation can be an itch, soreness, or a burning sensation in the vagina, vulva or upper parts of the thighs. Disorders may be caused by inadequate vaginal hygiene, irritation from chemicals such as vaginal deodorants and contraceptive foams, or by infection. Often they are caused by infections picked up through sexual contact.

The most common vaginal infection is trichomoniasis, caused by a microorganism called *Trichomonas vaginalis*. It is usually, but not always, caught through sexual contact. Its symptoms are a white, green-yellow or greyish discharge with a noticeable odor, red sores on the vaginal walls, pain during intercourse, and itching. The bladder may also become infected. If not treated in time it can spread to the Fallopian tubes and cause infertility. To avoid reinfection, the patient's sex partner should be treated simultaneously.

Candidiasis is caused by a yeast in the vagina. The resulting vaginal discharge is thick, white, and frothy, with a yeasty smell. There may also be severe itching, soreness, and pain when urinating. Yeast infections are not necessarily sexually transmitted. A large number of people carry the yeast without any symptoms, but under certain conditions it can flare up. These include taking the Pill, pregnancy, diabetes, anemia, or just general ill health.

Other infections which cause discharges are nonspecific vaginitis (NSV), which is really a name for any vaginal infection that cannot be attributed to a known microorganism, and *hemophilis vaginalis*, which has symptoms similar to those of trichomoniasis but requires different treatment. Any woman who has recurrent trouble with such infections even though she is scrupulous in her genital hygiene should check that her sexual partner takes similar care. Men can act as carriers of many infections without actually suffering from them.

Vaginismus is the name for a female genital malfunction which is not an infection, but which can cause lovers the most acute embarrassment. It is a spasmic, tight contraction of the muscles at the entrance of the vagina. It makes penetration during intercourse impossible, and if it occurs while the woman is being penetrated the penis can sometimes be so tightly gripped that the couple have to be taken to hospital for medical attention before they can be separated. The cause of the condition is psychological, usually the result of an early traumatic experience, a deep-rooted fear of or distaste for sex. It can be cured by psychotherapy.

Dyspareunia is the general name for painful intercourse, and it can have a variety of causes. The woman may have small and unsuspected lesions in her genital region or a congenital malformation which she does not know about. These can be treated surgically. In postmenopausal women dyspareunia often occurs due to a reduction of vaginal lubrication. It can be counteracted by hormone treatment. If intercourse is painful in any way and for any reason, a woman should always have her condition medically diagnosed.

Cystitis, the so-called "honeymoon disease" is not a disease of the sexual organs, but an inflammation of the bladder resulting in frequent and painful passing of water (and sometimes of blood). It is caused by the passage of a particular bacterium from the anus to the opening of the bladder, invariably during sex.

The symptoms and treatment of the venereal or sexually transmitted diseases common to both partners are discussed in the corresponding section in the previous chapter on male sexuality. The descriptions apply to males and females alike, but women have a disadvantage in that the symptoms are often internal and may go unnoticed.

Right : hygiene is important but it must be remembered that venereal diseases are no respecters of cleanliness.

Chapter 5
Techniques of Sex

The more liberal attitudes toward sex in recent years caused an immense demand for more information about the subject. Not only were there misconceptions to be cleared up, but it was also widely acknowledged that in sex, as in many other human activities, there is scope for variety. As a result, men and women wanted ideas and information on what had been almost a taboo subject. In the late 1960s manuals of sex technique became bestsellers. Of course, manuals of sexual technique were not new to the West. The most famous of these, the *Kama Sutra* was written sometime between 400 and 100 AD, and first appeared in English in 1883. It was as much a document on the social conditions of its time as a guidebook to sex, and although highly entertaining, its value to 20th-century couples was somewhat limited. Many of the positions required an expertise in yoga beyond the ability of most Westerners. Contemporary sexual manuals are more suited to the Western way of life. They are evidence that an interest in sex beyond its reproductive role is no longer considered sinful or degenerate. They also recognize the fact that women have an equal role to play in lovemaking, because most sexual techniques require both partners to participate actively. Some may shock us while others hold few surprises, but like this chapter they all have the same basic message – sex is fun.

Sexual Foreplay

The best known of the Western sex manuals, Dr Alex Comfort's *The Joy of Sex,* is subtitled *A Gourmet Guide to Lovemaking.* The analogy between sex and cookery is an extremely appropriate one. Both are forms of art requiring sensitivity, skill, imagination, and inventiveness, and in both cases should be performed with love and care. Likewise they both improve with time if the willingness is present. But just as one rarely wants to exist on a diet of *haute cuisine,* so sexual techniques serve to embellish and bring variety to everyday sex life. Comfort himself makes this point: "But still the main course is loving, unselfconscious intercourse. . . ." So while a staple diet is essential, variety is just as important if the palate is not to get jaded.

The permutations of lovemaking appear to be endless. The *Kama Sutra* and the *Perfumed Garden* list hundreds of methods, many of which differ only very slightly in their positioning of a single limb. G Legman, author of *Oragenitalism,* a modern sex manual, used a computer to arrive at his stunning figure of 3780. If all this suggests that lovemaking has been reduced to a

performance of sexual gymnastics or athletics, it should be stated that no sex manual can ever claim to teach love. For sexual expertise is not synonymous with good lovemaking, and the sexual technician is not necessarily a good lover.

There are several essential components in good lovemaking which no amount of sexual expertise alone will produce. These include compatibility between the partners; a similar degree of commitment which is understood by both; confidence in oneself, which ultimately produces confidence in the partner; sensitivity to one's partner's moods and reactions. Maturity (which is not the same as age) is also an important factor; a loving relationship involves responsibilities and a mature lover does not shirk them.

That notorious lover Casanova always maintained that he genuinely liked women. This is an important point because many people use lovemaking as their field of battle against the opposite sex. Egotism and a desire for conquest have no place in love, and no amount of sexual experience can compensate for their presence. Like-

wise, a repertoire of interesting sexual techniques acquired through a long series of relationships is also irrelevant if that is all that the lover has learned from his or her experiences.

So what place have sexual techniques in lovemaking? Well, firstly they introduce change and variety, and prevent sexual intercourse from becoming a routine, itself a potential destructive factor in any relationship. They encourage lovers to discuss and experiment, and so release any inhibitions. They present lovers with ideas and suggestions that may not have occurred to them before. After all, certain techniques will suit some couples more than others, depending on their relative sizes, their agility, state of health, degree of privacy, sensitivity and, of course, inclination.

A list of sexual techniques should be treated as a series of recipes. One is not expected to try them all, and some will undoubtedly be failures, but everyone should try at least a few.

Many lovers do get through life without running through all the refinements of eroticism, and there is much to be said for

the gradual enlargement of the repertoire of love by personal discovery. The discovery of oragenital sex at age 50 may be as exciting as the discovery of how to use the tongue in kissing at 17, and may bring new life to a marriage. But few relationships are continuously exploratory; passion does get spent, inhibitions do harden, and routine does creep in, and knowledge of the techniques of sex can help in such circumstances. Man and woman are, in many ways, a mystery each to the other, but how each functions sexually, how the other obtains his or her optimum sexual joy, should not be mysteries, for knowledge of these secrets is the key to lasting sexual happiness.

The most important elements of sexual foreplay are knowing your partner's sexually sensitive areas – erogenous zones – and how to stimulate them agreeably and progressively and without causing pain. During the arousal phase of sexual intercourse each partner stimulates the other alternately or simultaneously. If they are sensitive to each other's needs and can interpret the other's reactions, the pace of their arousal will keep more or less parallel and they will have a chance of attaining the plateau and orgasm phases together.

Men tend to be more genitally centered in their sexual stimulation needs than women, and often do not realize that the whole of a woman's body, as arousal progresses, becomes an erogenous zone. Direct and initial assault upon the primary erogenous zones, the breasts and genital area, will not bring her to climax unless she is already aroused. In fact, it would most likely have the opposite effect. Kissing, stroking and nibbling are the overtures to arousal, and initially a man should direct

his attention to the secondary erogenous zones, the face, neck, arms, back, base of the spine and buttocks. The mouth, of course, is particularly sensitive, and mouth kisses can escalate from the gentle teasing brush of lips to deep penetration.

Many people underestimate the importance of words in sexual foreplay. Expressions of admiration, wonder, and delight in the woman's body, and of feelings of tenderness and love for her, contribute greatly to her arousal. With many (but not all) women, expletives, in their erotic as opposed to insulting context, also have a powerful erotic effect. Loving sex is a union, and words can cement it. Talking, too, can bring an element of fun into foreplay, and can thus help dispel inhibitions and create a mood of relaxation. In this age of sexual outspokenness it is sometimes forgotten that most women do have inhibitions, shynesses, and maybe doubts about themselves, and there is nothing like loving words and admiration to overcome these.

No man will need to be told to pay attention to a woman's breasts, for as both literature and the advertising industry testify, these female assets have an unfailing fascination for the male. Breasts are highly sensitive glands, easily hurt or bruised. Cupping, gently squeezing, pressing together, and of course kissing them, are activities that both partners find highly erotic. When a man turns his attention specifically to the nipples he needs to do so with extra delicacy. He may squeeze or roll a nipple between thumb and finger, or he may take it in his mouth and suck or roll his tongue around it, or flick the tip of it repeatedly with the tip of his tongue. All these actions will excite the woman provided that they are done gently; many women find it painful to be bitten on this sensitive area.

Biting has its place in loveplay, as do nipping, slapping, and scratching. A small degree of pain can be exciting, and there comes a stage in the arousal process when a little bit of roughness has a positive effect, but lovers should usually confine their biting, slapping, and scratching to the less vulnerable parts of the body, the back, buttocks, legs, arms and shoulders.

When a woman is sufficiently aroused, her vaginal lips will be swollen and moist due to the secretion of lubricating fluid. When he turns his attention to her genital area he should first gently brush, hold, and rub the entire vulva, before delicately parting the lips. After a spell of caressing the vaginal lips, he will try to locate the clitoris, which is situated at the upper point where the vaginal lips join, just below the pubic bone. This sensitive organ needs especially careful treatment. It can be pressed against the pubic bone, rubbed with and up-and-down or circular motion, or very gently squeezed, and these movements may very well bring the woman to a first climax. If she does not wish to climax at this stage she may wish her partner to stop clitoral stimulation.

It is normal for the man to explore and stimulate the vagina with his fingers before introducing his phallus. Penetration with the middle finger, or the middle and index fingers together, with the palm of the hand upward, and gentle movement in and out for a time, will excite both parties to a point where they will no longer be able to delay final consummation.

Some couples feel that whatever the hand can do the mouth can do better, or more excitingly, and with much greater intimacy. Orogenital contacts are probably the most exciting of all the techniques of foreplay. A series of body kisses proceeding down to the vulva, followed by stimulation of the clitoris by the tongue, and then rapid tongue penetration of the vagina, is one of the most pleasurable means of bringing about a strong climax in a woman.

Arousal Technique

Men are generally more susceptible to visual stimulation than women, and this is an important point which a woman should always bear in mind during the preliminaries to lovemaking. Posing, teasing, and other aspects of uninhibited behavior are all potent seduction weapons, as is sexy clothing or lingerie removed provocatively.

Verbal expressions of feelings and admiration are as important to men as they are to women. Men do like being complimented on their bodies, in particular on their penis. Some of them are extremely sensitive about the size of their phallus, which they consider as an exemplification of their virility. Because a man is usually less sensitive to overall caresses, very early on in lovemaking he needs to have all the woman's attention directed at his genital area. Initially she can stroke or brush his phallus teasingly but it should not be long before she manipulates it with more ardor.

Experience tells a woman how to excite her man. If not, an open and experienced man will show her. Very often a relatively inexperienced woman will grip the penis with her whole hand and pull it roughly, a technique that most men find unpleasant, and certainly not erotic. A far more pleasurable technique is to place the thumb on one side of the penis and the fingers on the other and exert pressure, using slow up-and-down strokes, with occasional bursts of very rapid strokes.

After the initial stages of penis stimulation the woman can seat herself so that she is facing him, and use two hands. This way he can see her, and can also arouse her. She uses one hand to hold the root of his penis, at the same time gently gripping his scrotum, while the other hand stimulates the highly sensitive tip, or glans. This way she can give him a number of extremely exciting sensations. A light fingertip stroke of the very tip will make him shudder, as will a light scratching of the taut underside of the penis. Rolling the entire organ between the palms of the hands can be a highly effective means of arousal, while rolling it against or between the breasts is an even

more pleasurable variation.

If this loveplay is a prelude to intercourse, a woman has to be careful not to bring her man to the point of ejaculation. If he tells her to stop because he is at the brink of orgasm she should do so immediately. In any case, if the partners know each other well, the woman will recognize the signs and slow down her actions accordingly. When possibility of immediate orgasm has abated stimulation can be resumed, though after one buildup like this the man will probably want to take the initiative himself. One method which all women ought to be aware of is that pressing fairly hard with the fingers on the urethal passage right at the root of the penis, or alternatively just under the scrotum, will arrest an imminent ejaculation.

It is said that many married men who also use prostitutes do so because of frustrated "fellation libido." Fellatio is stimulation of the penis using the mouth. The excitement it induces in a man is due to the wide range of pressure and versatility of movement that the mouth is capable of. It should be thought of as an expression of love and not, as some might have it, a perversion. Provided that the man is scrupulously clean and has washed his penis thoroughly, the practice is in no way unhygienic. The woman may start by lightly kissing the glans and flicking it with the tip of her tongue; she may then run her tongue the length of the underside of the penis a few times before taking the organ into her mouth and simulating coital movements while exerting pressure with her lips. At this stage the man may be unable to call a halt even if he feels his orgasm coming, so a woman has to know how to read the signs if fellatio is intended as a prelude to vaginal penetration.

On occasions a woman may arouse her man through fellatio and swallow his semen. As an ejaculation comprises only about a teaspoonful of practically tasteless fluid, and as a woman salivates profusely if she has been working ardently with her mouth, she may not even notice the substance in her mouth. Some women do actually enjoy it.

The Missionary Position

Opinions vary as to how many positions of intercourse are possible. Some sex manuals propose hundreds, but many of these involve only slight variations in the positions of the limbs or require the participants to be contortionists. Shortage of space limits us to describing only the basic positions, but any couple can always introduce their own modifications. The important point to remember is that if a position is creating physical strain or is painful, it would be dangerous to continue it. Changes of position during intercourse not only give partners the chance to see the act and each other from different viewpoints; they also affect the angle and depth of penetration and thus produce different physical sensations.

The face-to-face position with the man above and woman below is the one most commonly used by Western lovers. It was the Polynesians who supposedly dubbed it the "missionary position," because they first saw it used by Western missionaries. The name gives the impression that it is unimaginative, inhibited and not profoundly satisfying. The latter opinion is certainly incorrect, and whatever other positions lovers go through they usually conclude their lovemaking in this position because it is the most comfortable for reaching climax. Its disadvantages are that it gives the woman little opportunity to make independent movements, and does not allow either party to stimulate the other's primary erogenous areas by hand, though such stimulation, of course, is not required in the final abandon of sex.

The second variation illustrated, with the man's

legs apart and the woman's together, is a useful one to bear in mind if the man's penis is small or his erection weak, or if the woman's vagina is large, as it may be for instance in women who have borne children, because the woman is able to exert pressure on her lover's penis by tightening her thighs.

A natural variation on the missionary position is for the man to raise his torso from the woman's by resting on his elbows or on the palms of his hands with his arms outstretched. This way he has a much better view of the woman's body; if he can support himself on one hand or elbow he can disengage the other to caress her breasts.

Variations

If, starting from the so-called missionary position, the woman draws up her knees to her shoulders, penetration will be easy and deep. Intercourse in this position also gives the woman the satisfaction of repeated stimulation of the clitoral area by the pressure exerted by

the man's pubic bone. She can also increase her sensations by moving the lower part of her body, and by clasping the man's body with her legs she can encourage and reinforce his thrusting movements.

A further variation, though one that demands a degree of suppleness that not all women possess, is for the woman to raise her legs further until her calves are resting on the man's shoulders. This position produces a more intense sensation than the previous one, but because penetration is very deep, it is recommended if the partners want intercourse to result in pregnancy. If this is the object, then it is a good idea for this position to be held for a short time after the man's ejaculation. To avoid strain a pillow can be put under the woman's buttocks to maintain the downward tilt of the vagina.

Flexion and Tension

Another natural development of the man-above, woman-below position is for the man to raise himself onto his knees and for the woman to arch her body so that he can enter her. The man helps her raise her buttocks by clasping his hands under them. By drawing her toward him simultaneously as he thrusts, deep and mutually satisfying penetration can be achieved. The visual stimulus that the man gets from seeing the woman's body tautly arched is one of the benefits of this position, and another is that it makes the woman flex her genital muscles. This position is difficult to maintain for any length of time, but as a variation during intercourse it can give both man and woman exquisite satisfaction. It goes without saying that a degree of physical fitness is required for this position, however, and it is not suitable for obese lovers.

Different Levels

Lovers who undress each other often discover for themselves the pleasure of intercourse on two levels, for example, where the woman is lying back over the edge of the bed and the man is standing or kneeling (depending on the height of the bed) on the floor.

As sex should not be confined to the bedroom, the dining room table will serve just as well for these positions. Apart from the excitement of

novelty, the man obtains a strong visual stimulus, and the woman the satisfaction of deep penetration.

If the woman leaves her legs dangling over the edge of the bed or table, all movements will be made by the man, with a combination of thrusting pelvic movements and pulling of the woman toward him by her hips.

The woman may, however, cross her ankles behind the man's back and thus be able to exert pressure to influence his movements. This will also have the advantage of freeing his hands so that he can stimulate her breasts and clitoral area.

A further variation on the dual-level position is for the woman to rest her calves on the man's shoulders. This not only allows the deepest penetration, but also enables the woman to use the muscles of her thighs and buttocks to tighten her grip upon the man's phallus.

The Superior Woman

The partner in the upper position in intercourse obviously has the greater freedom of movement and therefore will be the more active, but there is no reason why the partner in the so-called "superior" position should be the man. Both men and women can obtain great satisfaction, both psychological and physical, when the

woman takes the upper position and the initiative that goes with it. In some cases, where the man is very much heavier than the woman, it is even preferable for the woman to be on top. In the basic position in which the woman lies on the man and whole length of body contact is maintained, there are three possible variations. The woman's legs may be outside, inside, or on top of the man's; if they are inside or on top she will be able to exert pressure with her thighs.

All three positions enable the woman to determine the depth of penetration and control the movements of intercourse. They also have the advantage of providing continuous clitoral stimulation on the woman as the partner's pubic bones are pressed hard against each other. Penetration can be quite deep in these positions, and the hard pressure of the whole length of the phallus against the front vaginal wall will heighten the feeling to climax.

The "Horse of Hector"

One of the most versatile and satisfying positions is the one the Greeks called "the horse of Hector," in which the woman is astride the man and resting on her knees. Very deep penetration can be achieved in this position, and the woman can obtain various types of genital stimulation by making pelvic thrusting movements or rocking movements or by

rotating her hips. She may also lean forward, kneel upright, or lean back, supported either by the man's thighs or by her outstretched arms. Each of these variations has its advantages. Leaning forward, pressing her breasts against the man's chest and making coital movements, the woman is able to enjoy strong clitoral stimulation from the man's phallus and pubic bone. In the upright or backward position the clitoral region does not get such stimulation, but it is accessible to manual stimulation. These positions also provide the man with a very exciting visual stimulus and enable him to caress the woman's breasts. In the upright position the woman can control the depth of penetration by raising or lowering her buttocks. If she raises herself almost clear of the man's erect phallus, he or she can manipulate it so that the glans is rubbed vigorously against her labia and clitoris and in the vaginal vestibule, movements which will give great pleasure to both.

The "Lyons Stagecoach"

Some sex manuals call the woman-above positions "riding" positions, and when the woman, starting from the position illustrated on the previous page, stretches her legs out so that her feet are over the man's shoulders, she attains a position that the French call "the

Lyons stagecoach'' (*la diligence de Lyons*). Pressing against the man's thighs with her hands and against the bed with her feet, she can move up and down or rotate her hips. The man's excitement in this position is enhanced by the considerable pressure exerted on his phallus, and as in the previous positions he also has the stimulus of being able to see and touch the woman's breasts.

From this ''riding'' position it is a simple matter to shift to the close-embrace position illustrated here. This is not a position that allows movement, but as a resting position during intercourse it has the advantage of deep penetration and close intimacy.

By leaning back from this position and resting on their hands, the couple reach what is known as the ''X position,'' in which both have freedom to make slow movements and also have the highly erotic visual enjoyment of each other's bodies and of their activities.

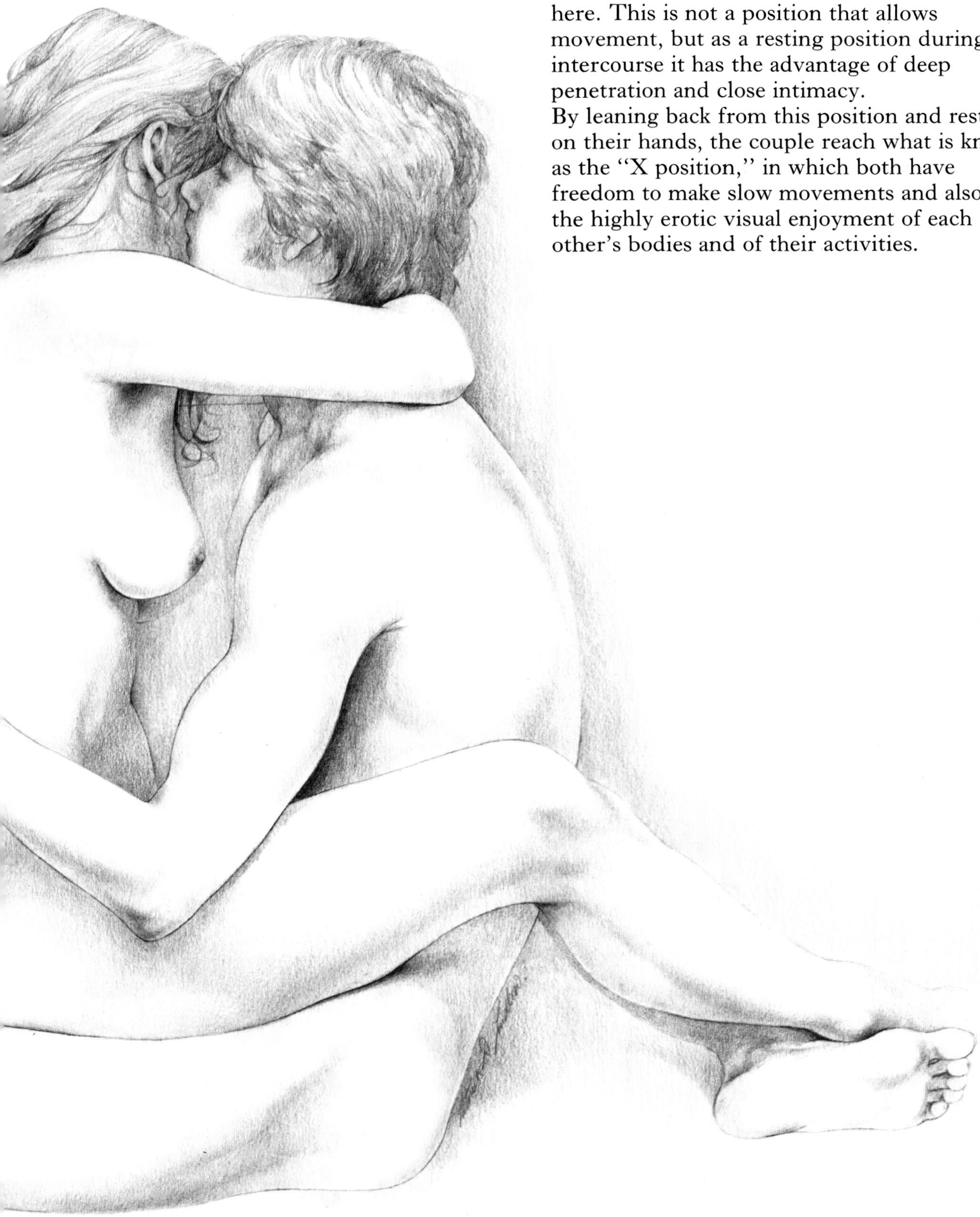

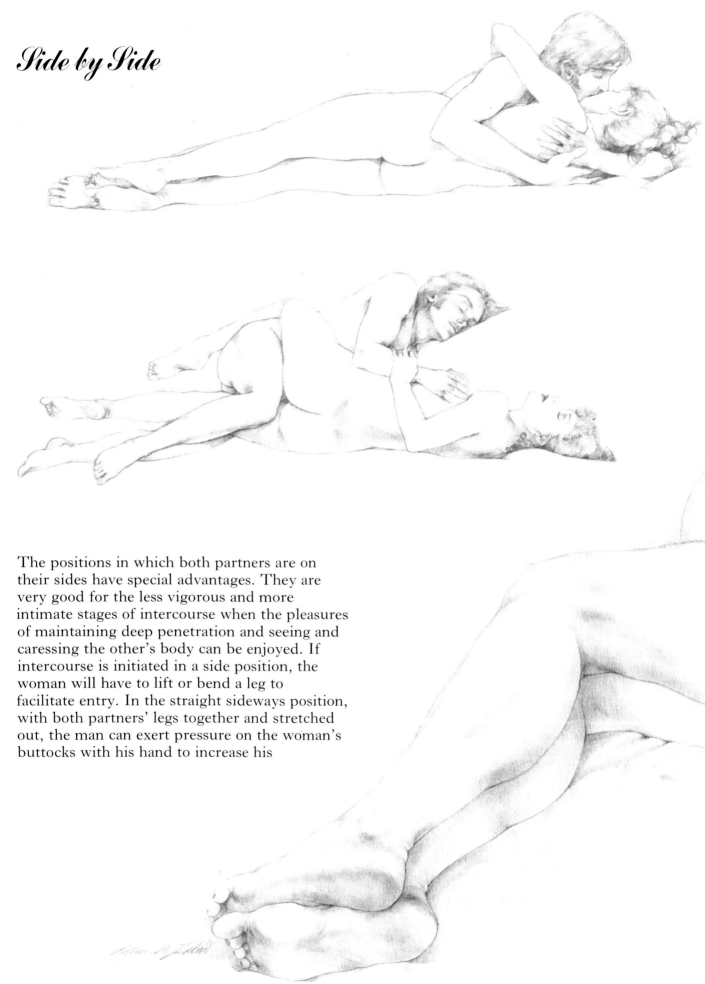

Side by Side

The positions in which both partners are on their sides have special advantages. They are very good for the less vigorous and more intimate stages of intercourse when the pleasures of maintaining deep penetration and seeing and caressing the other's body can be enjoyed. If intercourse is initiated in a side position, the woman will have to lift or bend a leg to facilitate entry. In the straight sideways position, with both partners' legs together and stretched out, the man can exert pressure on the woman's buttocks with his hand to increase his

penetration. Even deeper penetration will be obtained if the woman raises both her legs, one on each side of the man's body. There will be some direct clitoral stimulation in this position if the upper parts of their bodies remain in embrace. If they draw apart, however, the cessation of clitoral stimulation by the phallus can be compensated for by manual stimulation, and this position has the additional advantages of providing the man with an exciting view and also enabling him to make thrusting movements.

Cuissade

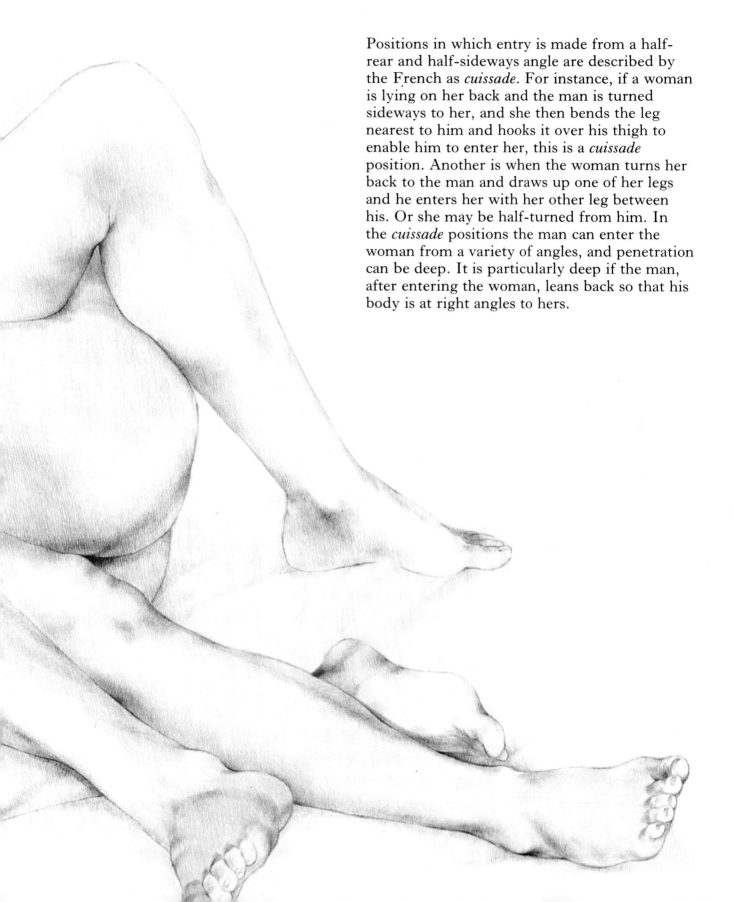

Positions in which entry is made from a half-
rear and half-sideways angle are described by
the French as *cuissade*. For instance, if a woman
is lying on her back and the man is turned
sideways to her, and she then bends the leg
nearest to him and hooks it over his thigh to
enable him to enter her, this is a *cuissade*
position. Another is when the woman turns her
back to the man and draws up one of her legs
and he enters her with her other leg between
his. Or she may be half-turned from him. In
the *cuissade* positions the man can enter the
woman from a variety of angles, and penetration
can be deep. It is particularly deep if the man,
after entering the woman, leans back so that his
body is at right angles to hers.

Flanquette

The so-called *flanquette* positions are those in which entry is made from a half-sideways and half-facing position. As in the *cuissade* positions, one of the man's legs is between the woman's legs and one of hers is raised. The advantages of the *flanquette* positions are the freedom to vary the angle of entry and also the ability to obtain deep penetration. The man is able to make slow and deep thrusting movements and the genital contact can be complemented with mouth and breast kisses.

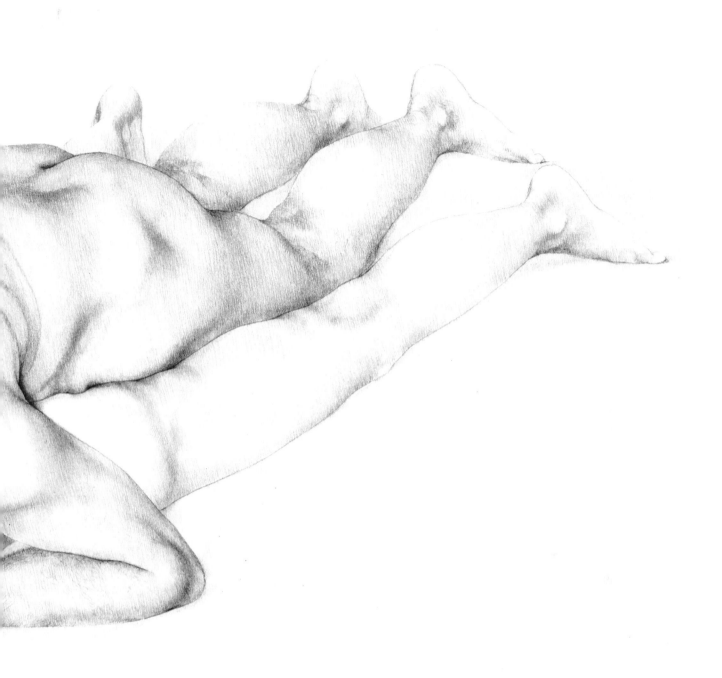

Rear Entry

Some couples are prejudiced against rear-entry positions because they feel it belongs to the realm of animal copulation, or that by foregoing face-to-face contact they are depersonalizing the act of sex. However, once rear-entry intercourse has been experienced such inhibitions usually disappear.

If the woman turns over on her stomach during lovemaking spreading her legs wide and the man mounts her, vaginal entry can easily be achieved. She may have to be helped by raising her pelvis a little, or else the man can put one hand under her to raise her and guide his phallus in. With all rear-entry positions, there is no stimulation of the clitoris by the phallus, but stimulation by hand comes about naturally as the man presses the woman's pubis to deepen his penetration. Penetration is not very deep from this position, but there is hard pressure against the front vaginal wall which can give both man and woman acute pleasure.

Turning Away

Rear entry is possible with the man lying on his back and the woman astride him and turned away from him. The woman has to lean forward to facilitate entry, but once entry has been achieved she has considerable freedom of movement and by rocking backward or moving forward she can control the depth of penetration and afford the man the sensation of hard

pressure against her vaginal wall. Alternatively, the man can control the coital movement by gripping the woman around the waist. Variations can follow naturally from this position and give both partners a wide range of enjoyable sensations. The woman can lean right forward between the man's legs and the man can raise his body a little, and each can grip the other's forearms and pull alternately to effect movements. Or the man can sit upright with his back against the wall or the head of the bed.

Kneeling

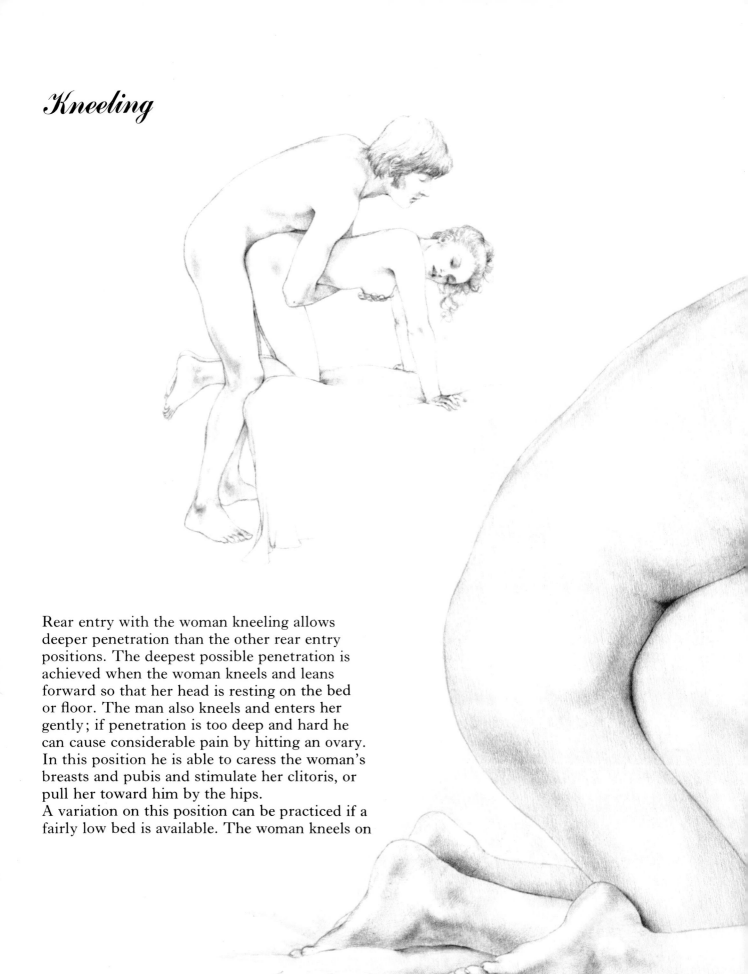

Rear entry with the woman kneeling allows deeper penetration than the other rear entry positions. The deepest possible penetration is achieved when the woman kneels and leans forward so that her head is resting on the bed or floor. The man also kneels and enters her gently; if penetration is too deep and hard he can cause considerable pain by hitting an ovary. In this position he is able to caress the woman's breasts and pubis and stimulate her clitoris, or pull her toward him by the hips.

A variation on this position can be practiced if a fairly low bed is available. The woman kneels on

the edge of it and either leans forward or
supports her body with her outstretched arms,
and the man enters by bending from a standing
position. The woman's feet may either be
hooked behind the man's knees or gripped
between them; in the latter position there will
of course be greater pressure exerted on the
phallus.

Standing

Intercourse in a standing position can be very
exciting, though a certain agility is demanded.
Sometimes a couple have reached such a peak
of excitement before undressing that once they
have taken their clothes off and embraced
standing up, union follows almost immediately.
Depending on the relative heights of the couple,
entry can be effected either by the woman
lifting a leg and turning it sideways, or by the
man bending at the knees, pulling the woman's
body toward him and entering her from below.
Needless to say, a hard upstanding erection is
needed to accomplish this. In the standing
position either partner can make strong coital
movements, and with her legs together the
woman can grip the phallus tightly.
Rear entry in a standing position is also possible,
particularly if the woman leans forward against
some object such as a chair in order to facilitate
it, but it is not possible to move much in this
position without the phallus coming out.
In general standing positions are not satisfying
for coitus to the point of orgasm, but they make
an exciting prelude to another more
comfortable position.

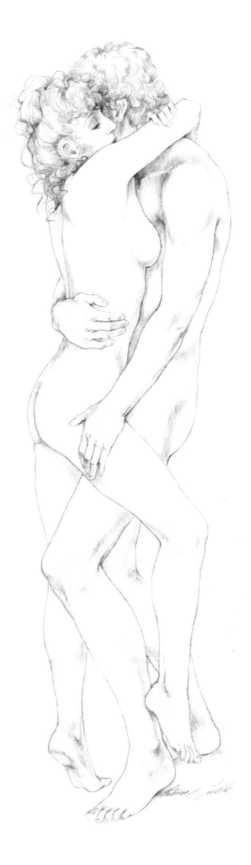

158

Poise and Balance

In oriental erotic pictures and sculptures a
variety of standing positions are illustrated
which would appear to be possible only if the
woman is light and the man strong. Starting
from the previous position, the man can lift the
woman by her buttocks into a position where
she can cross her legs behind his back, and he
can then rock back and forth and control the
speed of the movements with his hands. One
sex manual even recommends this position for
dancing! A variation which takes some weight
from the man and enables him to make vigorous
thrusting movements is for the woman to
release her grip on the man's neck and lean back
against a wall.

Sitting Comfortably

Intercourse can take place in sitting positions, and lovers throughout the centuries have been known to practice it covertly, while dressed of course, in public situations. The thrill of a clandestine experience might compensate for the necessary immobility of coitus under such circumstances and the need to keep a straight face. Immobility, however, is not necessarily a drawback of the sitting postures. If the man is seated and the woman straddles him, she will probably be able to keep her feet on the floor and thus move up and down. Obviously it is essential that the man maintains a strong erection. The facing position does not permit much manual stimulation, but if the woman turns her back the advantages of other modes of rear entry intercourse can be enjoyed. A further refinement is for her to turn sideways and raise the leg nearest the man's body. This position permits the deepest penetration, simultaneous manual stimulation of breasts and clitoris, and mouth-to-mouth kissing.

Chapter 6
Husbands and Wives

Marriage is intrinsically a cultural and sociological institution as well as a sexual partnership. A man and woman "related" to each other by love, common interests, and mutual respect take pains to learn about and gratify their partner's needs, wishes and desires. This is a continuing, ever-changing process as two people develop and grow. If they are both aware and understanding of these changes in the other, the marriage will be a success, a sound and satisfying background to the external activities and pursuits of life. But this describes an ideal situation. Today, in addition to the problems of psychological adjustment, married couples have to adapt their lives to radical social changes which have affected marriage, as well as to some fundamentally new ideas about what marriage is and should be.

The rituals of marriage reinforce and formalize the vows made between the husband and wife, and unite the two families together.

What is Marriage?

One result of the sexual revolution has been the airing of new ideas about marriage and the questioning of traditional customs and ideas. New lifestyles such as mutual polygamy, serial monogamy, and communal living have been advocated. It has also been predicted that the institution of marriage as we have known it will become obsolete in the 21st century. It is not surprising therefore that many young people are confused about whether or not they should marry and what they should expect if they do.

Right : tomb painting of Senejem and his wife, dating back to the 19th Dynasty (1166–1085 BC). During this period marriages were arranged by formal contract rather than religious ceremony, and monogamy was the rule.

People normally get married for private and personal reasons, but their action has social significance and consequences. By marrying they form an economic unit and become potential parents. Now, the private reasons why people in our culture marry – basically because they are in love and cannot bear to be apart – cannot change from generation to generation. But the traditional pattern of marriage, subjected to new social pressures, has undergone very marked changes.

We only need describe the traditional pattern for the changes to be obvious. At one time the roles of husband and wife were clearly defined and were conceived as complementary to each other. The husband assumed the dominant role of breadwinner, treasurer, and decision-maker, and the wife was expected to concern herself with pleasing her husband, dealing with domestic matters, and the bearing and rearing of children. In the Christian wedding ceremony the bride promised to "love, honor and obey" her husband and in doing so clearly accepted a subservient role, generally reinforced by her dependent economic status. In his home the man was sovereign. Any work he undertook there was generally the kind that required a certain amount of physical strength, or mechanical skill which he had learned from his father and would pass on to his sons. But the dependence was not one-sided: the many aspects of household management such as cooking and sewing were a total mystery to him.

This pattern of marriage with its strictly demarcated roles had to change when women became enfranchised, better educated, and economically independent. Today, with millions of married women working and contributing, often equally, to the family budget, it is inevitable not only that there is more financial equality in a marriage but also that husbands generally contribute to the housework and play a much bigger part in the caring for and rearing of their children. The male and female roles are now envisaged as supplementary rather than complementary.

Comparing attitudes to marriage expressed by a cross-section of the British population in 1950 and 1970, Geoffrey Gorer found significant differences in replies to the question: "What do you think tends to make for a happy marriage?" In 1950 people put far more stress on the importance of material circumstances than did the interviewees of 1970, while in 1970 much greater emphasis was put on the importance of comradeship and joint activity. Financial security and sexual compatibility seemed to be taken more for granted by the young marrieds of 1970 than by those of 1950. Asked what were the most important qualities that a husband or wife should have, the 1950 interviewees tended to speak of moral qualities or financial status, whereas those of 1970 were concerned more with psychological qualities. "This shift of emphasis," Gorer

Above: "Faults on both Sides" by Thomas Faed illustrates how a lack of communication between the partners of a marriage can totally undermine a relationship.

commented, "to husbands and wives being people who like one another rather than efficient executants of their roles as breadwinner and housewife would appear to confirm the shift to the ideal of symmetrical marriage."

Further confirmation came in answers to the question "What do you think tends to wreck a marriage?" In 1950 the most frequent causes were not having a home of one's own, bad household management, and the interference of in-laws. Also in 1950 untruthfulness and lack of trust figured much more significantly than in 1970 (mentioned by 33 percent of the sample as compared with 6 percent). For the young marrieds of 1970 the primary danger to a marriage was considered to be lack of communication, neglect, or one partner going out without the other, and far greater emphasis was put upon the hazards

of infidelity and personality conflicts. When asked what were the most serious faults a husband or wife could have there was also a significant change of emphasis from complaints about the characters of husbands and wives to complaints about their behavior; a change, Gorer remarked, "congruent with the hypothesis of symmetrical marriage. Formerly, if husbands and wives got on together this was sufficient for a satisfactory marriage; today they must do things together if the marriage is to be satisfactory."

Gorer's findings clearly show a change in prevailing attitudes to marriage over the two decades prior to 1970, but they do not support the idea that the institution was becoming obsolete. In fact, they suggest that it was still vigorous, and was successfully adapting to the changed social conditions of the modern world.

Types of Marriage

For a person in the mid-20s to be able confidently to promise to remain with and be faithful to another person "till death do us part" is a remarkable thing, for it can mean a commitment to 50 years or more of partnership. People inevitably change over a period of 50 years, particularly as that period spans such major events as parenthood, changes in economic status, menopause, and retirement. Any honestly made marriage vow must take account of this and express a confidence that a person will be able to accommodate himself or herself to the partner's development and changes over the years, as well as his own.

Psychologists distinguish between homogamous marriages and heterogamous marriages, that is to say marriages between people who are very much alike and between people who are very different (the attraction of opposites). The question of which form has the best chance of success cannot be easily determined, for there are so many different considerations. These include social class, religion, personality traits, intelligence levels, professions, and basic interests. However, some relevant observations may be made. It may be said, for instance, that the principle of "opposites attract" may work during the early stages of a relationship, but when the initial rapture has worn off a partner's opposite characteristics may cease to be exciting and become just irritating. On the other hand, if the partners in a relationship are very different, but feel that their characteristics complement each other, for instance if one is excitable and the other calm, or one is impulsive and the other cautious, they may have a bond of mutual need stronger than a homogamous bond. Also they may continue to find each other exciting because of

Above : the period of a marriage inevitably has to accommodate changes in individual personality and the way this affects the relationship between the husband and wife.

Left : "Marriage Contract" by William Hogarth. Marriages used to be arranged by the couple's parents, with economics being the main consideration. The couple themselves had little say in the matter.

Opposite page, right : in certain marriages the husband and wife develop their separate ways but are united by a single strong bond. Eric Berne calls this an "H" type of marriage.

their differences. Whereas when like marries like and in marriage they grow to be almost identical the result can be deadly boredom. The most successful marriages are probably neither exclusively homogamous or heterogamous, but those in which the couple have in common basic interests, values and attitudes to life, but different and complementary abilities and personality traits.

The psychologist Eric Berne made an interesting classification of types of marriage based on the shapes of letters of the alphabet. A: the couple start far apart, but eventually find a common bond (represented by the crossbar of the A), perhaps their baby, and then grow increasingly close together.
H: the couple start far apart, and although the marriage is held together by a single bond they really continue to go their separate ways.
I: they start and continue as a single unit.
O: they go round and round repeating the same patterns.
S: the marriage wanders around seeking happiness, which proves elusive.
V: they start off close to one another but immediately begin to diverge.
X: they start off far apart, experience a single period of bliss, and then begin to drift apart again.
Y: they start off together, but an accumulation of difficulties eventually leads to their going their separate ways.

Berne's classification does not claim to be a complete typology of marriage, but it is useful in that it emphasizes the time factor and the basic problem of two individuals joining their lives together for a lifetime. There are some people today who maintain that it is preposterous to ask someone in their 20s to make a solemn lifelong commitment. Instead they advocate the issuing of marriage contracts for five or 10 years, with an option to renew the contract if both parties are agreeable. There are advocates, too, of serial monogamy, whereby a person would be able to have a different partner for each stage of his or her life, maybe three, four, or five in a lifetime. Such proposals would appear to be based on a realistic understanding of human nature, and their advocates rightly claim that they are sensible and do not demand too much of a person. But love *does* demand much, indeed demands all, and a person in love wants to give to the beloved his or her all, unreservedly and unconditionally. To append one's signature to a 10 year contract with an option of a renewal clause is hardly a declaration of love. And the point about marriage is that it *is* a declaration that two people want to make, to each other, to the world, and if they are religious to God, that they feel their love is deep and strong enough to carry them through life together. And confidence in the marriage partner's commitment can give a man or woman the necessary secure foundation upon which a life and an individuality can be built.

Above: many marriages have been long and happy because the relationship was strong enough to adapt to changes. That of the British Liberal Prime Minister William Gladstone and his wife Catherine lasted 59 years.

Problems and Pitfalls

The feeling of being in love is one of the most profoundly pleasurable and exhilirating experiences. It creates an intense feeling for another human being, a feeling of closeness and being one with them, unable to live a day without expressing one's undying love.

But although falling in love may be the reason why two people marry, it is only a temporary stage. There usually comes a time when the need to make love daily is over and when the novelty of living together has worn off. If the partners are emotionally mature, they understand and accept this and pass easily from the "in love" stage into the loving stage, of working together and building a relationship which provides a secure background to the inevitable pressures and trials of life.

If one or both partners are insufficiently mature emotionally to understand and cope with this transition the first pitfall of marriage lies ahead. Forty percent of divorces occur in the first five years of marriage and one of the most frequent causes of the breakup of young marriages is simply falling out of love. When the rapturous phase is over there proves to be no sound basis of affection, common interests, or mutual understanding to sustain the relationship.

Another possible crisis stage is the birth of a first child. For most women, pregnancy and the birth and care of a child are major experiences in their lives. Unless they are shared joyfully and fully the man may feel left out in the cold, and that his wife has become another individual – a mother more concerned with this intruder than with him. If the woman becomes so absorbed in her experience that she fails to give as much attention and love to her husband, resentment, jealousy and loneliness can eventually drive him to seek first companionship and then even love elsewhere.

On the other hand, the infertility of either partner can lead to disappointment and anxieties which create tensions that can wreck a marriage. Only a very strong bond of love can overcome this problem,

so that the infertile partner does not feel guilty or a failure.

An aspect of being in love is finding in the beloved a fulfillment of one's emotional needs. A person may find his or her emotional needs fulfilled without knowing precisely what these are. With time such needs can change, and failure on the part of either to understand and accommodate them can create situations in which the partners gradually begin to go their separate ways. Eventually the gap can become too wide to bridge and both find that they are living with a stranger.

The one fault that predominates in a marriage is selfishness and its accompanying defects of intolerance and lack of give-and-take. Gorer found that selfishness is the second most common cause of marital breakup. Not talking over problems, especially emotional ones, neglect, or one partner going out without taking heed of the other's wishes, are faults mentioned more by women than by men. An important point is that a married couple should also see each other *socially*. Otherwise there is the danger that they may increasingly identify their partners with their roles of breadwinner or housewife rather than regard each other as individual personalities. How many times has a "housewife" protested that she did not marry a house?

Above : happy is the bride. But will the marriage survive the harsh realities of day-to-day living?

Opposite page : the arrival of a baby can be a crisis point in a marriage. It is important that the father participates in the routine care of the child. Otherwise he will find himself cast in the role of breadwinner, while being excluded from the intense mother-baby relationship.

Stresses and Strains

Practical as well as emotional circumstances can create pitfalls in a marriage. As we have said before, when a couple marry they form an economic unit, and the financial problems they are likely to encounter can represent a rude awakening from the romance of courtship.

One of the common problems of the past was a young couple being unable to afford a home of their own. They were obliged to live with one or the other's parents and the resulting lack of privacy accounted for a lot of tension and strain between a young man and his wife. Far fewer couples today have to face this problem. A large proportion of today's young married women continue to work, and it is when the wife stops work to have a child that financial problems often arise. Unless the couple have diligently saved to cater to the loss of part of their joint income and the extra expense of a baby they may find their lifestyles considerably changed. With less money to socialize and the added expense of baby-sitters, both have to make adjustments to the new situation.

The loss of a large part of their freedom can also cause strain and tension. A young wife now more or less confined to the house with the time-consuming task of caring for the child can become tired, irritable, and less of a companion to her husband when he comes home from work.

The same applies to the husband. A woman will feel let down and cheated if her man loses the characteristics that originally excited and interested her, especially if he devotes himself entirely to his work, to the point where he even "brings the office home with him." Nowadays there is less emphasis on the delineation of roles. The responsibility of looking after children can be shared and they are recognized as being of equal importance to those of providing the income.

The greatest cause of dissatisfaction in marriages in the early years, and of separations and divorces, is the incompatibility of the partners' sexual needs. In many cases the husband wants intercourse far more

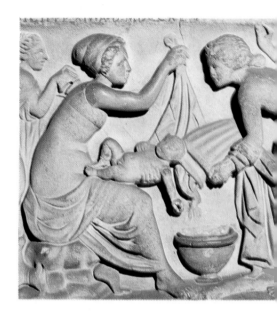

Right : for women who do not wish to be tied to looking after their children, and who can also afford it, the traditional answer has been to pay someone else to do it for them. This bas-relief from a sarcophagus shows a Roman nursemaid.

Below : most newly-weds would agree that privacy and a place of their own are essential for a happy start to the marriage.

frequently than his wife does, and if she too frequently refuses him or makes excuses he will feel that she has become frigid. He may even consider that he would be justified in seeking satisfaction elsewhere. When a man gets responses such as: "I've got a headache/toothache/backache," "It's too hot/cold/early/late," "I'm tired/not well/feeling sick," "We'll be heard by the neighbors/the children," "I've just been to the hairdressers'," or, most cutting of all,

"Don't you ever think of anything else?", before long he is likely to think that he has fallen into a trap. He will resent the fact that although he has kept his part of the marriage bargain his wife has reneged on hers. The fault may, of course, be his own; having got the courtship out of the way, he may feel that romance is no longer necessary and displays of love become purely sexual. On the other hand, the wife may not understand or sympathize with his sexual needs and make no attempt to do so. Wherever the fault lies, any problems should always be discussed; they rarely go away. Instead resentment and frustration will build up, and before long the marriage will be on the rocks. There are very few sexual incompatibilities that cannot be overcome by the understanding, genuine love, and the willingness to give that was the basis on which the marriage contract was made in the first place.

Above: excessive devotion to work, with the result that the husband and wife hardly see one another, can wreck a marriage.

Left: quickie divorce bureau in Mexico. Now that divorce is so readily available, the commitments taken on in marriage are far less binding.

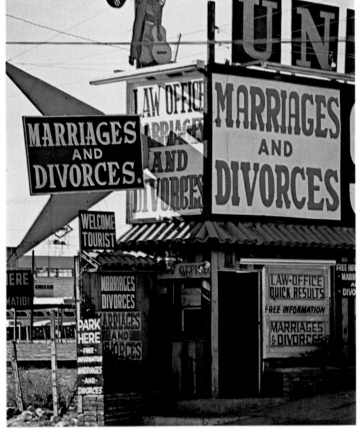

Sex within Marriage

Kinsey came up with some rather surprising findings about sex within marriage. Although his statement that "no other type of sexual activity is found in the histories of such a high proportion of an eligible population" seems almost like a comical statement of the obvious, since generally people get married on account of sexual attraction, certain other statements in his reports are surprising or even incredible. For example: "marital intercourse, although it is the most important single source of sexual outlet, does not provide even half of the total number of orgasms experienced by the males in the American population." And even more surprisingly: "Not more than 62 percent of the upper level male's outlet is derived from marital intercourse by the age of 55."

Let us take up this last point. The differences in sexual behavior between people of different classes or levels of society were among the most unexpected findings of the Kinsey team, and as corresponding differ-

Above: a sudden infatuation with an interesting stranger can temporarily eclipse a longstanding relationship.

Below: a cartoonist's view of how marriage changes people – for the worse.

ences are to be found in Geoffrey Gorer's English study we may assume that they are fairly common to Western societies. Kinsey found that for males of the lower income level, intercourse with the wife constituted 80 percent of the total sexual activity in the early years of marriage and 90 percent by the age of 50. On the other hand, men in the upper level derive 85 percent of their sexual activity from their wives in the early years but, by the time they had reached their 50s this had greatly diminished to 62 percent. "The general opinion that males become increasingly interested in extramarital relations as they grow older," Kinsey remarked, "thus proves to be true only of the upper level males." The reason for this, he conjectured, might be that upper level females are more inhibited than those of lower social levels. Their husbands become dissatisfied and get the urge to seek variety elsewhere before they get too old. Kinsey did not believe that a lowered sexual drive or preoccupation with professional or business affairs provided the explanation. The study assesses the proportion of the outlet and not its frequency, and the fact that the older upper level male gets *one third* of his sexual activity through ways other than marital intercourse. Masturbation and nocturnal emissions account for 19 percent of this, but this still leaves a substantial proportion of activity that must involve partners outside the marriage.

AFTER MARRIAGE

BEFORE MARRIAGE

Above: "Der heimliche Liebhaber" (the clandestine lover), by Jean-Baptiste le Prince. Lack of sexual fulfillment within a marriage often drives one of the partners to seek out extra-marital affairs.

One subject that all men are curious about is how frequently others have sex and whether they themselves are average or above average in the frequency of their intercourse. They feel that frequency is an index of their general virility, manliness, and well-being, and very often their self-esteem is tied in with their sexual performance. The fact is that in the population as a whole the decline in the frequency of marital intercourse proceeds at a steady rate as the years go by. Men who marry before the age of 20 average four times a week, and in this group many individuals have intercourse with their wives as many as seven or 10 times a week. By the age of 30 the average frequency has dropped to three times a week, by 45 to twice and by 60 to once. The physiological and psychological factors that contribute to this decline are not clear. A point mentioned in an earlier chapter, that women have orgasms more often in the later years of marriage, seems to indicate that although a married couple may have sex less frequently, they get more satisfaction out of it. The emphasis changes from quantity to quality.

This is obviously not true for those males who obtain one third of their sexual activity through extramarital sources. These outlets may be masturbation or other partners, or in a minority of cases through homosexual encounters. The fact that the wife is often responsible for the husband's behavior in such cases was suggested by another finding of Kinsey's: that the older women in the upper socioeconomic level to a large extent considered that they were already having too much sex. They wished that their husbands were not so demanding, while their partners wanted intercourse more frequently and believed they would have it if their wives were more interested.

The Problem of Monotony

Of all the ills that beset marriage, sexual monotony is one of the most common.

A correspondent of the sex counsellor Robert Chartham, a young woman named Jenny who had been married for three years, wrote to him describing how marital love-making had become for her an almost intolerable routine:

"As soon as David puts out his hand and passes it over my body and thighs, I know that he'll come back to my left breast, fondle the nipple for half a minute with his finger, then he'll lean over me and run his lips and the tip of his tongue up and down my throat, suck the lobe of my right ear for three or four seconds, come down over my shoulder and right breast, and caress the nipple with his lips, and so on – and so on – and on!

"I know every single move he's going to make and the order in which he will make them, and though I haven't the strength, or rather the control, to resist what he does, and we never fail to come off practically together, I could scream every time he comes to me. If only he would do something different! If only he could give me some new sensation, even if it was just a little one.''

David may have been a singularly unimaginative lover, but Jenny's problem was one that affects many marriages. Sexual encounters become routine, and although orgasms may still be achieved and enjoyed by both parties there is a feeling that something has gone out of the relationship, and that sex is not what it used to be. Some couples even accept this as an inevitable fact of life. This acceptance is a prelude to the onset of sexual apathy; erotic desire is repressed and resentment builds up against the marital partner. This can eventually surface and wreck the marriage.

Routine is a separation of consciousness from the activity. To be able to establish routines is a very useful human faculty, for it frees the consciousness from the immediate and the humdrum. We are able, for instance, to hold a profound conversation or think seriously about a problem while

There are sexual techniques which never fail to turn the partner on, but when they become routine the effect may be the opposite. When sexual boredom sets in, a change of technique is called for – otherwise either or both partners may seek variety elsewhere.

driving a car along a familiar route, because the driving and routing has become almost automatic. But automatic behavior has no business in an activity such as making love, where consciousness and concentration ought to be heightened, not lessened. The individual consciousness may become obliterated in the final stages of lovemaking where physical responses reach their peak, but throughout the arousal and plateau stages a person needs to feel that they are performing a spontaneous and meaningful action with another aware person, not a robot.

As Kinsey established, what distinguishes human sexuality from that of animals is that in humans sexual arousal is dependent not only upon physiological but also upon psychological factors. This means that consciousness must be involved in the sexual act, and therefore it is essential that there be spontaneity and variety in the act. Otherwise boredom sets in and sex becomes mechanical and joyless.

The answer to this problem is ridiculously simple. Both partners have a tremendous scope for introducing variety and being enterprising in their sexual encounters. For a start, the time and place may be varied. The usual time and place, last thing at night and in bed, is not necessarily the ideal. When the body is tired sex drive is going to be low and bed becomes a place to sleep. Sex can take place in any room in the house or even outside the house provided there is sufficient privacy. For some the very factor of lack of privacy adds another dimension of excitement. The important point is that it should be a response to a spontaneous urge and not allocated to a specific time and place in the same way as having breakfast or taking the dog for a walk.

With so many techniques and positions available there really is no excuse for monotony in marital sex. The permutations are innumerable and no two sessions need be the same. Nor need the mood be the same, a point usually overlooked by advocates of sophisticated techniques. Loving sex can be fun or it can be solemn, it can be violent or gentle, short and sweet or long and languid, accompanied by laughter and talk or enjoyed in silence. Married couples who are relaxed with each other, uninhibited, and knowledgeable about sex will find too much to do to ever allow themselves to fall into a routine.

Many sexual games turn out to be enjoyable once a few inhibitions have been overcome. But a partner's fears and loathings must be respected – after all, the game is for the benefit of both players.

The Value of Sex Games

Many couples introduce variety by playing games. The games range from simple play-acting through the kinky to the bizarre. There is a line to be drawn between sexual games and fetishes or obsessions. For game-players it is the variety which is important, and the occasional game adds spice and interest. For fetishists the actual play or the fetish object itself is of primary interest and there is no other route to sexual fulfillment.

Sexual games can be fun and they can also be immensely exciting. On an impulse a man offers his wife money if she will make love with him. He is casting her in the role of a prostitute, and she takes the money, and submits to his desires. He can carry her off and take her by force. Or she may take the initiative by playing the vamp and seducing him. Many couples also enjoy doctor-and-nurse games.

Some people will not participate in play-acting games because they think that they depersonalize sex. They believe that the other partner is indulging in a fantasy of making love to somebody else, which implies that their normal lovemaking is unsatisfactory. In fact it is simply bringing out another aspect of the partner's personality. Shakespeare's Mark Antony spoke of Cleopatra's "infinite variety," expressing a feeling that every lover has toward the beloved. To explore each other's infinite variety can be a lifetime's occupation for a couple, and play-acting can be a highly effective method of exploration. Drama liberates hidden potential and under the cover of pretense lovers can probe each other's personalities.

Familiarity, the saying goes, breeds contempt. We would prefer to say that it tends to breed indifference, but it is certainly true that unfamiliarity breeds excitement, and casting one's partner in an unfamiliar role can be very exciting sexually. There is a short Harold Pinter play which begins with a scene of a wife seeing her husband off to work in the morning. Everything they say and do down to the dutiful kiss on the cheek before departure is an unvarying daily routine, which they both enact mechanically. But when the husband has gone the wife prepares to receive her lover. She makes herself seductive and creates in the room an atmosphere for lovemaking. The lover duly arrives, and he is gay and passionate – a man who makes a vivid contrast to the departed husband. But the point is that he *is* the husband, returned in the role of the lover. The couple make love, and they keep the pretense up: the lover departs and at the end of the day the dull husband returns and the unvarying daily routine is resumed. The play very effectively makes the point that play-acting and make-believe can be potent aphrodisiacs in marital sex.

There are elements of dominance and submission, and often violence in sexual love. Romantic lovers may find these incompatible with their tender feelings for each other. But sexual games are a way of expressing these elements in such a manner that they need not be identified with them. For instance some couples occasionally play a game of rape. Dominance and submission are also the basic stimuli in the bondage games recommended in Comfort's *The Joy of Sex*. Bondage games can be an effective means for a couple to explore and express aspects of their sexuality, but they do require a strong element of trust. As Comfort writes, "The rules (in sexual games) are only those of childplay – if it gets nasty or spiteful or unhappy, stop the game: while it stays wild and exciting, it has a climax children's games lack; that is the privilege of adult play."

There are those who will maintain that game playing is infantile and has no place in mature sexuality. Freud has a lot to answer for in bringing the concept of infantalism into human sexuality. We prefer to go along with the American psychologist Abraham Maslow, who maintained that it took a mature, self-confident and "self-actualizing" adult to engage in childlike play, and that such play is a "regression in the service of the ego" – a means of maintaining psychic health.

Personal Taste and Distaste

Game playing may not always be for both partners a matter of doing what comes naturally. When one wants to do something the other finds distasteful serious problems can arise. A woman wrote to the Swedish sex counsellors, the Hegelers:

"A couple of years ago, while we were having intercourse, my husband asked me

to do something for him. It wasn't anything difficult or tiring, or anything that hurts, or in any other way unpleasant, but it scared me – and I just couldn't bring myself to do it.

"We talked about it afterward and he apologized for having asked me to do it, but he'd been thinking about it for a long time and it was something he wished very badly. We haven't talked about it since, but I have thought about it a great deal, and have actually tried and tried to be more broad-minded, but it's somehow against my nature, or my upbringing.

"The unfortunate thing is that, as a result, I no longer dare to be so relaxed when we make love together nowadays as I would like to be. I feel restrained by a fear that he may ask me to do something or other that I won't be able to bring myself to do."

This is a situation that crops up in many marriages, and, as in this case, although the man is respectful of his wife's sensibilities and does not press the matter, the situation can have an adverse affect on the harmony of the marriage. It is usually the man who harbors the desire and ventures the proposal, and therefore it is the woman who is confronted with the dilemma, "Should I or shouldn't I?" The Hegelers remark that there are many middle-aged women who quite happily perform certain types of love play that as teenagers they would have thought perverse and even revolting. Many of these have started the practice with great trepidation and urged on, not by their own desire, but by love for their partner and willingness to please him, have found that not only were their apprehensions groundless but that they actually enjoyed themselves. But some cannot bring themselves to comply with the request; consequently they feel guilty and suspicious of their partners. Their subsequent sex lives become tense and miserable.

Of course, a wife cannot be regarded as a sexual slave and obliged to do things she considers unnatural or finds esthetically repugnant, nor should she be in any way victimized if she declines to do something. On the other hand, in such a situation where she reacts instinctively and negatively she ought to stop and try to analyze the reasons. Sometimes an overprotective, strict and puritanical upbringing, which associated sex with dirt or sin, is responsible. In this type of situation sound reasoning will almost always prevail. Or it may be that the woman considers that her husband's sexual appetite has become jaded and he is seeking sensation for its own sake rather than expressing love through sex. If so, she could be quite wrong, because there is no incompatibility between loving and wanting novelty and spice in the expression of love. As we have already said, variety is essential to the vitality of a long-term loving relationship.

Of course, it must depend to a great extent on what the demanding partner wants. If he wants to indulge sadomasochistic tendencies which his wife finds repellant even though she may understand their cause, she is bound neither by love nor by the marriage contract to submit to pain and humiliation to gratify him. If he wants to insert something other than his phallus or fingers into her vagina (not an uncommon practice, as any hospital casualty department will testify), she is being perfectly reasonable in refusing to agree to a practice which is not only crude but dangerous. One wife who wrote to the magazine *Forum* did say that she discovered a delightful new pleasure when her husband took to putting ice-filled condoms inside her before making love because he liked the sensation of a cold vagina. On the other hand, if her husband is turned on by rubberwear or boots or black lingerie, a wife is not going to be either humiliated or injured by obliging him, and she might reasonably be expected to do so, at least provided that compliance does not positively turn her off.

Many of the things that husbands most commonly want done or want to do, and that cause marital problems because of the wife's reluctance, are not on the whole either extraordinary or unnatural. The idea that the woman may take the initiative and active role in lovemaking has been widely canvassed over recent years, and although female inhibitions have by no means been swept aside wholesale, men are inclined to think otherwise. They feel sexually deprived if their wives will not perform acts that they think most other wives do. This is particularly true of fellatio, which has had such enthusiastic promotion in literature, sexual and otherwise, that today it can hardly be regarded as unnatural or perverse. And yet a request for it is probably the most common cause of the kind of unhappy situation described by the Hegelers' correspondent.

Biorhythms and Sex

We do not wish to fall into the error that we consider many marriage manuals make — that of overstressing the importance of

sexual satisfaction at the expense of love. After all, marital sex has no chance at all of giving lasting joy and satisfaction unless it is based on love. To concentrate on sexual variety, techniques and games without attending to the matter of being and remaining lovers is to distort the priorities.

Many young couples expect each and every one of their sexual encounters to be a tremendous experience and start getting worried if one or two of them are not. Or

they may get worried if they run into periods when they do not make love as frequently. But these are experiences common to every couple, and real lovers will set no importance by them. When the love foundations of a relationship are utterly stable, variation in the intensity of particular experiences have no significance. They will enjoy ecstatic sex on one occasion, have fun on another, and on some nights sex will be companionship. The point about married love is that there is a lifetime to experiment.

Scientists have recently discovered subtle rhythms and cycles involved in human biological functioning. The female's 28-day menstrual cycle is the most obvious example of a biological rhythm, but it is now known that males as well as females have a 23-day physical energy cycle, a 28-day emotional cycle, and a 33-day intellectual or cerebral cycle. Each of these cycles has its peaks and troughs, so it is natural that sexual desire and sexual expression will vary in intensity. A married couple may find that they make love passionately for several days in succession and then enter a sexually quiescent period. This is not something to worry about; on the contrary, one of the advantages of sex in the context of marriage is that it can ebb and flow, or trough and peak, in its own natural rhythm. Lovers become aware of this and derive a particular satisfaction from the interaction of their biorhythms.

"Marriage," the actress Mrs Patrick Campbell is supposed to have said, "is the result of the longing for the deep, deep peace of the double bed after the hurly-burly of the chaise-longue." To find a partner with whom one can experience that peace, can utterly relax and be secure, is one of the aspects of falling in love. But one can have too much of a good thing, and from time to time nostalgia for the challenge and the passion of the first encounter will crop up. The art of being and remaining lovers involves satisfying that nostalgia. Marriage brings security but this is not synonymous with the routine of boredom. The interests, outings, discussions and special events, including seduction, should not be abandoned. After all, getting married does not mean accepting a life-sentence at home. Marriage is an organic, dynamic process; it needs stimulation and excitement to prevent it from stagnating, as well as love to sustain it.

Sex and Pregnancy

Leaving aside the various religious, cultural, and social taboos, let us take a practical and realistic look at the complex and many-sided question of sexual intercourse during pregnancy.

The physical, psychological and emotional aspects of the subject must be discussed. As Dr Van de Velde pointed out in his book *Ideal Marriage* (1928), "It is extraordinarily difficult for a doctor who possesses not only clinical and scientific knowledge, but also experience of life and human nature, to decide on which to take his stand and what advice to give." Van de Velde then went on to admit that at a time in his career when his knowledge of life did not match up to his medical expertise, he took account solely of the *physical* welfare

of his female patients and expressly forbade sexual intercourse – only to regret it later as his experience of life and knowledge of human nature expanded.

There are possible physical reasons why a pregnant woman should abstain from intercourse during the first three months. During this time a woman is most vulnerable to miscarriage and if she has already miscarried, vigorous sexual intercourse should be avoided. Nature seems to have some extent taken care of this, for in Masters and Johnson's investigation of 101 pregnant women, most of those experiencing their first pregnancy said that they were less interested in sex than before pregnancy. But both those pregnant for the first time and women who had already had babies became more interested in sex in the middle three months, their desire for intercourse decreasing again in the last three months.

Another physical danger is the possibility of puerperal (during and just after childbirth) infection if the male introduces germs into the vagina. But this can of course be avoided if both husband and wife are scrupulous about hygiene.

There are far more basic concerns in life than physical dangers. Through their research into the sexual lives of pregnant women, Masters and Johnson reached the conclusion that too many physicians tend to prescribe too long a period of sexual abstinence before and after birth – sometimes as long as three months each side of the event, and they considered that such prescriptions were wrong and irresponsible because they took no account of the psychological effects of sexual deprivation, and the way it could damage a marriage.

In a marriage where there were sexual problems before the wife became pregnant, her desire for intercourse often diminishes considerably as soon as she becomes aware that she is pregnant. At this point, the husband may take to leading his own life and even finding temporary gratification elsewhere. Regrettably, this is not an uncommon situation. On the other hand, if the sexual and emotional relationship was strong before the wife's pregnancy, she will consciously and subconsciously desire to continue her sexual relationship with her husband during her pregnancy. She will even knowingly and willingly risk the possible physical dangers, which anyway are minimal in a normal pregnancy, because at this time more than ever she needs her husband's love, understanding, and affectionate gestures of tenderness. But of course full sexual intercourse is not the essence of the husband's love and tenderness. The loving husband will find little difficulty in abstaining from sex in the last stages of his wife's pregnancy and for a time after the birth, for the whole process is a joint emotional experience. And there are, of course, alternatives to full intercourse by means of which a husband and pregnant wife can make love. For the woman, however, it may be unwise to experience orgasm during the final stages, for it can precipitate labor.

As to when normal sexual activities can be resumed after birth, this is variable and depends on the particular couple. Three to four weeks after is probably the average. Masters and Johnson found that women who breast-feed their babies tend to resume intercourse sooner than those who bottle-feed.

Woman's New Role in Marriage

Today's woman has been made aware of her new freedom and her right to full sexual expression and satisfaction. But few of the exponents of these ideas made the point that she also has responsibilities. If she thinks that sexual happiness and satisfaction, whether marital or extramarital, is going to be given to her on a plate without any obligation on her part, she is courting unhappiness and frustration in her relationships with men.

The concept of what should constitute a happy and balanced marriage has changed in many ways. And the importance of maintaining sexual compatibility and learning how to maintain it, has been widely publicized. The subject of sexuality, for so long a mixture of myths and facts which a woman was expected to be ignorant of before marriage, is now openly and freely discussed and written about. And straightforward terminology, formerly permitted only in medical journals, has replaced the coy and misleading euphanisms from which the majority of women gleaned a hazy knowledge of what to expect of their own or their husband's physical, psychological, and emotional needs.

So there is no excuse for ignorance. Nowadays a wealth of serious and well-researched literature by sexologists, scientists and psychologists has provided women with the opportunity to learn about all aspects of sex, and it is her responsibility to do so before embarking on marriage. We have heard the argument that all the probing and analysis of sexuality takes the romance out of a relationship, but in fact the opposite is true. Sexual intercourse is, at its best, an expression of romantic love, and if a woman knows and understands her man's body and what gives him pleasure, the experience can only be enhanced for both of them. The sexual side of love can be joyous and truly satisfying if both partners respond to each other and the delight is mutual.

Many young men as well as women still enter into marriage with high ideals of the significance and beauty of sex within marriage and expect more than they usually

Right : active participation in lovemaking is now considered the norm for a woman. She can initiate sexual intercourse without fear of being branded a rampant nymphomaniac.

Below : it is now recognized that women also respond to visual stimulation, although this fact has yet to be catered for commercially.

find. Both partners should face the fact that successful and gratifying sexual intercourse does not "come naturally" but is a sophisticated art the techniques of which must be learned, and like any art it cannot be learned overnight. And here lies the woman's new responsibility: not to simply submit to lovemaking, but to participate.

It used to be primarily the man's responsibility to make sure that sex did not result in an unwanted pregnancy. With the advent of the pill, the intrauterine device and the diaphram this responsibility has passed to the woman. Some women apparently consider that this change constitutes a shift of power as well as of responsibility, and in a sense this is true for a wife can theoretically now choose whether and when to give birth. But with new powers there always come new responsibilities and,

paradoxical though it sounds, it has become the modern woman's responsibility not to bear a child unless both partners are prepared for it.

Woman's control of contraception also makes her freer to initiate sexual activity. Gone are the days when a woman might hesitate to signal her sexual readiness lest the man was unprepared. Gone too are the days when the onus of instigating sexual activity always fell on the man. A wife can say "let's make love" without being thought a nymphomaniac. It is now recognized that a woman has sexual appetites and desires, and it is also acceptable. The elaborate rituals of make-up and perfume are no longer just a way of supposedly driving a man wild with desire without his realizing its premeditated instigation, but simply one of the many techniques of seduction.

Marital Responsibilities

The idea that the male had sexual responsibilities toward the female would have been generally regarded as somewhat eccentric not very long ago, for woman was regarded as man's sexual convenience and not considered to have sexual needs herself. But female emancipation and the discovery of the female orgasm have changed this situation. The husband who mounts his wife, takes his pleasure, then rolls over and goes to sleep without a thought for her feelings is rare today, not only because men know that women can have orgasms but also because few women would let a man get away with such conduct.

But there is a tendency in this age of enlightenment for husbands to think that by giving their wives orgasms they have adequately fulfilled their sexual responsibilities. *The Hite Report* interviewee who said, "Orgasm is important, but not as important as *he* thinks: my orgasm is actually more important to my husband than to me!" was expressing a feeling that many modern married women have. Some husbands get so fixated on giving their wives orgasms that they become more like sexual performers than lovers. Some become so anxious about the matter that they lose the ability to have orgasms themselves, and instead just ejaculate. In such situations true sexuality is sacrificed to the achievement of a supposed norm. Neither the female orgasm nor the mutual orgasm should be the object and criterion of conjugal love. Although intense sensations can elicit impressive manifestations of emotion, sensation and emotion are not the same. The emphasis on the importance of the female orgasm has tended to detract from the woman's equally important need for emotional satisfaction from sex, for love, tenderness, admiration, close communion and intimacy. The same is true for men, often portrayed or expected to respond like sexual machines instead of human beings.

If a man today is no longer burdened with what used to be his primary sexual responsibility toward his wife – to "take precautions" and insure that she does not get pregnant unless they wish to start a family – he is certainly not relieved of responsibility toward her when she is pregnant. This is a time when a relationship can be greatly strengthened by the husband showing love and understanding, and sharing the experience, or irremediably damaged by his being insensitive. As we have seen, a couple's sex life need not be disrupted much by pregnancy. With all the emphasis today on the joys and techniques of sex and the importance of sexual satisfaction to psychological health and marital harmony, the significance of the fundamental fact that sex is also for procreation can easily be ignored. For a man to become a father requires a psychological adjustment that he needs to understand in advance and be prepared to make.

Marriage involves mutual responsibility, personal involvement, and sharing of problems. Communication is of the essence.

189

What Makes for a Lasting Marriage?

In conclusion, let us consider what the components are of a sound and lasting marriage. We suggest that there are eight basic ones: communication, affection, shared interests, sexual compatibility, zest, a constructive approach to problems, full acceptance of each other, and mutual growth.

Communication. Psychologists have found that one of the common characteristics of unhappy marriages is an extreme difference in talkativeness between the partners. Marriage should be a dialogue, and considering the length of time involved a couple should be wary of marriage unless they find that they can talk to each other on a variety of subjects and that they have an interest in each other's views. But they should also be sure that they are comfortable being with each other in silence. Sometimes compulsive talk is not communication but a cover for a fear of emptiness, and between lovers there are channels of communication other than verbal.

Affection. In marriage, it is not enough for a couple to love each other; they should like each other as well. It has often been observed that friendships can be more enduring than marriages, and unless there is a strong element of friendship in a marriage the foundations of the relationship will be very insecure. Purely erotic love, of course, is possible without basic affection and liking for the sexual partner, and the soundest reason why potential mates should delay making love is that they need a chance to discover if they really like each other before passion clouds their capacity for judgement.

Shared interests. The importance of comradeship and shared activities was stressed by twice as many people among Geoffrey Gorer's interviewees in 1970 as in 1950. Doing things together implies having shared interests. Common interests may have existed prior to marriage and indeed may have brought the couple together. Very often they are developed within a marriage, by one partner taking up the interests of the other. It is not necessary for them to have everything in common, indeed it is probably a good idea for each to have some independent interests, but it certainly helps if they have some common ones, for communication has to be about something.

Sexual compatibility. It goes without saying.

Zest. The sense that life and marriage are things to be enjoyed and not merely lived through is a quality invaluable in both partners. The problems of family and married life, particularly in the early years, can undermine a person's sense of life as an adventure, but it is important to try to keep this sense alive. Hard times do not generally last long, and a couple who maintain a zestful approach to life and who seek and develop new ways to enjoy themselves together will be more likely to come through even the hardest times with their marriage intact.

A constructive approach to problems. In the best of marriages there are going to be problems, difficulties, and tensions which, if not dealt with intelligently and constructively, will cause disaster. Interpersonal conflicts and differences of opinion are bound to occur, but if they are not brought out into the open and tackled positively, resentment builds up and trouble follows.

Full acceptance of each other. This means acceptance in spite of all the partner's faults, weaknesses, and shortcomings. Marriage cannot be based on romantic idealism, and love must always be for the whole person, realistically observed. To marry someone with the expectation that they will change certain undesirable aspects of their personality is asking for trouble.

Mutual growth. Stagnation brings death and this applies to people too. Growth, change, and development are the law of life, and to expect people to remain always the same is to betray a basic insecurity. Marriage partners who are secure with each other will each delight in the other's growth and development as they go through life together.

These, then, are some of the features of a sound and lasting marriage. Others will occur to the reader. We do not say that all successful marriages necessarily have all these elements, but only that the more they have the better their chances of success.

A lasting relationship requires that both members cease building up images – of themselves and the partner – and accept each other for what they truly are. This is one of the crucial differences between being in love and loving.

Chapter 7
Patterns of Relationships

The dictum of St Paul – better to marry than to burn – was a grudging recognition that human sexuality must express itself, and marriage, the institution within which it might be allowed to express itself, was accepted if not actually blessed by the Church. Paul's attitude has had a profound influence through 2000 years of Western civilization. Even in the last century the great Russian novelist Leo Tolstoy could take it a step further and declare that all sex not specifically aimed at procreation is unnatural and sinful. But human beings have always sought sexual satisfaction outside marriage, and they always will, and no expression of disapproval, however strong, is going to alter it. In recent decades, fortunately, the circumstances and problems of premarital and extramarital sexual activity have been considered more broadmindedly and sympathetically. The studies and views of psychologists and sociologists have also helped to soften a moral intransigence that in the past has brought unnecessary tragedy and distress into many human lives.

Sex before Marriage

A recent study of a hundred societies with different cultures throughout the world revealed that 70 percent of them took a permissive attitude toward premarital sex. It also revealed that those that condemned it tended to be the most developed societies. In the Western society of the last century excessive value was placed upon premarital chastity, supposedly for religious reasons but probably more for fear of unwanted pregnancies and because fathers were concerned about the preservation of their line. With the advent of reliable birth control these reasons no longer apply. Although belief in premarital chastity for other reasons can be found in some sectors it is broadly true that Western society now takes a more indulgent view of premarital sex than it did at the beginning of the century.

Sociologists are divided, however, on the question of whether there has been very much significant change in behavior as a result of the general change in attitude. The popular view seems to be that young people today obtain sexual experience earlier, more casually, and more promiscuously than earlier generations. But the data available suggest that the change has not been so dramatic as most people believe. A survey in a coeducational college in the United States came up with the interesting discovery that 20 percent of the students were sexually experienced, but 75 percent of them believed that most of their classmates were. Even the young people themselves tended to exaggerate the sexual lives of their contemporaries.

Reliable data are difficult to obtain because adolescent sexual behavior varies so much in relation to nationality, social class, and educational level, and also because boys are inclined to be boastful about their

Below left : this scene from a French tapestry, made for a wedding in the late 1400s, illustrates the traditional emphasis on chastity before marriage. According to medieval legend, the unicorn (a symbol of virility and strength) could only be captured if a virgin lured it to put its head in her lap, thus stressing the power of purity and symbolizing the sexual awakening of the virgin bride by her husband.

Left : in medieval times husbands insured that their wives remained faithful by locking them inside a metal chastity belt.

sexual life and girls to be reticent about it. But when the findings of a number of researchers are compared a picture emerges of a steady increase in premarital sexual activity over the successive decades of the present century. But the magnitude of the increase is more consistent with the relaxation of social and religious restraints, enabling people to express and develop their natural sexuality more freely, than with a collapse of moral standards resulting in an age of unbridled licentiousness.

The major change took place after World War I, in the 1920s. Kinsey found that among women still unmarried by the age of 25, only 14 percent of those born before 1900 had experienced sexual intercourse, whereas 36 percent of those born between 1900 and 1909 had. In a study conducted in 1938, the psychologist L M Terman found that the incidence of premarital intercourse was increasing with "extraordinary rapidity" and predicted that "intercourse with future spouse before marriage will become universal by 1950 or 1955." His prediction proved wrong, however. Kinsey found that only about 50 percent of the women in his sample who had married before the age of 25 had had intercourse

Above : at one time the chastity of a young lady was considered so important that she was not allowed to be in the company of a man without the presence of a chaperone.

before they married. Among men on the other hand, the figure depended on educational level. It was 67 percent for college graduates, 84 percent for high school graduates, and 98 percent for those who only attended grade school. In a study carried out in England in 1969 by the anthropologist Geoffrey Gorer, 26 percent of the men and 63 percent of the women said that they were virgins at marriage. Furthermore, of those who had premarital sex 20 percent of the men and 25 percent of the women had experienced it only with the person they eventually married.

These findings suggest that in spite of the greater permissiveness of modern attitudes to premarital sex, for many people, particularly women, virginity is still valued and preserved for their ultimate marriage partner. Of course, we have to discount from the figures a proportion of people who had no opportunity or no inclination to participate in premarital intercourse. But, when considering the behavior of the general population the indications are that chastity is not that outmoded. Whether it is a good idea for people to be virgins when they marry is another question, which we shall come to shortly.

Sex and Adolescence

In the the mid-1960s the magazine *Seventeen* conducted a survey among a sample of its teenage female readership, and found that 25 percent in the 18–19 age group had experienced intercourse. In the Kinsey survey the figure of 25 percent was not reached before the 20–21 age group. It would appear that in the intervening 15 years girls had been engaging in sexual relationships at progressively younger ages. The recent propaganda campaign in Britain for a reduction of the age of consent from 16 to 14 might be seen as another indication of this fact.

The controversial British educator A S Neill, is reported to have said that the only reason he did not make contraceptives available to the pupils in his school was that it was illegal. Children, he believed, would grow up to be happier and better adjusted adults if they were brought up to have no feelings of guilt or shame about their sexuality and were allowed to express it naturally when they had both the desire and the opportunity. Some of Neill's critics argued that physical development and emotional maturity were two different stages and that while children should not be made to feel guilty or shameful about sex they certainly ought not to be actively encouraged to engage in it. There is a far greater likelihood that the physical and emotional aspects of sex will be integrated if a person begins his or her sex life when they are sufficiently mature to understand their sexuality.

But the problem is how to define maturity, and it is further complicated by the fact that sexual experience itself can precipitate maturity. Certainly one particularly relevant aspect of maturity is that it involves the abilities to appreciate, care for, and be responsible for another person. Perhaps today's parents of teenagers would contribute more to their children's happiness and development if they took note of the trend toward sex at younger ages and instead of adopting strict moral attitudes

Left : Western society enforces a prolonged childhood on adolescents, and for that reason sex among the young is generally disapproved of. Many young girls express their powerful sexuality through romantic dreams and infatuations which often end with a broken heart.

stressed the importance of mutual appreciation, caring, and responsibility in sexual relations. Adolescents living in an environment where their sexuality is unrecognized or condemned are more likely to have traumatic first experiences under inappropriate conditions than those who are allowed to express their sexuality naturally when they are ready to do so. And note we say "express" and not "indulge," for there is a world of difference in attitude implied by the two words.

Above : romantic settings assume an exaggerated importance in young love affairs.

The Double Standard

In nothing is the double standard of sexual conduct, the idea that there is one rule for men and another for women, so prevalent as in attitudes to premarital sex. Asked the question, "Do you think that young men should have some sexual experience before marriage," 64 percent of the men and 40 percent of the women canvassed by Geoffrey Gorer's researchers in 1969 answered "Yes." When the same question was asked about women, only 47 percent of the men and 24 percent of the women were in favor. The notable point about this was that women as well as men tended to support the double standard.

Kinsey accounts for the double standard by tracing it back to Chaldean and Jewish legal codes of 3000–4000 years ago, according to which a male had property rights in the woman he proposed to take as his wife. If she was violated while he was betrothed to her he could exact retribution in the form of cattle or other goods from her family because her value had depreciated. This may be true up to a point, but it is doubtful that such an explanation accounts for the following opinions expressed by some of Gorer's female interviewees:

"Men should have experience . . . Women do not need experience."

"I think most men do, and I think it helps them to choose the right woman when they want to settle down." [And for women?] "No; you find all this out when you get married."

"A man is different, and he wouldn't feel a man unless he had sown some wild oats." [And a woman?] "Just with the person that she is to marry; this is just to see if they are physically suited."

"Men are built this way, and have not got as much control as women."

"Young men should make love to one person or persons; he then understands how a woman feels the first time she's married and has intercourse." [And young women?] "I'm still old-fashioned in that way. You should be a virgin when you get married."

"It's not so good for a woman to have experience; she can learn from her husband."

"It gives men more confidence and they can probably satisfy their wives when married." [And women?] "Will get a bad reputation, and there is danger of disease."

"I think it makes him less nervous of sexual relations when he eventually marries. [And women?] "No. I think it is up to the individual. I personally don't approve, though."

These expressed opinions break down into two groups: the condescending attitude to men as sexual "animals" and the acceptance of the unequal status of women. They also imply that the male libido is stronger and more demanding than the female, and that young women do not need sex as much as young men do. Perhaps the reason for this is that women generally reach their sexual prime some 10 years later then men do. But there is no justification for either the condescending or the submissive attitude to male sexuality that would appear to be the most common female rationalizations of the double standard.

Above: a succession of scandalous love affairs gave Giacomo Casanova a place in history; a female counterpart would have been unacceptable.

Left: "The Outcast" by Richard Redgrave, showing an unmarried mother being thrown out by her father. It illustrates the Victorian attitude to women who transgressed the traditional code of morality.

Men who uphold the dual standard tend to rationalize their opinion in a different way. They argue that women are more vulnerable than men, not only because they can get pregnant but also because they are more idealistic and become emotionally committed during sex. To quote some examples:

"If a man doesn't get quite a lot of experience before, he'll want even more after marriage." [And women?] "They are more idealistic than men, and it is better if they think they're in love. They shouldn't make themselves too cheap."

"It's a question of practice; this is essential . . . the only way to learn is with a person one is not mentally involved with." [And for young women?] "If she falls in love with the right person she is going to marry he will – or should – have all the experience she will need."

"It's a man's way of proving himself a man and the development of masculine instincts is natural and healthy." [And in women?] "A woman risks so much more than a man so it's better that she is in love."

"Young men should have experience with just anyone. Before you marry you should have your fling. But women should have no experience. Most men would not like to marry a woman who had intercourse with someone else."

These are representative minority opinions, but fortunately not typical of the population as a whole. They express the most bigoted and ignorant type of male chauvinism, in which a misconceived idealization of the female results in a denial of her sexuality while at the same time the man claims the right to sexual license as essential for his education, and for the ultimate stability of his marriage. These opinions, backward though they are, still exist in Western society, just as the double standard still exists. The more widely held view, however, among both sexes, is that premarital sex is equally right for both sexes, particularly when it occurs in the context of love. And perhaps the most telling point concerning this subject is the fact that 77 percent of the married females in Kinsey's sample had no subsequent regret about their premarital sex lives, and a further 12 percent only had a very minor regret.

The Value of Sexual Experience

Right : in Chaucer's poem "Canterbury Tales," the wife of Bath prologues her tale with an account of her life with five husbands in succession.

Some years ago the writer Stephen Vizinczey enjoyed international success with a novel titled *In Praise of Older Women*, which told of a young man's initiation into and instruction in the arts of sex by a series of mature women. As we have seen, the most common argument for the dual standard put forward by both men and women is that a man needs to learn the techniques of love. It is logical therefore that he learns not by trial and error with inexperienced partners but through the instruction of an older and more experienced partner.

The question of the proper relative ages of sexual partners is controversial. While marriages between people involving a wide age gap may be approved, at least provided that money is not the motive, less permanent liaisons are generally frowned upon,

for the older person is thought to be exploiting the younger. In actual fact, when the relationship is between a young man and an older woman it may be quite ideal from a biological point of view. Both partners may be at their sexual peak and able to satisfy each other sexually much better than other members of their own generations could. With an older man and a younger woman the difference in libido may cause some difficulties, but these can be compensated for by the understanding and expertise that the man brings to the relationship. Different types of relationships suit different partners, and it is only convention and not any natural law which considers the relative ages of the partners.

Nothing disrupts relationships, in particular marriages, so much as sexual ignorance. And as theory is no substitute for

experience the inescapable conclusion must be that premarital sex benefits the stability of marriage. It might also be argued that the best and quickest way to learn about sex is through an experienced partner, in circumstances uncomplicated by emotional involvement. This is a contentious point. Should sex be divorced from love and, if so, can the two be reconciled again? But the fact that premarital experience makes for marital success and happiness is indisputable. Young people have to learn to love and learn how to make love, and if they do so before marriage there is less likelihood of sexual incompatibilities. As we noted previously, Kinsey found that, on the whole, women with premarital sexual experience were more successful in achieving orgasm in marital sex.

There are other arguments in favor of premarital heterosexual intercourse. Unlike the alternative sexual outlet, masturbation, intercourse develops people emotionally and enables them to make emotional adjustments to others. Also, as people get older they have more difficulty in making emotional and physical adjustments, so it is preferable that they make them at an early age. And if a relationship is going to founder because of sexual incompatibility, it is better that it does so before marriage than after. Last but not least, a person enjoying a full sexual life, untroubled by guilt or frustration, is able to function and concentrate more effectively in other, nonsexual fields. The psychologist Wilhelm Reich argued that most of the world's troubles and crimes are attributable to people's frustration through not being able to achieve satisfactory orgasm.

Above : brothels have provided a convenient place of sexual initiation for many young men, as well as catering for sexual outlets and diversions.

Reasons for Promiscuity

The Victorian idea of the "fallen" woman who lost her virginity, developed an addiction to sex, and became promiscuous, was a double-standard myth designed to inspire in young women a fear of sex and sin. Which is not to say that promiscuity does not exist.

In her book, *The Sexual Side of Love* (1973), Maureen Green reports a typical case. Audrey, an attractive teenage student, was famed for her promiscuity. At every party she turned her attentions on some attractive young man she had selected. Invariably she left with him and they would spend the night together. Her conduct puzzled many of her friends whereas in fact it was based upon insecurity. Her parents had died in a car crash when she was four, and a grandfather had brought her up. She had never felt certain of his love, and when she grew older she found that she could use her sexual appeal to gain the attention of men. In all her casual liaisons she was look-ing for a deeper and more secure love than she had ever known. But her method spoiled her chances of finding genuine love. It was only when she met an older man who understood and could make her understand the reason for her conduct, and could give her the emotional security she craved, that Audrey gave up her promiscuous life.

If promiscuity is as rife among young people today as some people would have us believe, then it is a terrible indictment on the lack of love and security in the home. The much-publicized young "drop-outs" of the 1960s and early 1970s were often vehement about the lack of affection shown by their parents. Many tried to compensate for the poor quality of the love in their lives through communal living and sex.

There can be no doubt that promiscuity in men takes different forms and has different causes than in the woman. Kinsey's statistics on the number of partners that men and women had had in their premarital petting and intercourse, reproduced in the form of a table, establishes this point quite clearly. Kinsey suggests some reasons for the greater potential for promiscuity in the male:

"The male is aroused at observing his potential sexual partner, as most females are

Right: prostitution has long catered for sexual needs without any love or commitment.

Opposite page, center: men are regarded as the more promiscuous sex because they are supposedly more easily aroused.

In both heterosexual and homosexual relationships, promiscuity may depend, in many instances, upon the male's anticipation of variation in the genital anatomy of the partner, in the techniques which may be used during the contacts, and in the physical responses of the new partner. None of these factors have such significance for the average female.

"Male promiscuity often depends upon the satisfactions that may be secured from the pursuit and successful attainment of a new partner. . . Once having demonstrated their capacities to effect sexual relations with the particular individual, they prefer to turn to the pursuit of the next partner. . .

"As far as his psychological responses are concerned, the male in many instances may not be having coitus with the immediate sexual partner, but with all of the other girls with whom he has ever had coitus, and with the entire genus Female with which he would like to have coitus."

For all that Kinsey says about the differences between male and female promiscuity, ultimately, insecurity and the quest for a profound and fulfilling relationship must be at the root of both. There is no symptom of insecurity more obvious than a need for conquest or to prove oneself. Again, Wilhelm Reich had some very pertinent observations on this subject. "People who have acquired the ability for orgastic satisfaction are far more capable of monogamous relationships than people who suffer from sexual stasis" he wrote. "And the monogamous attitude of these people is not due to the inhibition of polygamous impulses or to moral scruples; it is based on the sex-economic principle of experiencing again and again vivid sexual pleasure and gratification with the same sexual partner. This presupposes full sexual harmony between the sexual partners. There is, in this respect, no difference between the healthy man and the healthy woman. If, on the other hand, a suitable partner is lacking, which under present sexual conditions is the rule, the ability for monogamy turns into its opposite, an irrepressible search for a suitable partner. If he or she is found, the monogamous attitude reestablishes itself automatically and continues as long as there is sexual harmony and gratification. Thoughts of and desire for other partners either do not appear or, because of the interest in the partner, are not put into action."

Above : in the 1960s many young people rejected what they considered to be the isolation and exclusivity of monogamous relationships, and lived in communes.

not. The male is aroused because he has been conditioned by his previous experience, as most females have not. The male is aroused by anticipating new types of experience, new types of sexual partners, new levels of satisfaction that may be attained in the new relationships, new opportunities to experiment with new techniques, new opportunities to secure higher levels of satisfaction than he has ever before attained.

License or Restraint?

Some observers of contemporary life are fond of making a comparison with Rome in its period of decline and arguing that a permissive society marks the end of a civilization. If this is true we ought to take it into account in considering the relative merits of license and restraint. We have generally taken the view that sexual repression is bad for a person. Sexual expression and fulfillment are not only good in themselves but also make a person more effective in nonsexual activities, thus benefitting society. Whether the sexual activity is obtained within the institution of marriage or outside it is irrelevant. This could be seen as the advocacy of promiscuous behavior, so perhaps we should reconsider our attitude in the light of the evidence from anthropology and history.

The argument for sexual restraint was put by Freud as follows: "We believe that civilization has been built up by sacrifices

For the ancient Indians the cultivation of erotic techniques was of major importance. Sexual pleasure dominated their art and culture.

Right : miniature of Shah Jahan and his mistress.

Below : sculpture from the Temple of Deri Jagadamba, Khajuraho.

in gratification of the primitive impulses, and that it is to a great extent forever being recreated as each individual repeats the sacrifice of his instinctual pleasures for the common good. The sexual are among the most important of the instinctual forces thus utilized; they are in this way sublimated, that is to say, their energy is turned

aside from its sexual goal and diverted toward other ends, no longer sexual and socially more valuable."

In 1934 an English scholar, J D Unwin, published a book titled *Sex and Culture* in which he tested this Freudian hypothesis. He undertook a massive investigation of more than 80 societies, both contemporary and historical, primitive and advanced, and considered how the sex regulations and behavior in each correlated with its degree of cultural advancement, or in the case of advanced societies with its degree of "productive energy." He found that societies with regulations prohibiting sex before or outside marriage were more evolved culturally than permissive societies. Also the early and vigorous stage of the advanced societies that had built the world's great civilizations had believed in and practiced monogamy. Furthermore, "the group within the society which suffered the greatest continence displayed the greatest energy, and dominated the society." Any human society, Unwin concluded, "is free to choose either to display great energy or to enjoy sexual freedom; the evidence is that

Above : "A Bacchanalian Revel before a Team of Pan," by Nicolas Poussin. One of the supposed factors contributing to the decline of the Roman Empire was the total collapse of moral standards and restraint.

it cannot do both for more than one generation."

Unwin's study is virtually unknown today, possibly because of its conclusions, and was only recently rediscovered by the American writer Vance Packard. In his book *The Sexual Wilderness*, Packard also quotes a relevant passage by the British historian Arnold Toynbee: "I myself believe, on the historical evidence, that the later we can postpone the age of sexual consciousness, the better able we are to educate ourselves. . . But today while we are lowering the age of sexual awareness, we are prolonging the length of education. How can the young be expected to give their minds to study during these sex-haunted years?. . . I admire the 19th-century West's success in postponing the age of sexual awakening, sexual experience, and sexual infatuation far beyond the age of physical puberty. You may tell me that this is against nature; but to be human consists precisely of transcending nature – in overcoming the biological limitations that we have inherited from our prehuman ancestors."

Toynbee's point appears to be borne out by Unwin's findings. And it is undeniable that although the Pilgrim Fathers and the Victorians were puritanical in their attitude to sex, they were tremendously energetic in other fields, such as creating and expand-

ing empires and businesses. John Cuber and Peggy Harroff, two sociologists from Ohio University, studied the marriages of 437 highly successful Americans. The survey, published in 1965, revealed that on the whole sex was an unimportant aspect of their lives, and the authors remarked that "Many of these career-dominated people had channeled almost the whole of their energies into success aspirations." All of which suggests that sexual self restraint does not necessarily produce frustrated, repressed, and twisted people. Instead it can generate and direct creative work which is beneficial to society. Of course a code of practice that would be intolerable if imposed from outside can be extremely rewarding when voluntarily embraced, and a lot of evidence points to the fact that the higher human achievements, both in individual lives and in entire civilizations, have come about in an atmosphere of voluntary sexual restraint. Total abstinence is of course rare, and always has been. The form of restraint most commonly accepted has been the institution of monogamous marriage. Unwin's finding of a clear correlation between monogamy and "productive energy" in his far-ranging study suggests that modern liberal and permissive attitudes to sex outside marriage may not be so enlightened after all.

Sex for its own Sake

An argument that contradicts the views against sexual license put forward by Freud, Unwin, and Toynbee, is that it is not sexual activity that reduces man's capacity for other activities, but the feelings of remorse and guilt, the time and energy consumed in fixing clandestine sexual meetings, and the doubt and confusion resulting from the contravening of society's generally accepted rules. According to this view conventional sexual rules are more or less arbitrary and are based upon such reprehensible premises as regarding another human being as exclusive property. Therefore if the rules were changed, emotions such as jealousy and possessiveness would eventually disappear from human nature.

A champion of this point of view, the American psychologist Albert Ellis, writes that "Sex without love . . . is hardly a heinous crime, and appears to be quite delightful and to add immeasurably to the lives of literally millions of individuals." Others have cited the Samoan attitudes to sex as recorded by the anthropologist Margaret Mead in her book, *Coming of Age in Samoa* (1967). The Samoans, apparently, considered sex as a very agreeable way to pass time, and young people enjoyed it without inhibition. Jealousy was unknown, and although they married they would continue to have affairs with others quite openly.

There is evidence, however, that in our society the divorce of sex from love and the pursuit of the uncommitted lifestyle eventually creates problems for their advocates. Many of the communes established in America and Europe in the 1960s and 70s broke up because guilt and jealousy made them unworkable.

A University of Illinois psychologist, Hobart Mowrer, has pointed out that in Hawaii the native people, who have the same carefree approach to life and sex as the Samoans, are right at the bottom of the economic ladder in a mixed society that also includes descendants of Chinese plantation laborers. This type of lifestyle, he says, may be "okay for a stone age technology in a favorable environment," but in the modern world young people need the second decade to acquire their culture and technology. His view is supported by the Kinsey researchers' finding that in American society males in the lowest educational stratum had five times as much premarital sexual intercourse as the males who went to college.

Furthermore, it appears that the sexually adventurous do not enjoy life any more than those who are celibate or have a single relationship. Speaking from his experience as a university psychiatrist, Seymour Halleck of the University of Wisconsin told the American Psychiatric Association: "Students who are psychiatric patients are likely to be promiscuous. Many of these patients both male and female can be described as alienated. . . While the alienated student seems to be leading a stimulating sex life, he frequently complains that it is unsatisfying and meaningless."

Consideration of anthropological and historical evidence does suggest that an ethic of license not only fails to develop in individuals in a society the qualities of responsibility and maturity, but also diminishes a person's capacity for intensity of feeling and for establishing a profound loving relationship, and often undermines his sense of personal integrity. The institution of marriage may be under attack today, and other forms of relationship than lifelong monogamy may become established as norms, but all the evidence points to the fact that if social institutions and the prevailing ethic fail to impose sexual restraints, neither the society as a whole nor the individuals within it can be expected to realize anything like their optimum potential achievements.

Left : a monogamous relationship is often portrayed as a trap that many unfortunate men fall into.

Right : monogamous relationships will always exist because a powerful love bond can overcome the strongest sexual drive.

Attitudes to Adultery

In all societies throughout the world and throughout history extramarital sex has been more severely condemned than pre-marital sex. The reason is obvious – it threatens the security of the family, in particular the upbringing of children. Yet most societies have allowed the man some discreet extramarital sexual activity on the grounds that his sexual drive cannot be satisfied by one woman alone. Few societies, however, extend the woman this right. The most frequent rationalization for this is that the husband had to be sure that his heirs were in fact his own .offspring and not his wife's lover's. For this reason, in many cultures adultery on the part of the woman was always more harshly punished, in-variably by divorce and sometimes by death. It was also considered that a woman was more likely to become emotionally involved with her lover, and this constituted a threat to the stability of the family.

Kinsey reported that many men were very curious to know how many members of their sex had extramarital intercourse. He thought that the reason for this interest was the fact that they either had or wished to have extramarital relationships themselves and wanted to reconcile this with their consciences by establishing that it was a common practice. He found that 50 percent of the men in his sample had sexual inter-course with women other than their wives at some time in their married lives. He also found distinctly different patterns in extra-marital sexual activity which depended on age, social class, and level of education. In the lower socioeconomic brackets the highest incidence of infidelity occurred at a younger age, steadily decreasing as the subjects got older. On the other hand, men who were socially and educationally more privileged tended to be more faithful when they were young but considerably less so as they got older. Men in the lower socioeconomic brackets got 12 percent of their total sexual activity in the early years of marriage from partners other than their wives, but only 6 percent when they were in their 40s, whereas in the higher levels the figures were 3 percent in the early years of marriage and 14 percent by the time they were 50.

The incidence of infidelity among women in Kinsey's sample did not show such marked social and educational differences. Extramarital sex accounted for 3 percent

Left : "The Killing of the Earl" by William Hogarth. Having mortally wounded the Earl, the Countess' lover flees through the window, while she begs for forgiveness from her dying husband.

of the total activity of married women in their early 20s irrespective of their social or educational level, though by their 30s the women in the higher levels were in general more unfaithful than their poorer, less educated contemporaries. Overall, the incidence of infidelity among married women rose as they got older, with 6 percent of women having had extramarital relations in their late teens, 14 percent in their late 20s, and some 26 percent by the time they were 40 (compared with 50 percent of men). One obvious reason for this rise is that women reach their sexual peak later than men. Also, in their 30s they are often loosening the ties with their children. But the main reason appears to be a dissatisfaction with their marital sexual lives which leads them to seek from another the emotion and affection that the husband no longer provides. Forty-two percent of the adulterous women in Kinsey's sample reported that they experienced orgasm more frequently with their lovers than with their husbands, and the majority of the rest said

that there was no difference; very few rated their husbands more satisfying lovers than their extramarital partners.

Other common reasons for a wife's infidelity were a conscious or unconscious attempt to acquire social status, retaliation for the husband's infidelity, assertion of independence, an accommodation to a respected friend, and the search for a new source of emotional satisfaction.

A considerable number of women had been encouraged to engage in extramarital activities by their husbands, sometimes because the man wanted to do likewise himself, more rarely because he obtained satisfaction from watching his wife's extra-marital coitus, but most often because he wanted to extend his wife's opportunity for sexual satisfaction. The latter motive also accounted for the fact that 42 percent of husbands who had discovered that their wives had extramarital relations had accepted more or less the fact, and made no difficulty about it. On the other hand, in cases of marriages that ended in divorce,

Above : Paolo and Francesca were a pair of young lovers whose affair was immortalized by Dante. Francesca was the wife of Paolo's brother, seen here about to kill him.

51 percent of males said their wife's infidelity was the main cause of the breakup, so a complacent attitude to the wife's extramarital activities is not the rule. But in yet other cases marital relationships have been improved as a result of one of the partner's extramarital adventures. Kinsey quotes the 17th-century writer Samuel Pepys, who confided to his diary the fact that in the 20 days since he had had an extramarital affair he had made love to his wife more times than in the previous 12 months, "and with more pleasure to her than I think in all the time of our marriage before." People's attitudes and reactions to their own and their partners' extramarital sexual activities are varied and unpredictable. Perhaps the only point that can be made about the practice with any certainty is that if a person values his or her marriage, extramarital affairs are dangerous.

The 1960s was supposed to be a decade when sexual attitudes changed radically and marital fidelity came to be considered old fashioned, but to judge by the evidence collected by Geoffrey Gorer's researchers in Britain in 1970 the effect of this new wave of ideas was only superficial.

Whereas Kinsey collected data about behavior, Gorer was concerned with beliefs and attitudes, and the answers to his questions about fidelity and adultery were not such as to suggest that morality in marriage had broken down.

Asked whether husbands and wives should be faithful to each other throughout their married lives, 90 percent of the married respondents said that husbands should be, and 93 percent said that wives should be. Interestingly, the percent that allowed husbands a license they did not extend to wives were predominantly women. Only 7 percent of the sample explicitly said that husbands need not be faithful and only 4 percent that wives need not be.

Another question was: "How do you feel about a married man [woman] who has an affair with a woman [man] he [she] does not really love?" Strong disapproval was expressed by 71 percent of the women and 53 percent of the men. Typical of such answers were: "He wants shooting;" "Disgusting – immoral – does not love his wife, does not respect his wife, and does not respect other women or himself," "It is horrible in a man and it is vile in a woman," "I think it's animalish, really; just to satisfy their baser instincts; it's disgusting." Only 4 percent of the men and 2 percent of the women expressed the opinion that it was natural and permissable for a man to have a casual affair, and only 1 percent of the men and none of the women thought it was natural for a woman. More men than women (16 percent) accepted the possibility of extenuating circumstances, and were less willing to pass judgement. Typical of such expressions of opinion were: "It all depends. There must be a reason why, so it's hard to judge without knowing all the facts." "Perhaps her husband is so absorbed in his work she just wants amusement. Perhaps she's getting a little older and wants to prove something to herself." The attitude that a casual affair implies that there is something lacking in the marriage, and therefore that the person is more to be pitied than condemned, was expressed by an equal proportion of men and women (15 percent). Some samples were: "He's probably not getting enough at home;" "There's something wrong with the wife. Perhaps she is not interested in sex or something;" "I'd look to myself to see why he'd gone; he must have been desperate."

A third question asked by Gorer's interviewers was: "If a husband [wife] finds his wife [her husband] having an affair with another man [woman] what should he [she] do?" The same question had been asked in Gorer's 1950 survey, so the answers were also indicative of changes in

Below left : an illicit affair can reawaken passions that have long been stifled by the routine of marriage.

Below right : unfortunately adulterous relationships always carry with them the possibility of discovery.

attitude between the 50s and 60s. The most notable change was the reduction in the number of people who proposed drastic measures. In 1950 there were 47 percent who spoke of divorce or separation, but only 32 percent in 1970. Also while the number who had recommended talking things over and attempting a reconciliation was 38 percent in 1950, by 1970 it had risen to 48 percent. There was a marked fall over the period in the number of people who recommended physical violence as punishment, and also a fall in the number who spoke of simply forgiving, ignoring the situation, or doing nothing. Both these factors indicate a more intelligent attitude to marriage. Another very notable difference was in the number of people who felt if their husband or wife were unfaithful the fault might lie with them. In 1950, 22 percent of the women had said they would

try to get the husband back by making themselves more attractive, but in 1970 only 1 percent said this: and again in the earlier sample there were 20 percent of the men who said they would examine their own faults if their wives had an affair, but only 5 percent gave this answer in 1970. Gorer considered that this was related to the declining importance of religion and particularly the idea that a person's misfortunes are the result of sinful behavior.

Generally speaking, the changes in opinion about adultery as expressed by this sample of the British population indicated the development of a more intelligent attitude but certainly not a more permissive one.

Sex for Sale

A fair number of Gorer's interviewees who disapproved of extramarital sex later admitted that they had experienced it themselves. And Kinsey, if you will remember, found that probably every other man and one woman in four experienced it at some time in their married lives. So let us take a closer look at some forms of adultery.

The mistress or "kept woman" figured prominently in history. In European society, from the 17th century onward men had mistresses quite openly and many enjoyed status and power. Today the situation is different. Status is no longer equated with sexual prowess and many political careers have been ruined by revelations or flauntings of such liaisons. With the emphasis on respectability and discretion, it is difficult to ascertain whether the phenomenon of the mistress is rapidly disappearing or has simply gone underground. However, there are far fewer women nowadays who expect to be supported, and, in Western society, fewer men who can afford to do so in addition to maintaining a home and children.

With more women being employed, both partners have more daily contact with members of the opposite sex, other than their spouse, and the place of work offers more opportunity for adultery than ever before. This is especially true of the traditional workplace relationship between the male employer and one of his female employees, such as his secretary. The expansion of the female work force has not been matched by a corresponding rise in women's promotion, and consequently even in those areas of employment where there are a large number of women, there are invariably more men at the higher end of the hierarchy. And while few men could nowadays expect to presume upon a woman because of their status, power still has its attractions. "Even though a man expects his wife to stop dating after the wedding, he merely transfers his womanizing from evening to midday and goes right on dating until retirement time," writes Marion Meade in her book, *Bitching*,

(1976) and she goes on to recommend ways that a female can exploit married males to obtain free meals, valuable gifts and uncomplicated sex if she wants it. It is calculatedly outrageous and cynical, but the philosophy of exploitation had to elicit some response from embattled women, and this is it.

Daytime or office affairs, however, are not necessarily so exploitative and sometimes relationships can develop that satisfy both partners, particularly if they occur between colleagues rather than employer and employee. The office party is an occasion when inhibitions can be overcome and long-nurtured feelings displayed. The problem with a sudden affair of this type is that the parties may not have had time to explore each other's feelings at depth and may have different ideas as to why they have become involved. Where one may be gratifying simple lust, the other may see it as the beginning of a deep and meaningful relationship. The result can be embarrassing, if not actually very unpleasant, especially as the two will not be able to avoid seeing each other during the day. It is precisely to avoid such complications that many men prefer to use prostitutes.

Kinsey found that 69 percent of the men in his sample had sexual relations with prostitutes at some time in their lives. They go for a variety of reasons: because they have insufficient sexual outlet elsewhere; because they are seeking a type of sexual activity that is not easily available in normal circumstances; because they can obtain instant satisfaction without any of the time-consuming formalities of courtship; because it is cheaper than seducing a woman by wining and dining her and giving her presents, and above all because they can be anonymous and uninvolved socially, legally, or emotionally. This lack of involvement, however, works both ways. Kinsey found that men in the upper social level particularly were often disappointed by the prostitute's lack of warmth, affection, and erotic response.

Mutual Affairs

In Manhattan in 1978, *Time* magazine's behavior writer John Leo reported that there were at least half a dozen "swingers" clubs operating openly. These are places where couples can go to take part in sexual exchanges. Leo and a female friend (unattached males are not admitted) visited one named *Plato's Retreat* and he described the scene there. There is a bar, swimming pool, a steambath, a discotheque, a "mat room" for orgies, and 20 "mini-swing" rooms to accommodate up to three couples. He noticed about 200 couples, all naked, presumably enjoying the amenities and each other's company. Leo found the proceedings "amiable, but flat," and noted that many patrons looked bored. A young woman standing at the bar said, "I don't know why I'm here. I'm only nude because there's nothing to do here with your clothes on."

The proprietors of *Plato's Retreat* estimated that some 65 percent of their patrons were married suburbanites, and sociologists have observed that over recent years the practices of group sex, swapping of partners, and troilism (sex involving three) have been greatly on the increase among middle-classes of North America and Europe. There are even a number of specialized publications that carry advertisements for swapping partners. When a California researcher, Paul Avery, put the following in a San Francisco paper: "Attractive couple in late 20s, bored with conventional friendships, wishes to meet with couples or singles to exchange unconventional experiences in the unusual/exotic/unique," he received 300 replies, 100 of them from married couples. He and his wife followed 100 of these up with correspondence and in some cases meetings. They found that the typical "swinger" couple regard themselves as broadminded and justify their activity by saying they enjoy having a good time. They also claim to have found that changing partners has put new life into their marriage. Psychiatrists would be highly dubious about this last point; one who has known several such

couples has reported that "in each instance, unhappy and tragic complications have ultimately arisen and the marriage has broken down;" and another has gone on record as saying that although these couples are not necessarily sick people an unusually high proportion of them are undergoing therapy. In many cases one of the partners is a reluctant participant, invariably the woman. There have been many cases in which men have sought to advance their careers by inducing their wives to sleep with a senior colleague. Compared with such cynicism and exploitation, the events at *Plato's Retreat* appear almost like harmless fun, although it is difficult to conceive that their married participants have not simply given up or have never had the intention of building a profound and lasting relationship.

There are cases in which a person might give his or her mate sexual license out of pure generosity. A 56-year-old correspondent of the Hegelers, the Swedish sex counsellors, wrote that as he was incapable of satisfying his 50-year-old wife, who had recently become sexier than ever as postmenopausal women often do, he had agreed to her obtaining satisfaction from other men. "She's got a couple of regular lovers," he wrote, "and has sexual intercourse a couple of times a week. It's made her as happy and lively as a 20-year-old. She says herself she's happy to be able to enjoy life. I benefit from all this too. Is it wrong of me to let her?" The Hegeler's reply was that they thought he had arranged matters in an admirably sensible and tolerant way which had their whole-hearted approval.

The right of a person to seek extramarital sex if he or she is not getting enough sexual satisfaction from the marriage partner raises certain moral questions, but it can scarcely be regarded as reprehensible for one partner to engage in extramarital sex with the other partner's approval. In circumstances where there is a considerable discrepancy in age or in sex drive, or where one partner has been sexually incapacitated by injury or illness, such arrangements can be highly beneficial.

Although sexual compatibility is the bedrock of the normal marriage, marriage does not consist entirely of sex, and people can in certain circumstances enjoy companionship, security, affection, mutual interests, and even parenthood while having their sexual needs catered to elsewhere.

The Dangers of Adultery

A seemingly reasonable extramarital affair, arranged to the satisfaction of both partners, can still backfire because suppressed feelings, such as jealousy, possessiveness, or shame, awkwardly assert themselves. Although mutually condoned adultery, whether in the form of mate-swapping, group sex, troilism, or allowing one's partner to have lovers, would appear morally preferable to deception, its consequences can sometimes be more disastrous for a marriage and for a personality than those of the furtive affair.

It must be acknowledged that possessiveness is a component of sexual love. The lover feels that the loved one belongs to him [her] and is part of him [her]. Consequently, removal of the loved one constitutes a form of theft and a threat to the personal integrity of the lover. This is one form of jealousy. Another quite distinct form is based on insecurity and self-doubt. Just as love can consolidate and stabilize a personality, so its withdrawal can do drastic psychological harm. With the ego so bat-

tered, it is not surprising that psychiatrists have found a very high failure rate in mutually permissive marriages. Although sex correspondence magazines like *Forum* often carry letters from people who claim that their marriages have been strengthened and enhanced by their affairs, they are probably exceptions.

Therefore, in most cases, if a person is going to indulge in extramarital affairs, and at the same time wishes to preserve the marriage, discretion is of the utmost importance. If the 50 percent of men and 25 percent of women in the Kinsey sample who had been unfaithful had all confessed, there would no doubt have been many more broken marriages and deeply distressed people. It is inexcusably selfish to confess for the sake of one's conscience and expect indulgence for honesty when such action can only cause the partner distress, and disrupt the marriage and the family.

It would be impossible to calculate how much distress was alleviated and how many marriages were saved by the adulteries of the men and women in the Kinsey sample. Although it must always be a very hazardous resort, adultery can in certain circumstances stabilize a marriage and restore self-confidence. As a personality can base its stability and growth on a good marriage, by the same token, it can be stunted by a bad one, especially when it involves daily marital conflict.

The rights and wrongs of extramarital sex are beyond the scope of simplistic moralizing. All we can say is that it may be therapeutic but is more likely to be disastrous. A person intent on an affair should scrutinize his or her motives, and consider whether alternatives within the marriage have been adequately explored. It may well be that the problems within the marriage need to be solved jointly or even that the relationship has broken down irrevocably.

Chapter 8
Birth Control –
the Chance to Choose

Safe, reliable methods of birth control have been
available for some years now, yet for many young
couples, lovemaking – which should be a carefree,
joyous experience – ends in the frustration and
emotional trauma of an unwanted pregnancy or
abortion. One of the main reasons for this paradox
is still, incredibly enough, ignorance of what sex is
all about. Another basic problem is that so many
young people are still shy and inhibited about
admitting that they need to protect themselves
against the possibility of conception. Some people
feel, consciously or unconsciously, that it is *wrong*
to make love without risking pregnancy, and yet
others consider it cold and calculating to
deliberately prepare for the possibility of
spontaneously making love. Whatever the reason,
a great many people are needlessly denying
themselves the sheer beauty and pleasure that free
and safe loving can give.

*An unwanted pregnancy has
always been the greatest
barrier to spontaneous
lovemaking. With the
availability of safe and
reliable birth-control methods,
this obstacle has been removed.*

A History of Hypocrisy

Attempts to research the history of the birth control "revolution" lead into a fog composed of dogmatic religious prejudices, the silence of some of the medical profession, the extraordinary "head-in-the-sand" attitude of the law, and sheer hypocrisy. Male contraceptives, the most common being the condom, have been used for centuries but were frequently obtainable only through indirect methods. The subject of birth control of any sort brought forth a fever of moral indignation from some of the

Below : magic played an important role in the birth-control methods of ancient India.

Below left : contraception has a long history. The ancient Greeks developed a number of methods, classifying them according to effectiveness and safety.

groups mentioned above, but the very idea of birth control for females was likely to cause a particularly rabid backlash. For example, in 1897 a doctor published "The Wives Handbook," a birth control booklet addressed mainly to women of the poorer classes. According to E S Turner, author of *Call the Doctor* (1958), the writer was prosecuted and struck off the General Medical Council Register, but "had it been a more expensive publication he might have escaped punishment."

As late as 1928, when *Ideal Marriage* was first published in London by William Heinemann's Medical Books Ltd, Dr T H Van de Velde stated in his personal introduction: "This book will state many things which would otherwise remain unsaid. Therefore it will have many unplea-

sant results for me. I know this, for I have gradually attained to some knowledge of my fellow human beings and of their habit of condemning what is unusual and unconventional." He continued, " . . . for that reason, this book could not be written earlier. So long as a doctor has to meet the requirements of his practice, he cannot permit himself to transgress the bounds of custom."

Of course, Van de Velde was not alone in putting forward the idea of birth control. Among other modern pioneers who faced the storms of abuse and hysterical criticism were Dr Marie Stopes, Havelock Ellis, Margaret Sanger, and Maud Royden. Marie Stopes' famous "dutch cap" for women was even lambasted as "sexual dictatorship!" In the early 1930s Lord Dawson of Penn, the court physician, told churchmen

that "sexual intercourse in marriage might be enjoyed for its own sake, not merely as a means of procreation." A generation earlier he would have been removed from office.

In the last few years an impressive amount of literature openly discussing the subjects of sexuality, pregnancy, and birth control has appeared, but to what effect? A survey quoted by Dr David Delvin in his book *Carefree Love* (first published in 1976) and conducted by *Doctor* magazine among British general practitioners, showed that 70 percent of those answering felt it their duty to give advice on family planning. But a number of doctors still do not prescribe any methods of birth control for the *unmarried*, and many Roman Catholic doctors believe, based on the principles laid down by their church, that it is wrong to prescribe any "artificial" method of contraception to anyone at all.

In Britain local family planning clinics are now staffed by specialists trained to deal with sexual and contraceptive problems, but a great deal of controversy still surrounds the concept that birth control methods should be made easily available. The most obvious argument against such availability is that it would encourage greater promiscuity among young unmarried people. This may be true in a certain number of cases, but little evidence exists that the lack of efficient birth control methods ever *discouraged* promiscuity, which in any case is not a mode of behavior that is attractive to everyone.

Parents and doctors who consider it their duty to explain or prescribe contraceptives, particularly to the young unmarried, show a more realistic understanding of the power of the human sexual drive. It is surely essential that people should not only learn about their own bodies and how they function, but also understand their sexuality in all its aspects – physical, psychological, and emotional. As Dr Van de Velde wrote: "There is great need of this knowledge; there is too much suffering endured which might well be avoided, too much joy untasted which could enhance life's worth."

Today a woman can expect many years of active life in which due to birth control, she can choose freely whether or how many children she wants. Consequently women can express ambition and take up careers, interests, and activities outside the home. Before effective birth control became widely available, every sexual approach by a wo-

man's husband meant the risk of another pregnancy, and many wives must have come to dread sexual intercourse. Yearly pregnancies also brought health problems, and neither of these factors could have made for much happiness in marriage for either partner.

It is all too easy to gloss over the horrors and terrors that were the lot of most women in a romantic, nostalgic view of the past. In a television interview about her life, the youngest surviving daughter (the thirteenth child) of Russian author Leo Tolstoy recalled that she had been brought up with the knowledge that her mother had, during her pregnancies, often jumped off cupboards in the desperate hope of bringing on an abortion. As she was an upper class woman, it can be imagined what the lot of the less privileged was like. In fact, one woman aged 80 described as common practice mothers of large families sitting in a hot bath and drinking a bottle of gin for the same desperate reason. When such stratagems failed and desperation (if she had the money) drove a woman to an abortionist, she put her life at serious risk. Small wonder that before the birth control "revolution" the joys of sex for a woman were severely limited.

Above: without reliable birth-control methods yearly pregnancies were an inevitability for many families. In 19th-century industrialized Europe this aggravated the already appalling, overcrowded living conditions that working-class people had to endure.

The "Rhythm Method"

Under the general term "contraception" there are three main types – natural, mechanical, and chemical. Each couple must decide which best suits them physically and emotionally, and which is most compatible with their moral beliefs.

The natural "rhythm method" is based on the idea that a couple who wish to avoid pregnancies only indulge in sexual intercourse during the woman's "safe" or infertile period during each month. Assuming that the woman has the average 28-day menstrual cycle, she ovulates – produces an egg that if fertilized would develop into a baby – in the middle of the cycle, about the fourteenth or fifteenth day after her last period began. With the rhythm method intercourse is avoided on the four days on each side of the probable fertile days, i.e., between the eleventh and the nineteenth days of the cycle.

The rhythm method is not considered very reliable because women vary a great deal in their menstrual cycles from month to month and at different times of the year. In calculating the "safe" period the woman considers her longest and shortest cycles over a period of at least six months and allows a longer period of abstinence if she is particularly irregular; it is also possible to buy a calculator which can be programmed with this information to show at a glance the days of abstinence in any month. But even with such help mistakes very often occur. This is the method recommended by the Roman Catholic church, which on the one hand maintains that God and only God can decide who lives and who dies, and on the other hand teaches that "nature" has provided her own method of family planning.

Apart from the dubious efficiency of the rhythm method, an obvious objection is that it inhibits spontaneous lovemaking. Also, it limits sexual love to those days when a woman's desire for intercourse may be at its lowest ebb, a fact which in itself can cause anxiety and tension.

Another natural method is the temperature method. Although this is more scientifically accurate than the rhythm method, it is fairly difficult in practice. When she is ovulating a woman's temperature rises slightly, so in this method she takes her rectal temperature every morning at precisely the same time and under the same conditions. The readings are scrupulously recorded on a chart and the times of "safe" intercourse are planned very carefully. But minor disorders such as a cold, emotional upset, or travel sickness can create temperature aberrations and thereby cause errors. This method also has the disadvantage of taking the spontaneity out of lovemaking, and it has the additional drawback that to interpret the chart accurately it is necessary

222

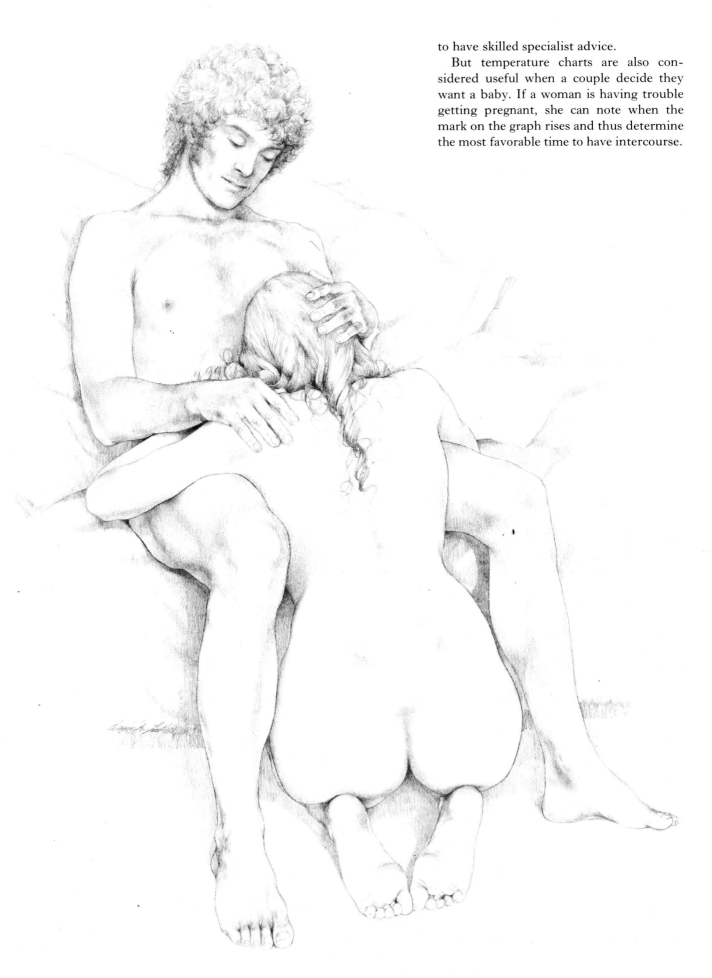

to have skilled specialist advice.

But temperature charts are also considered useful when a couple decide they want a baby. If a woman is having trouble getting pregnant, she can note when the mark on the graph rises and thus determine the most favorable time to have intercourse.

Coitus Interruptus

The natural method known as *coitus interruptus* is still used by considerable numbers of married couples because of fears, phobias, and prejudices against other methods of birth control. Dr David Delvin says that as many as *one in seven* of all married couples employ this method.

In practicing coitus interruptus, the man withdraws his penis from the woman's vagina before he reaches a climax and ejaculates. Most doctors and sexologists are not in favor of this method of birth control for two reasons. First of all, it is very frustrating, because the most psychologically and physically significant moment for the man in the final stage of lovemaking is when he "pours himself into" the woman. Secondly, as a method of contraception it is not at all safe. This is not only because it is extremely difficult, particularly for a young man, to exercise the necessary control over his orgasm to be absolutely sure of withdrawing before he ejaculates; also, most men produce drops of seminal fluid at their peak of sexual excitement before ejaculation, and these few drops contain active sperm which can travel through the vagina to the uterus.

The only advantageous use for this method of contraception is when a couple are desperate to make love and have no other means available. If practiced regularly it is likely to make one or both partners

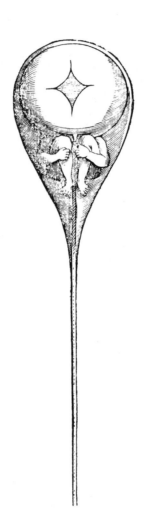

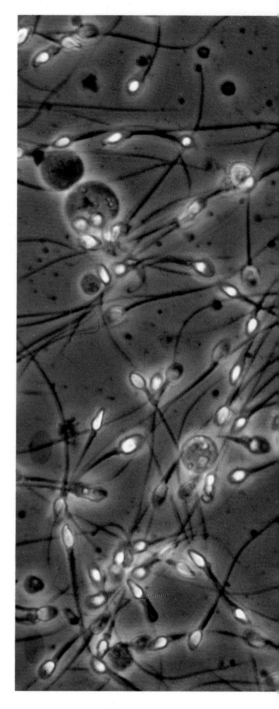

Above left: John Humphreys Noyes, founder of the Oneida Community.

Above: the importance of sperm in reproduction has long been recognized. In the Middle Ages it was thought to contain the fully developed embryo.

Above right: the average ejaculation contains between two and three hundred million sperm, and only one is needed for fertilization.

nonorgasmic, for an essential element in the orgasm is the clouding of consciousness and surrendering of the body to its involuntary movements.

Coitus reservatus is quite a different thing. Here the man does not withdraw his penis – he simply avoids reaching a climax inside the woman, or reaching one at all. He inserts his erect penis into her vagina and they lie together, resting. The man makes just enough occasional movement to maintain his erection and stops when the tension mounts. Some couples, though only a small minority, find this feeling of

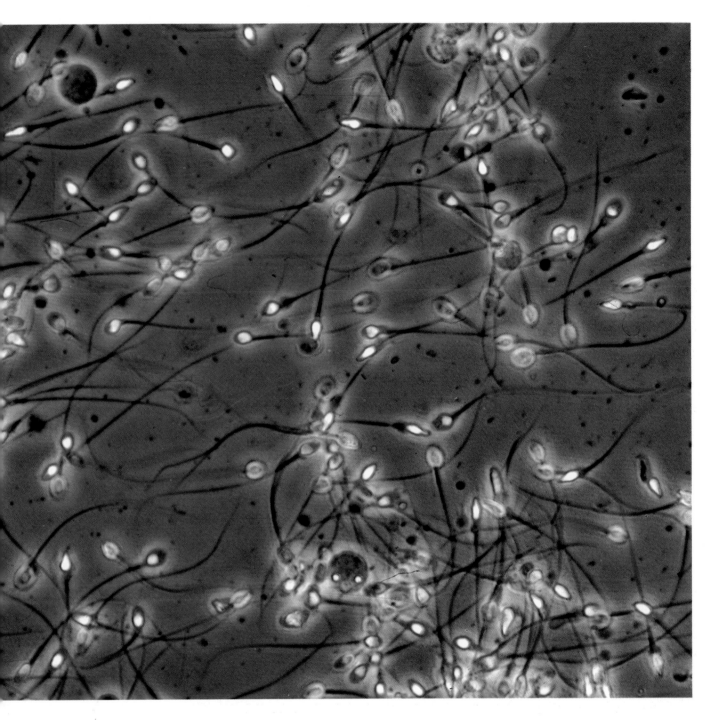

"togetherness" fully satisfying. This method, alternatively known as "Karezza," has been recommended and deliberately practiced in some societies. The Oneida community of New York, which sought to live according to a fundamentalist reading of the Bible, practiced coitus reservatus. It is also recommended in certain Oriental cultures, which consider sexual intercourse a useful meditation technique. Claims are made by some yoga experts that it is emotionally and spiritually helpful for a man to lie calmly with his penis inside a woman. They further claim that a very experienced yogi can reach a climax without ejaculating, or can draw the seminal fluid back up through his penis using extraordinary muscle control, thus retaining the precious liquid of the "life force." In fact, what happens in this very difficult feat is that the semen goes into the bladder and is excreted in the urine.

Coitus reservatus is not recommended as a method of contraception. Very few men are able to stop once they have reached a near-orgastic state of arousal, and the risk of pregnancy still exists through the possible leak of semen into the vagina.

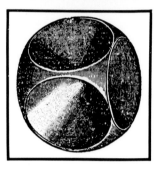

Above : the condom first appeared in literature in 1564. It rapidly gained popularity as a contraceptive and prophylactic.

Above center : block pessary, the prophylactic equivalent for use by women.

Left : the somewhat absurd incongruity of the condom led to its use in less serious matters.

Opposite page, above : Gabriel Fallopius, the 16th-century physician credited with the invention of the condom.

Using the Condom

The mechanical male contraceptive that the British and Americans sometimes call the "French letter," "prophylactic," or "rubber," and that the French call the "English hat" is still very widely used. Medically known as the condom or sheath, it was available in England by the 17th century. It is a sheath of very thin latex

rubber, usually with a teat on the end to hold the ejaculated semen. Normally the man rolls it over his erect penis immediately before intercourse and after the preliminary arousal stage. Sometimes the woman may put it on for him, thus incorporating its application into their foreplay.

The advantages of the condom are that it is cheap, quick and easy to use, fairly reliable, obtainable without fuss, and does not affect the body chemistry. These factors naturally make it the most popular contraceptive among young people. Its most obvious disadvantage is that the rubber is a barrier to the most intimate of body contacts, and consequently both partners may experience a certain loss of sensation. Perhaps even more important, the woman's accumulated sexual tension may slacken when foreplay is interrupted to put the condom on, and she may return to a state of low arousal in which she is not ready for coitus.

Manufacturers of condoms are generally scrupulous about the testing of their wares before they are put on the market, but vigorous use can reveal weaknesses that may not have shown up during tests. Many young men have found with dismay upon withdrawing that the condom was torn or had slipped off inside the vagina, and uncounted pregnancies have resulted from such failures. The chances of this can be minimized if condoms are used with care. The user must insure that all air is excluded from the teat when he puts it on, and that there is sufficient vaginal lubrication to allow easy movement. Most important of all, he should withdraw before he has lost his erection. To be extra cautious he can doublecheck the condom for weaknesses or leaks before use by filling it with water. He must also bear in mind that thin latex deteriorates under conditions of excessive heat or moisture (as in a wallet carried in a trouser pocket), and be sure to replace older ones with freshly manufactured condoms.

The reliability of the condom has been estimated as anything from 85 to 93 percent. The figure rises if the sheath is used in combination with a spermicidal cream, jelly, or suppository. But combination methods tend to be messy and to inhibit spontaneity, and couples who settle into a regular sex life frequently stop using condoms and cream and instead opt for one of the more reliable modern methods of contraception.

Below : early condoms were usually made of animal gut. The development of Vulcanized rubber in the 1840s, and latex in the 1930s, provided a more acceptable, hygienic and safe material. Rubber technology enabled condoms to be manufactured on a large scale and gave them their popular name.

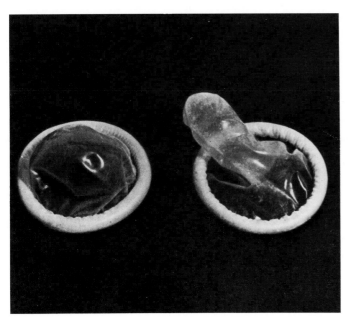

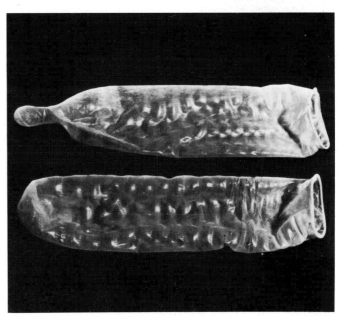

The Diaphragm

Until the introduction of the pill and intra-uterine device into large-scale use in the 1960s, the most commonly used female contraceptive was the diaphragm or dutch cap. A diaphragm is a small, circular rubber device like a membrane with a thicker outer rim. It is inserted into the vaginal passage to shut off the entrance to the uterus so that no sperm can get in to fertilize the egg. It is unwise to use a diaphragm without first covering it with a spermicidal jelly or cream to kill the male sperm, because the highly active sperm can not only live for several

Left : Dr W P J Mensinga, German inventor of the diaphragm (1880).

Above : Dr Aletta Jacobs, who in 1882 established the first birth-control clinic in Amsterdam. It was the enthusiastic promotion of the Dutch birth-control pioneers which caused the diaphragm to be called the "Dutch Cap."

Right : the mass production of pessaries also developed in the late 19th century. They proved very popular but were not very effective on their own.

Opposite page, right : there are three different types of diaphragm: (1) the true diaphragm or Dutch cap ; (2) the larger bowl-shaped vault or Dumas cap ; and (3) the smaller cervical cap. This last is suitable for women with limited previous sexual experience.

hours but can work their way around the rim of the diaphragm.

The greatest advantage of the diaphragm method is that the device can be inserted several hours before lovemaking so that there is no interruption in loveplay. The diaphragm cannot be felt by either partner during lovemaking. It is an effective method of contraception, but allowance must be made for the fact that the spermicidal cream or jelly is only effective for about three hours; if sexual intercourse has not taken place within that time, fresh cream or jelly must be applied. The diaphragm should be fitted properly by a doctor, and frequent check-ups are necessary to make sure it is still the right size, particularly when sexual activity is resumed after the birth of a child. There is also the danger that, if a couple make love in certain positions, the penis

may dislodge the diaphragm. Once a woman is sexually aroused, internal changes in her body take place, and as these physical changes vary in different women, the diaphragm may lose its efficiency at this stage.

Another possible disadvantage of the diaphragm method is that a few women are sensitive to the rubber or the chemical spermicide. Some women, particularly younger ones, complain that it takes the spontaneity out of lovemaking – they claim it is "cold and calculating" to prepare oneself for a possible lovemaking session, but that rushing off to insert the cap in the middle is unromantic and counterproductive. This point of view is particularly applicable to unmarried women, but within the framework of marriage, when a happy and well-adjusted couple are attuned to

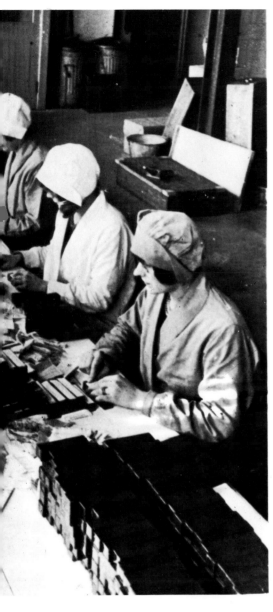

picking up signals from each other, the woman will probably know when it is appropriate to make the necessary preparations. Some couples even make the preparation part of their initial loveplay. Of course, a woman who makes love regularly can simply make a habit of inserting her cap nightly.

It must be clearly stated that chemical barriers such as spermicidal jellies and creams are reliable only in conjunction with a cap or diaphragm. Some manufacturers of certain creams and jellies claim that they are effective when used alone, but it would be unwise to take the risk. The pessary, which is simply a spermicidal tablet inserted into the vagina to kill sperm, should only be used when the man wears a condom or as added protection if the woman has been fitted with an intrauterine device.

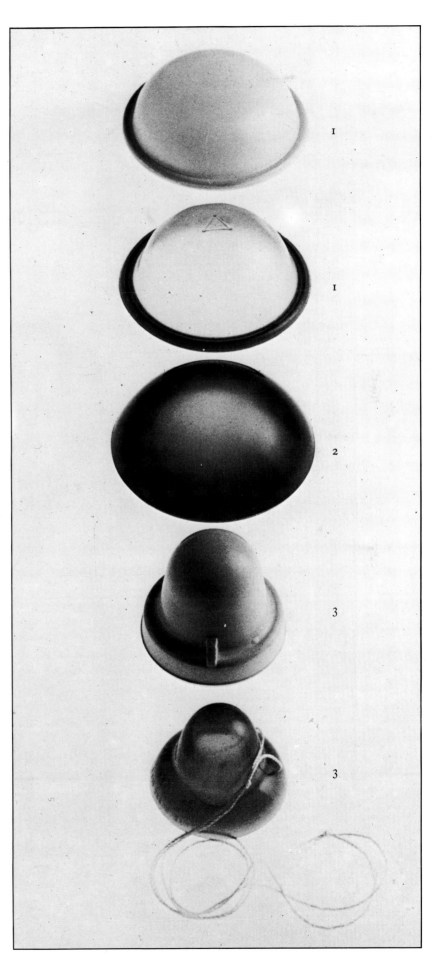

Intrauterine Devices

The intrauterine device is a small loop or coil of variable size and shape, usually made of plastic. It is inserted into the womb to prevent conception, and should only be fitted by a doctor or trained person in a clinic. IUDs are available compressed in a thin plastic tube which can be slipped easily through the cervical canal into the uterus, where, as the container is withdrawn, the loop or coil resumes its correct shape. The best time for the device to be inserted is during or immediately after a period. Some women experience temporary pain and slight bleeding for a few hours or days after insertion.

The greatest advantages of the IUD are that it is simple to insert (by someone properly trained), it may be left in the uterus for a long period of time (doctors advise renewal of some types every two or three years), and once in place it needs little attention. It can usually be easily and quickly removed and does not affect fertility. Its effectiveness as a contraceptive is considered second only to the pill, although

Left : Dr W Oppenheimer of Israel (above) and Tenrei Ota of Japan (center), the pioneers of the modern IUD. Although the first practical IUD, made from silk-worm gut, was developed in 1909, it was generally ignored because of the current antagonistic attitudes to family planning. Some research on the contraceptive effects of devices placed in the womb did continue, notably by Ota and Oppenheimer, who both published their results in 1948.

Left : a selection of Ota rings devised and developed between 1927 and 1966. Initially they were made of metal coils. Ota then introduced the use of plastics as a less toxic and more acceptable form of IUD material.

Above : a selection of IUDs. Reading clockwise from top left : Copper T, Dalkon Shield (now no longer generally available), Copper 7, Saf-T-Coil, Lippes Loop.

some doctors suggest that a spermicide be used as well during the monthly time of ovulation. It is also relatively cheap and allows complete spontaneity in lovemaking, because neither partner needs to make any particular preparations.

There are many types of loops and coils including the Lippes loop and the Saf-T-Coil ((illustrated), which are most commonly used by women who have already given birth. For those who have not, the Beospir, Copper-7, and Copper-T are most frequently recommended.

All types of IUDs have thin nylon threads which are left hanging through the cervix into the vagina, so that the woman can check regularly that the device is still in place. These threads are also used by the doctor to remove the IUD when necessary.

How an IUD works in preventing conception is not quite certain. Several possible theories have been put forward, as follows:

a) It makes the egg pass so rapidly down the Fallopian tube that it cannot be fertilized or arrives too early to be implanted in the wall of the uterus.

b) It interferes with the composition of the lining of the womb so that implantation cannot take place.

c) It directly prevents implantation. The various types of loops and coils have all been exhaustively tested and proved effective, despite the uncertainty as to how they work. Should pregnancy occur, the device must be removed, as otherwise the risk of miscarriage or other complications may be higher; most types of IUD, however, have no effect on the baby.

IUDs have several disadvantages. They can fall out, especially the smaller types used by women who have not had children. Secondly, many women – about 25 percent of those fitted with the device – must have them removed due to acute discomfort, heavy bleeding, and pain, although some who persist in their use find that these symptoms cease after three or four months. Another drawback is that IUDs may cause or aggravate infection of the uterus. There is also a slight risk that the device can perforate the wall of the womb, but this is rare, and only in a very few cases is any significant damage caused. In addition to the small (2 percent) but definite risk of an ordinary pregnancy, an IUD does not protect against ectopic pregnancy, in which the fertilized egg starts to grow in the Fallopian tube.

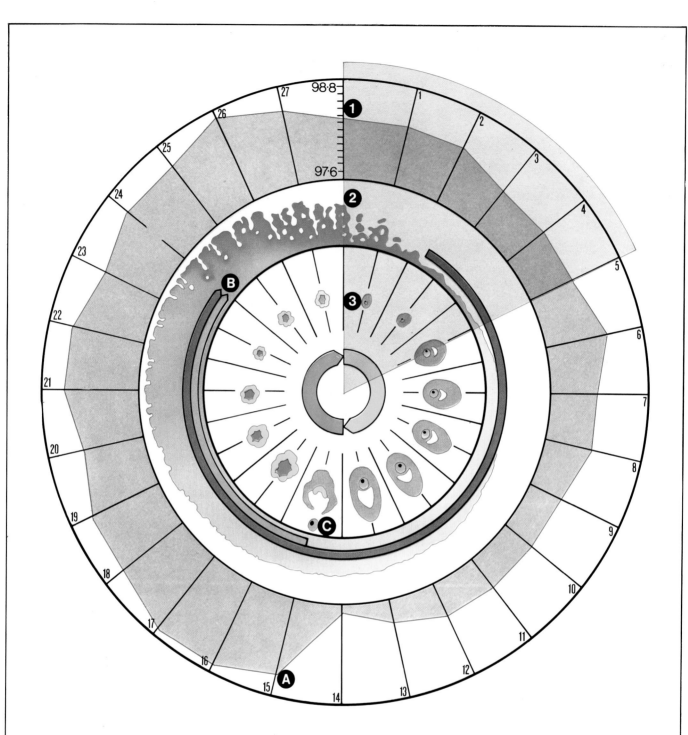

The secretions of the reproductive female hormones follow, on average, a 28-day cycle. The Pill works basically by interfering with this process. The ovarian follicles (innermost circle) start to develop when the brain stimulates the pituitary gland to secrete Follicle Stimulating Hormone (FSH), indicated by the yellow semicircle. The follicles begin to secrete estrogen (olive-green line). A few days later the pituitary begins to secrete Luteinizing Hormone (LH). About day 13 the level of LH rises dramatically (blue semicircle) and causes the largest follicle to release its egg (C). This is the point of ovulation. The body temperature, indicated by the purple outline (1), rises sharply (A). Stimulated by LH, the burst follicle develops into the corpus luteum (yellow body) which secretes progesterone (turquoise line). Progesterone and estrogen inhibit the production of LH and FSH, and complete the building of the uterine lining in preparation for the embryo. However, if the egg is not fertilized, estrogen and progesterone secretions stop, and the lining starts to break down (B). This is released as the menstrual flow (pink wedge). Meanwhile, FSH and LH production restarts. But, if the egg is fertilized, estrogen and progesterone production continue and no FSH and LH are produced, thus preventing overlapping pregnancies. The Pill mimics this effect: by maintaining a constant level of estrogen and progesterone, no further follicles are produced.

The Pill

No other method of birth control has proved as revolutionary in its effect or as controversial in its reception as the oral contraceptive known as the pill. It is composed of synthetic forms of the sex hormones estrogen and progesterone. The levels of these hormones vary naturally in a woman's body during each menstrual cycle. They help to insure that no ovulation occurs when a woman is pregnant, and the contraceptive pill is designed to have the same effect – i.e., to inhibit ovulation – so that no ovum is produced for possible fertilization by the male sperm.

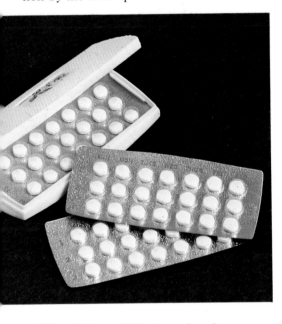

The pill is available in packs of 21, 22, or 28 tablets depending on the type. One pack is used during each menstrual cycle. There are now three main types of pill:

a) Combination pill, so-called because each pill contains both estrogen and progesterone. It is the most commonly used and most effective type. With most a woman starts taking the first course of tablets on the fifth day after her period begins. She then takes one each day for 21 or 22 days, after which she stops taking them for six or seven days, according to the directions. A menstrual period usually begins two or three days after the last pill, and a new pack of pills is taken for the next cycle. In addition to inhibiting ovulation, the combination pill also affects both the lining of the womb so that no implantation of an ovum can occur and also causes the cervical mucus to become thicker, thereby forming a chemical barrier against sperm.

b) Sequential pill, the effects of which are more similar to a woman's own natural cycle of hormone production. However, it is considered less effective than the combination pill. Again the woman takes one pill a day for 21 days, starting on the fifth day after the start of a period, but the first 14 pills contain only estrogen whereas the remaining pills contain both estrogen and progesterone. Although ovulation is prevented, the sequential pill has no effect at all on the lining of the uterus or the cervical mucus.

c) Continuous pill, which is taken each day for 28 days even during menstruation. Each pill contains progesterone only, and its main function is to prevent implantation of an ovum in the uterus lining. It also affects the cervical mucus to form a barrier against sperm, but has little effect on ovulation, and is considered slightly less effective than the combined pill.

Some women have difficulty remembering the sequence of days in the cycle, so combination and sequential pills are also available in packs of 28, though the extra pills contain no hormones.

When a woman starts taking the pill it is important for her to know that she may not be fully protected during the first cycle, and she or her partner should use a secondary method of contraception during the first two weeks of the cycle.

If she forgets to take one pill a woman should take it before the next one is due; if, however, the gap is greater than 12 hours, or if she misses more than two, she should

Above: Dr Gregor Pincus (left) and Dr John Rock (right) who developed the first contraceptive pill in the 1950s. Following a series of studies on the effects of orally administered progesterone, they developed a pill which appeared to prevent ovulation. Pincus and Rock performed their first trials in 1956 in Haiti and Puerto Rico – two areas where overpopulation was a problem. The result of this first ovulation-inhibitor was a 96-percent reduction in pregnancies.

233

finish the pack but use a second contraceptive as well. It is particularly important
not to forget to take the continuous pill,
which must be taken at the same time every
day. Laxatives and emetics, which result
in the emptying of the contents of the
stomach, can also cause the loss of a pill and,
if taken over a period of time, would
render the method ineffective.

The greatest advantages of the pill as a
method of contraception are, of course,
that it is the easiest, least embarrassing, and
least inhibiting of all methods because it is
self-administered. It is also virtually 100
percent effective as a contraceptive, and its
introduction in the 1960s has signified a
major revolution in family planning.

The freedom to make love at any time,
without fear of an unplanned or unwanted
pregnancy, is a benefit to women's psychological and emotional life that scarcely
needs emphasizing. Physically, too, the
pill has helped many women through its
beneficial side effects. For example, the
pill can regularize the menstrual cycle and
reduce the pain of periods for a number of
women. In fact, the pill is often prescribed
for this reason to young girls who experience
irregular periods at the start of their
menstruation.

However, the pill does not suit every
woman. Some suffer from certain unpleasant physical and emotional side effects
such as headaches, depression, sickness,
swollen or sore breasts, or vaginal discharge.
In most women these symptoms disappear
after the first few months, during which time
a woman's system adjusts to the intake of
the hormones. If the symptoms persist,
another type of pill with less estrogen can
be tried. Other side effects of the pill in
some women may be overweight due to

*Above : a mass propaganda
program was required to
educate women about the
availability and effectiveness
of the Pill.*

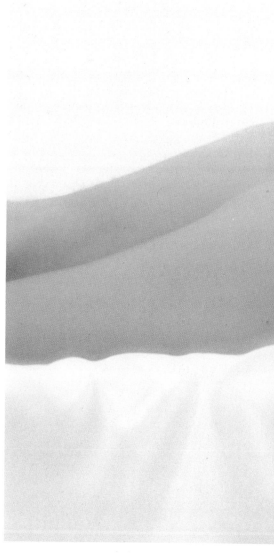

fluid retention, loss of sexual desire, bleeding, and in rare cases blood clotting, or
thrombosis.

It is extremely important that no woman
should take the contraceptive pill without
the advice and supervision of a doctor. The
risk of thrombosis is higher in a woman
over the age of 35, as indeed are the risks
involved in pregnancies. Other factors that
a doctor will take into consideration before
prescribing the pill, in addition to any
history of blood thrombosis disorders,
include hepatitis, diabetes, migraine, epilepsy, and high blood pressure. Regular
cervical smear tests are essential for women
taking the pill in order to detect possible
cancer of the cervix. Discovered in time, the
chances of a complete cure are very good.

Doctors and specialists differ in their
opinions as to how long a woman should
stay on the pill. There seems to be no

scientific evidence to support the practice of those doctors who take young women off the pill for short periods to "reestablish their natural rhythms." A woman who stops taking it in order to have a baby should wait two or three months (using another method of contraception) before trying to conceive; it may be some months before her ovaries are ovulating normally and conception can occur.

Can taking the pill make it more difficult to have a baby later? A major survey of the effects of the pill on fertility, in which the pregnancies of at least 16,000 women who had babies were monitored, reported these findings: "For the vast majority of women, fears of possible effects on future pregnancies need not deter them from taking the pill." It also concludes that the pill is perfectly safe, especially for women under 35. And other studies indicate that 60 tò

75 percent of women who stop taking the pill to become pregnant achieve their aim within three months of taking the last pill, and 90 percent become pregnant within one year. Babies do not seem to be affected in any way by their mothers past use of the pill. However, some recent surveys show various negative aspects of the pill's effect on a woman's overall health, and this information should be seriously considered by doctors who prescribe the pill.

In conclusion, a vast majority of doctors and specialists point out that pregnancy and childbirth carry higher risks than taking the pill. So for most healthy young women who have regular medical check-ups, the advantages of the pill probably outweigh the disadvantages and possible risks involved, although much more long-term research into such areas as vitamin deficiency and overall endocrinal balance is needed.

Above : the health of the woman is as important as the avoidance of pregnancy. There are many brands of the Pill available and they suit different women in different ways. If one Pill produces unpleasant side effects the woman should switch to another brand.

235

Sterilization

The most effective and drastic method of contraception is sterilization. As it is not usually reversible, sterilization is normally chosen only by couples who have a large or grown family and are absolutely certain that under no circumstances will they want to have any more children. In fact, a responsible surgeon will not undertake the operation until the doctor or an experienced counsellor has had a serious talk with the couple and been satisfied that they fully understand the consequences of their decision and are emotionally mature enough

to make it. The possibility of the death of one of the partners or their permanent separation must be taken into account. If they are still convinced, then the question arises of which of them should undergo the operation.

It is much easier to perform male than female sterilization. It is known as vasectomy because it involves severing and tying the *vas deferens*, the tubes that conduct sperm from the testes to the outside of the body. The vas deferens are easily accessible – all the surgeon has to do is make a small incision in the scrotum, perform the operation (which takes only minutes), close up the incision with a stitch or two, and send the patient on his way with a few cautionary words. Usually only a local anesthetic is needed, and the man can resume his normal activities, if they are not too strenuous, the next day. And this includes sexual activities,

Below : most parents would agree that there is an optimum size for their family. Apart from economic consideration, a smaller family means that more attention can be devoted to each child. At this point sterilization is sometimes considered to be a sensible step.

although other contraceptive measures must be used for a time because live sperm are still present in the genital system, particularly in the seminal vesicles above the point where the tubes were cut. It has been estimated that it takes 12 ejaculations to rid the body of all the sperm, and normally a vasectomized man is not medically cleared until he has produced two ejaculations containing no sperm (about three months after the operation).

Simple though the operation is, most men, even some of those who volunteer for it, have fears and apprehensions about it. They may associate it with castration, even though neither the penis nor the testes themselves are touched in the operation, or they may be apprehensive about how their subsequent sex lives will be affected. Most men are unaware that much of their seminal fluid comes from the prostate gland, and that the testes only contribute sperm to each ejaculation. The intensity of orgasm and the volume of seminal emission will not be affected. A very few men do have erective or orgasmic potency problems after a vasectomy, but the cause is psychological, not physical, and the majority find their sexual experiences unchanged or enhanced due to their new freedom from worry about pregnancy.

Female sterilization is a far more major operation, but some men prefer their wives to submit to it rather than have the operation themselves. The reason for this choice may not be that they anticipate having intercourse with and impregnating someone other than their wives, but a basic (and perhaps outmoded) feeling that where procreation and its problems are concerned, responsibility should ultimately devolve upon the female. Most commonly, although a man may be absolutely certain that his family is complete and his child-raising years are over, he still relates potency to manliness and enjoys the knowledge that he remains capable of fathering offspring.

Until recently female sterilization was usually effected by tubal ligation, or cutting and tying the Fallopian tubes through which the eggs travel from the ovaries to the womb. The principle is simple, but to get at the Fallopian tubes the surgeon has to go through the lower abdomen, and as in all major surgery this can have a traumatic effect on the nervous system and complications can arise, though these occur only rarely. After the operation the woman is

MALE STERILIZATION

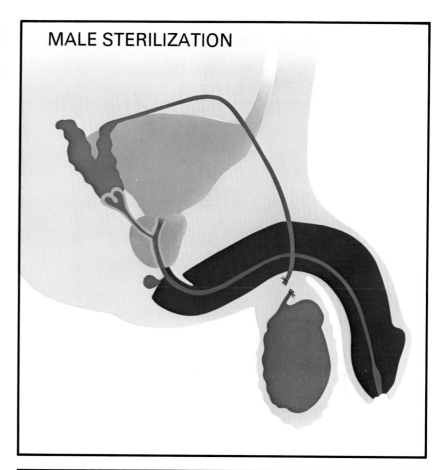

FEMALE STERILIZATION

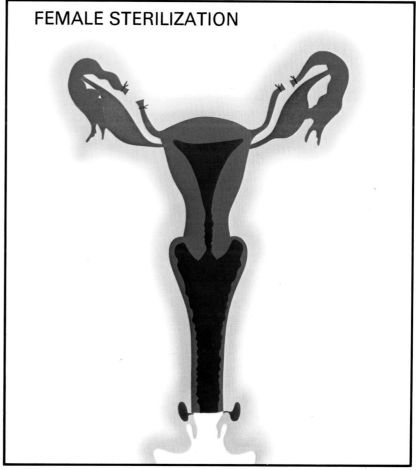

usually kept in the hospital for about a week. She is then advised to take things very easy during her first week home and to get back to her normal routine only gradually, over a month or so.

Today a simpler, safer, and faster method called laparoscopic sterilization is used. In the early 1960s two surgeons, Raoul Palmer in France and Patrick Steptoe in England, described a way of looking directly at the internal body organs by inserting a small telescopelike instrument called a laparoscope through the abdominal wall just below the naval. Sterilization is performed under a general anesthetic through another small incision in the lower abdominal wall. Looking through the laparoscope, the surgeon grasps each Fallopian tube with a special pair of forceps and turns on an electrical current to burn the tubes closed. The two small wounds can be closed with a single stitch or a special skin staple, and the entire operation takes about 15 minutes. In most cases a woman can leave the hospital a few hours afterward.

As with male sterilization, there should be no after effects on sexual activity and enjoyment, and if there are, the probability is that they are psychological. Such repercussions can be particularly severe, of course, if the operation is combined with the termination of a pregnancy, as it sometimes is. But most women find that the subsequent freedom from worry about contraception and pregnancy more than compensates for the pain, fear, and inconvenience of being sterilized.

Methods of Birth Control		What is it?
	Pill	Pills containing synthetic estrogen and progesterone hormones.
	Coil or Loop Intrauterine devices (IUD)	Small flexible devices of different sizes and shapes, inserted into the uterus.
	Diaphragm (together with spermicidal cream or jelly)	Soft rubber cap with flexible metal rim that fits over entrance to the uterus.
	Condom	Thin, strong rubber covering fitted over the penis.
	Spermicidal agents (1) Jellies, creams, soluble tablets, vaginal suppositories.	Chemicals put into the vagina.
	(2) Aerosol vaginal foam.	Foaming cream in aerosol can.
	Rhythm method ("safe period")	Finding out time of ovulation by keeping record of period dates and temperature changes.
	Douche	Syringe filled with water or other special solution.
	Withdrawal (coitus interruptus)	
	Sterilization	Surgical operation.

Coping with an Unwanted Pregnancy

With modern techniques of contraception most couples ought to be able to enjoy carefree lovemaking in the knowledge that their chances of an unplanned or unwanted pregnancy are remote. But "accidents" do happen, and they happen more often through carelessness or incomplete protection – for instance, using a diaphragm or condom without a spermicidal cream or jelly – than by the failure of any method properly used. Pregnancies probably occur most frequently when a couple has simply been carried away or trusted to luck and made love with no protection.

What can be done under these circumstances? In fact, there are four methods of controlling fertility after sexual intercourse:

a) Morning-after pill, a five-day series of pills containing an artificial estrogen called diethylstilbestrol (DES). If the DES pill series is begun within 24 hours of sexual intercourse, it is almost 100 percent effective in preventing pregnancy. It is widely used in the United States but is not

How it works	Advantages	Disadvantages	Effectiveness
Taken daily for a certain number of days each month, prevents release of egg.	Easy to use. No interference with enjoyment.	May cause unpleasant side effects. Prescription required.	0.5% pregnancy rate.
Prevents fertilized egg from implanting in uterine wall.	Usually stays in place indefinitely. Cannot be felt. Does not reduce pleasure.	Temporary discomfort after insertion. May be expelled without knowing it.	With newest types of IUD 1% pregnancy rate.
Used in conjunction with cream or jelly, prevents sperm from entering the uterus.	No side effects. Cannot be felt by either partner. Can be inserted up to three hours before intercourse.	Must also use cream or jelly. Should not be removed for at least six hours after intercourse.	With correct fit and good cream, 95-98% effective.
Prevents sperm from reaching the uterus.	Easy to obtain. Simple to use.	Can be felt. May slip off. Must be put on at time that interferes with enjoyment.	5-6% pregnancy rate. If woman uses spermicidal cream or jelly less than 5% pregnancy rate.
Immobilizes or kills sperm.	No prescription needed. Usually easy to obtain.	Must be applied again before each intercourse. May cause irritation.	Not reliable unless used with diaphragm or condom.
Forms a chemical barrier against sperm.	No prescription needed. More effective than creams or jellies when used on its own.	Must be inserted again before each intercourse. May cause irritation.	At worst, 20% pregnancy rate. At best, 90-98% effective.
Intercourse is limited to woman's infertile period, just before and just after ovulation.	No pills or devices involved. Only method approved by Roman Catholic Church.	Keeping careful records required. Limits intercourse. Not reliable if periods are irregular.	About 20% pregnancy rate.
Washes out vagina to remove semen before it enters the uterus.	None.	Must be done *immediately* after intercourse. Unreliable. May cause infection.	Least effective of all methods.
Man withdraws penis before ejaculation.	No product required. No cost.	Interferes with sexual climax. Unreliable.	Poor.
In a man, prevents sperm from being released in seminal fluid. In a woman, blocks the passage of eggs from the ovaries to the uterus.	Almost always permanently effective. No need for any other birth control method. Does not interfere with sexual desire or enjoyment.	Cannot be undone.	Virtually 100%.

favored by doctors in Britain or in many other countries.

One such pill is called stilbestrol. Taken within two or three days after intercourse, it will bring on a period. But it has serious disadvantages. It produces acute nausea and vomiting in many women, in addition to undesirable changes in body metabolism. Some of these can be alleviated by anti-nausea drugs.

A more serious drawback is that if the morning-after pill is not successful in preventing pregnancy, the effect on the baby can be harmful. It can cause a rare disease, vaginal cancer, in a daughter once she reaches puberty. Advocates of this morning-after pill therefore insist that a woman who has taken it must be offered an abortion if it does not work.

b) Morning-after coil, an ordinary intra-uterine device which is inserted the morning after intercourse to prevent implantation of a possibly fertilized egg. The advantage of this method over the morning-after pill is that it causes no unpleasant side effects and the woman is left with a reliable contraceptive once it has been inserted. However, insertion of an IUD if a woman is pregnant can cause serious and even fatal infections, and this form of post-intercourse contraception is not often used in Britain.

c) Menstrual extraction (or interception), a technique in which a period is brought on by using a suction device. A thin tube is inserted into the vagina, through the cervix, and into the womb. A syringe is attached to the end of the tube to draw out the contents of the womb. This only takes a few minutes and is usually painless.

Most doctors in many countries have reservations about this method, because unless the operation is carried out within a day or two of intercourse, it may be simply an early abortion, about which there are strict laws. A doctor carrying out a menstrual extraction on a woman whose period is already overdue might be exposing himself or herself to prosecution for illegal abortion.

However, those in favor of this method claim that, performed early enough after intercourse, it is neither contraception nor abortion, which is why the term "interception" is often used.

d) Abortion, the removal of the fetus from a pregnant woman's uterus early in the pregnancy. This is not a method of con-

traception but an indication of its failure. It must be stressed that no woman, however desperate the circumstances, should ever consider going to an illegal or "backstreet" abortionist. Before the introduction of abortion legislation in Britain in 1967, which gave qualified gynecologists a certain amount of freedom to terminate pregnancies in cases of genuine need, a terrifying number of women ended up in hospitals suffering from the after effects of an amateur's efforts – intense pain, heavy bleeding, dangerous infections often resulting in infertility, and even death.

A woman who suspects an unwanted pregnancy must not hesitate to go to her own doctor immediately. The law in Britain states that once a pregnancy is confirmed, two doctors must agree that to continue the

Above : the arrival of a child is a joyful experience only if the child is wanted.

240

pregnancy would result in any of the following:

a) a risk to the woman's life;

b) a risk to her physical or mental health;

c) a risk to her dependants; or

d) a child born physically or mentally handicapped or deformed.

Legally a gynecologist in a clinic or hospital can perform the operation up to 28 weeks after conception, but in practice many will refuse if the woman is more than 20 weeks pregnant.

In the United States until quite recently abortion was illegal except in cases where the pregnant woman's life was endangered. Then in 1970 the state of New York passed a law making abortion during the first 24 weeks of pregnancy legal and strictly a matter between the woman and her doctor. Similar but slightly more restrictive laws were passed in 1970 by three other states (Alaska, Hawaii, and Washington). But on January 22, 1973 the U.S. Supreme Court decided that all American women had the right to an abortion, although certain restrictions were placed on that freedom in the interests of safeguarding the woman's health. During the first 12 weeks of pregnancy any woman may obtain an abortion performed by a licensed doctor without interference from the law; from week 13 to 24 the state may specify the conditions under which the abortion is performed for

the sake of the mother's health, and after this period abortion may be restricted to cases where the life or health of the mother is in danger. Abortion is now widely available throughout the United States.

In Britain the most commonly used method of abortion is the dilatation and curettage method, generally known as a D and C. A general anesthetic is usually given. The surgeon enlarges (dilates) the cervical canal and then inserts a long, pencil-thin curette, an instrument with a spoonlike tip, into the womb. Its contents are then scraped loose and withdrawn. The patient may stay in the hospital or go home the same day, advised to take things easy for a week. She will experience vaginal bleeding and perhaps pain similar to an ordinary period.

In America suction abortion, also called vacuum curettage, has now replaced the D and C for abortions performed up until week 12. It is a simpler, safer, and faster technique in which the fetus is sucked out of the uterus through a narrow hollow tube or vacurette which is inserted into the womb through the cervix. Usually only a local anesthetic is required. The whole abortion takes 5 to 10 minutes and can be performed in an out-patients' clinic. As with the D and C, most women experience some discomfort or cramps after a suction abortion, but normally they are not severe and disappear within a few hours.

Above : when a casual relationship results in an unwanted pregnancy, abortion may be the only wise solution.

241

Birth Control in Today's World

The choices people make in respect of birth control affect not only their own lives but also society and the world at large. It has been estimated that less than one-third of the fertile women in the world today regularly use any method of contraception, and of course the ones that do are in the most industrially advanced countries of North America and Western Europe. Thus it is in the Third World of Africa, the Indian subcontinent, South America, and Southeast Asia that the current population explo-

sion is taking place. The rate of increase is alarming indeed: the 1972 Club of Rome report, *The Limits to Growth*, projected that there would be 7 billion people in the world by the year 2000, and that unless stringent measures of population control are taken, in 60 years there will be four people in the world for every one today.

Taking stringent measures may mean interfering with individual people's freedom to choose. Some commentators foresee the day when couples will have to have a license to procreate and will be taxed on their offspring. Already in India and elsewhere government schemes are in operation that give cash benefits to men who volunteer for vasectomies. But formidable barriers re-

Above: poster from Pakistan stressing the economic benefits of a smaller family. On the left the family has seven children, and their condition is miserable. On the right, with only three children, they can afford to buy a car and enjoy themselves.

Center: Turkish family planning poster, part of a worldwide campaign to promote contraception.

Opposite page: the point of fertilization: the sperm fuses with the egg.

main to be broken down before any worldwide birth control plan can be effective.

There is first of all the barrier of ignorance. A story is told of someone who was shown how to move one of 28 beads on an abacus from one side to the other each day, and to abstain from intercourse when the red beads were moved. The person impatiently moved all the red beads across at once. This may be an apocryphal tale, but it points up one of the difficulties which attend centralized attempts at population control. In addition there is the barrier of religious prohibition, which affects hundreds of millions of people the world over.

How should these sociopolitical considerations affect young people embarking upon family life today? Parenthood and the cementing of a heterosexual relationship through it are rich life experiences that promote growth and maturity, and it would be sad if, because of the overpopulation of this small planet, the freedom to procreate were one day curtailed. But only if people exercise voluntary control will the necessity for such legislation be avoided. Small families and planned parenthood are the responsibility of everyone; certainly no unwanted children should be born into today's world. The ethics of the abortion question are intractable, and the opinions of those who hold it to be inadmissible for religious reasons must be respected, but tomorrow's world will be difficult enough without launching children into it with the disadvantages of being unwanted or becoming an intolerable strain on the parent's resources.

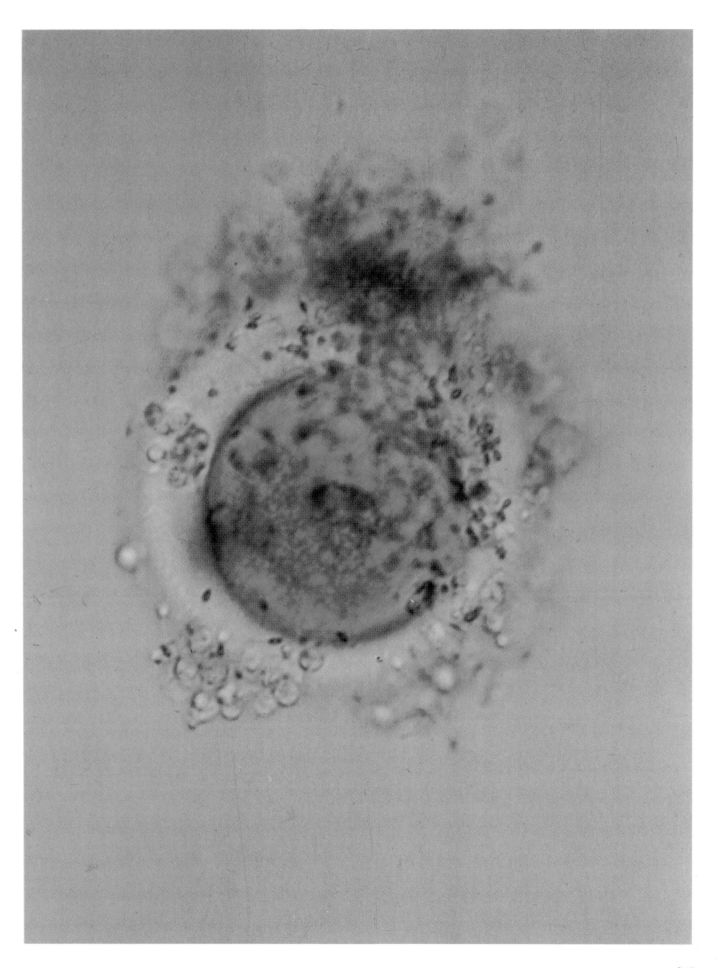

Sex Education

A teenager participating in a public forum on the subject of sex education is reported to have said, "We should educate the adults for sure. It seems to be what they need to be happier." This statement brings out one of the anomalies of sex education today. Often the supposed educators are less well-informed and more inhibited than the young people they are supposed to be teaching. Sex education, for a majority of

Right : educational aids, such as lifelike models, play an important role in young children's sex education.

Above : Elise Ottesen-Jensen, one of the Scandinavian pioneers of sex education. She highlighted the importance of adequate sex education in overcoming such problems as venereal disease and unwanted pregnancies.

people responsible for it, still means instruction in reproductive biology. Obviously many other important things must be known about human sexuality aside from analogies to the reproductive mechanisms of birds, bees, and the beasts of the field, and these subjects are precisely what conventional sex education ignores. Reproductive biology can be taught at primary and secondary school level, but in many sex education programs it is introduced much later, and the more advanced aspects of sex education, those which are appropriate to adolescence and young adulthood, are never broached, let alone explained.

Subjects which should be part of a curriculum of sex education are masturbation, homosexuality, the physiology of sexual response, contraception, and the differences between male and female sexuality. Sex should be discussed, too, in various contexts – for instance, in the context of interpersonal love, in relation to the family, to society, and to contemporary world problems. Within advanced sex education programs some of the difficult ethical questions should be aired, such as sexual deviancy and abortion. In fact, sex education should continue so that, as with any other subject, more advanced aspects are presented at different levels of education as they become appropriate. But very few of the people responsible for organizing sex education in schools take so broad a view of the subject.

To carry out such a program would require substantial numbers of teachers comfortable and happy enough in their own sexuality to be capable of uninhibited, balanced, and unopinionated instruction. So as the teenager said, sex education should begin with educating the educators.

Furthermore, it must be realized that every adult, and particularly every parent, is a sex educator. It is not only that parents have to answer children's questions about where babies come from, and at puberty prepare their sons for the occurrence of possible wet dreams (nocturnal emissions) and their daughters for menstruation. Parents give sex education daily in their own lives, in their reactions to anything from a nude pin-up in the newspaper to local gossip and dirty jokes. If they try

to exclude sex from the home and frown upon every allusion to it, sex education is still taking place in the sense that their conduct endows children with attitudes to sex which will influence their own future sex lives. When parents touch each other, admire each other physically, caress, and let it be seen that their sexuality is a joy to them and certainly nothing to be ashamed of, even though its most intimate expression occurs in private, this in itself is a form of positive parental sex education.

Possibly most important for teachers and parents is to understand the sexuality of the infant, the child, and the adolescent. Through the bodily intimacy that occurs between a baby and its parents the child undergoes a learning experience that will affect its later adult life. Experiments with monkeys have shown that infants brought up in isolation and without mother contacts were completely disorganized sexually upon reaching maturity, and this analogy certainly holds for human beings as well. Sexuality is an attribute of humans that not only manifests itself in different ways from the cradle to the grave, but can become twisted and tangled at every stage of life. To understand it in depth, and understand all that it

Above: Chilean women receiving instructions in contraception. Instructions in birth-control techniques are a major part of adult sex education, even in Catholic countries where the Church's view (right) that nothing must interfere with the procreative purpose of sex, has to be reconciled with the social need for effective family planning.

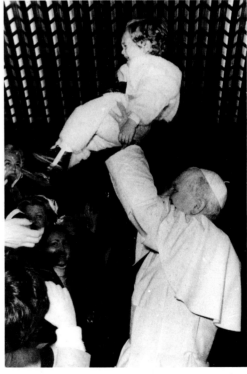

involves in the contexts of human relationships, personal growth, physical health, and social implications, is a learning process that cannot begin too early in life and that will never be completed.

Chapter 9
When Sex Goes Wrong

In 1970 Masters and Johnson published their second book, *Human Sexual Inadequacy*. "A conservative estimate," the American researchers wrote, "would indicate half the marriages in this country as either presently sexually dysfunctional or imminently so in the future." They thereby revealed a crying need for sexual therapy which, though it could be met at Masters and Johnson's own clinic for the relatively small number of couples who could spend two weeks in St. Louis, Missouri, called for the provision of help on a much larger scale. With the publication of their book, however, other therapists could share the fruits of their 11 years of research into sexual failure and inadequacy. For couples with serious and long-standing problems the help of professional sex therapists can be vital, for they are unlikely to be able to achieve complete frankness with each other except through intermediaries. People who are more open with each other but still find that problems develop may find the Masters and Johnson findings helpful without outside intervention, and even couples who have not experienced any sexual problems may understand themselves better in the light of their pioneering work.

Benefits of Sex Therapy

In comparison to the frequency of failure in sexual functioning and the great amount of distress it causes, the number of specialist sex therapists is incredibly low. The majority of people with such problems still turn to doctors and psychiatrists for help.

These medical and psychiatric practitioners can be helpful, but they must first grasp a concept that runs counter to their normal practice — the "patient" in sex therapy is the *relationship* between the partners, not either individual specifically. Furthermore, psychiatrists are often trained to consider sexual dysfunction as symptomatic of deep-rooted psychological problems, whereas Masters and Johnson's basic tenet is that most sexual problems are attributable either to ignorance or ambivalent attitudes to sex. Of course, some sexual problems spring from childhood or adolescent traumas, but the frequency of sexual inadequacy suggests that Masters and Johnson are basically correct. This is fortunate, because education as a cure is a simpler process than the uprooting of psychological trauma.

The basic idea that it is their relationship that is to be treated is explained to patients at Masters and Johnson's sex therapy clinic at their first interview. There are always two therapists, a man and a woman, and at this interview they explain the procedure to be undertaken in the first four days. They then go to separate rooms where the female therapist interviews the woman patient and the male the man. They begin by asking what the problem is and how the couple have tried to deal with it previously, after which they proceed to more general questions, such as what the patient considers normal sexual functioning and the appropriate roles of male and female in an intimate relationship. Then follows a series of searching questions about the couples' own relationship.

Although they have come voluntarily for therapy and are paying to receive their treatment, patients do not always tell, or even know, the whole truth. The co-therapists are skilled at detecting when a person is holding back the truth, and after they have listened to the tape recordings of the first interview they hold a second one the next day, at which the female therapist questions the man and the male the woman. At this session specific areas of the sexual history that the therapists have agreed are particularly interesting or relevant are further explored. Sometimes a patient will find it easier to volunteer information to a therapist of the opposite sex.

The nondemanding schedule of these first two days is intended to create an atmosphere conducive to therapy, one of relaxation, friendliness, and confidence in the therapists. On the third day the patients undergo a physical examination and their medical histories are recorded. Next is what is known as a "round table discussion," during which the patients and both therapists sit down together and discuss salient points which have arisen so far. At this point the co-therapists will probably have arrived at a possible explanation of the causes of the couple's problem, and this is now presented to them and talked over. "When we hold up the 'mirror' for them," Masters and Johnson wrote, "give them back verbally what they have said to us, they look at each other as though they didn't know each other and are just seeing each other in focus for the first time." This new awareness and insight is the beginning of the therapy. The therapists hope by the end of this discussion session to have accomplished the major task of reopening communication between the patients.

Two points are made to virtually every couple at this stage. The first is that a dysfunctional partner must get out of the habit of taking a "spectator role" in sexual activity, i.e., observing his or her responses. Most people with sexual problems do this out of anxiety, and it only increases the problem. The second point is that sex must not be goal-oriented, that neither partner should feel under pressure to "produce, perform, and achieve." As William Masters put it, "Other therapy has usually been directed at teaching the individual to do something. We insist he [or she] doesn't have to *do* anything."

This point is applied in the first directed physical encounter between the couple. They choose two periods in the day when, in the privacy of their room, they undress and spend time simply caressing each other, taking turns massaging and fondling each other so as to give pleasure purely through the sensation of touch. They are specifically instructed not to touch either's genitals or the woman's breasts during these first "sensate focus" sessions, for the purpose is to encourage sensory awareness in an atmosphere of relaxation in which there is no pressure to proceed to intercourse.

Day four begins with a discussion of the partners' responses and feelings evoked by the sensate focus sessions of the previous day. Two further sessions are then held during which touching of the genitals and breasts is permitted, provided that it is done in a manner that does not demand a sexual response. Having thus learned to be relaxed together and to give and receive sensuous pleasure without sex, the two are now prepared for therapy to treat their specific problem.

Hairtrigger Trouble

What is known commonly as "hairtrigger trouble" and medically as premature ejaculation among men is probably the most common sexual problem. If a man cannot control his rate of arousal and finds himself ejaculating before he achieves vaginal penetration or very soon after, he will be unable to bring his partner to orgasm through intercourse, and constant repetition of this pattern results in both people feeling sexually frustrated and disappointed.

Every man ejaculates prematurely sometimes. If he has anticipated sex with a particular partner for a long time and psychological and physical stimulation has been intense, any man may have difficulty containing himself and prolonging coitus on a first occasion. Anxiety or overeagerness can also cause the problem; if the thought enters a man's head that he might come too soon, he probably will. Overeagerness is easier to control than anxiety, for it naturally

A man can learn to overcome hairtrigger trouble by learning to control his sexual response. The treatment requires the active participation of the woman.

abates somewhat with familiarity, whereas anxiety feeds on itself. Patterns of sexual response very quickly become habitual, and if a man once feels anxiety about his performance or if his first sexual encounters are hurried for fear of being caught in the act, he may find it extremely difficult afterward to control his ejaculations.

There are certain things he can do. Many men first try turning their minds to something else – a domestic or business problem, for instance, or counting backward from 100 – but this is not necessarily effective. Also the technique precludes the total abandon essential for full orgasmic satisfaction. Another obvious stratagem is to enter the woman very gradually and gently, and to lie still in a state of deep penetration for a time. The phallus can remain virtually motionless while the pubic bone is moved from side to side against the woman's clitoral area, thus bringing her closer to a climax. To help retard his own climax he might also try applying an anesthetic to the glans of his penis before intercourse. Sprays for this purpose can be bought at any sex aid shop. Such methods enable a man to delay his ejaculation for a time, but as they may diminish his own enjoyment they are not completely satisfactory. A complete and effective cure, on the other hand, can be achieved if the female partner plays an active part in the therapy.

Men with acute hairtrigger trouble often try to diminish their arousal by discouraging their partners from touching their genitals during foreplay. Many doctors and sex advisors once counseled this procedure, but in 1956 Dr James Semans of the Duke University School of Medicine, in Durham, North Carolina, published a paper in which he refuted this solution. In "Premature Ejaculation: A New Approach" he recommended direct and controlled genital stimulation by the woman as part of a cure for premature ejaculation. Masters and Johnson adopted his approach with a refinement or two of their own, and of the 186 patients over the 11-year research period who had this problem only four failed to respond to the treatment.

The technique is very simple and can be practiced by any couple on their own. In fact, even couples with no premature ejaculation problem may profit by it, since increased ejaculatory control can add to their own enjoyment.

First the couple must set apart a time for sex play with the primary object of training the man's response. The session may end with intercourse, but only after a period of 20 to 30 minutes in which they can concentrate on the problem. To start, the woman can sit with a pillow between her back and the head of the bed. The man lies on his back between her legs with his head toward her and his own legs crooked over her thighs. The woman then manipulates the man's penis until it is erect and continues stimulating him until he signals that ejaculation is imminent. At this moment the woman performs "the squeeze." With her thumb on the frenellum (the underside of the penis) just below the tip, and two fingers opposite on either side of the ridge of the glans, she squeezes quite hard and holds the pressure for about four seconds. This causes the urge to ejaculate to abate, and after about 30 seconds stimulation can be resumed. When the man again signals that his orgasm is imminent, the women again applies the squeeze. They may repeat this procedure 15 or 20 times before the man finally ejaculates, which it is important he should do because otherwise the accumulation of prostate fluid can cause inflammation of the gland. If the man's control fails and he ejaculates earlier, this should be accepted as part of the learning process.

When the couple have learned a certain degree of control they proceed to vaginal insertion. This is done in a position with the woman above and without any thrusting. The idea is for the man to become used to the feeling of insertion, and if he signals that he is nearing ejaculation the woman can just raise her body and give his phallus the squeeze. After a few such sessions the man can try some thrusting movements, and after a few more sessions he will probably find that he can prolong coitus long enough to enable both partners to reach a climax.

Ejaculation Problems

Some men have the opposite problem to premature ejaculation. They cannot ejaculate intravaginally at all. They may be quite capable of reaching orgasm through masturbation or fellatio, and may be able to maintain an erection during coitus for a long period, but they cannot release their seminal fluid. The reason may be a strong fear of impregnating his partner, inhibitions due to religious or parental restrictions, basic dislike of women, or a blockage caused by a single traumatic experience.

Some men are unable to ejaculate into their wives, but have no difficulty doing so in intercourse with other women. This was the case with one young man who married for money and social status, whose problem would have had little likelihood of responding to therapy anyway, since it was not purely physical but was a result of a combination of "unloving" emotions. However, if the blockage is caused by a fear of making the wife pregnant, for instance, then treatment may be effective. The fear can be allayed in the discussion sessions, during which instructions for contraception can also be given, and the nonorgastic response pattern can be gradually broken down in the couple's "sensate focus" sessions. In these sessions the woman is first instructed to stimulate the man's phallus in whatever manner helps to bring him to orgasm, and to do so several times so that he comes to identify the pleasurable sensations of orgasm with her. When they can achieve regular success at this the woman is directed to adopt a coital position above the man and, after bringing him close to orgasm manually, to slip his phallus into her vagina and move demandingly until he ejaculates. If he fails to do so and his orgastic feelings abate, she resumes manual stimulation until orgasm is imminent again and then makes another attempt. In order to break down the mental blockage Masters and Johnson report that in many cases it is enough for the man to allow just a few drops of his seminal fluid to reach the inside of the woman's vagina. They treated 17 men at their clinic for ejaculatory incompetence, and only three of these failed to respond. Among the successes was a man who not only disliked his wife intensely but was a practicing homosexual.

The problems of premature ejaculation and retarded ejaculation can become so acute that they result in impotence, which

Many ejaculation problems have a psychological cause which affects the way the man views his partner. Therapy sessions have proved the most successful form of treatment.

was briefly discussed in Chapter 5, to which the reader is referred for basic definitions. Erective impotence is a fairly obvious condition, but some men suffer from the less noticeable condition of orgastic impotence. Such men are able to have intercourse up to the point of ejaculation, but they find that ejaculation itself is an anti-climax not attended by any particularly intense feelings. Or they may have what Alexander Lowen called a "local climax" as distinct from a full orgastic response, i.e., a climax confined to sensations in the genital area. Lowen specifies two common causes of this type of impotence. It may occur as a result of the man's unwillingness to surrender himself completely to the sexual act, an unwillingness that could be rooted in a fear of or hostility toward his partner or toward women in general. Another cause in a few men may be their undemanding attitude toward their own sexual needs. A man may be orgastically impotent because he has internalized an idea of himself as a "family man" that excludes his other roles. The remedy for the condition begins with understanding its cause and then hopefully changing the basic attitudes and behavior patterns involved.

Treating Impotence

In addition to the distinction between erective and orgastic impotence, Masters and Johnson distinguish primary and secondary types of impotence. A man who has never been able to have intercourse is considered to suffer from primary impotence, while in secondary impotence a man only has erective failure in 25 percent or more of his sexual encounters, or goes through a period during which he fails to achieve erection. Secondary impotence is more common than primary, but the treat-

ment for both conditions is the same.

The Masters and Johnson treatment requires the understanding cooperation of a sexual partner, and the most controversial aspect of their clinical work was the use of "partner surrogates" as third members of the therapy teams that treated impotence in unattached males. However, the manner in which the selection of these surrogates was made, and the attitudes, knowledge, and compassion that these people brought to the therapy sessions, insured that the treatment was far from the licentious activity that a few people may have suspected.

If a man's impotence springs from deep-seated feelings against sex or from religious prohibitions, these are talked over in the interviews of the first days, and the therapists endeavor to impart the understanding that such feelings and prohibitions are culturally determined and not set down by natural law. If, on the other hand, the impotence is attributable to excessive use of alcohol or a preoccupation with career or business concerns, the therapists emphasize that the patient's cooperation in combating his drinking problem or minimizing his worries is a precondition of successful treatment. Three basic goals must be accomplished: removing his performance fears, discouraging his tendency to adopt a spectator role, and encouraging his partner's confidence in him.

The "sensate focus" sessions are the means employed to achieve these ends. When a couple are expressly forbidden to consummate their "pleasuring" of each other they have no grounds for fears or apprehensions. The man cannot adopt a spectator role because there is nothing to watch. At this stage the therapists emphasize the importance of the man's concentration on giving his partner pleasure, on the principle that this initiates the "give to get" cycle. As a rule, after one or two pleasuring sessions the impotent male finds that erection occurs, but the couple are still not permitted at this stage to have intercourse. They must continue the pleasuring sessions until erection occurs regularly; then they go through one or two sessions during which the woman stimulates the man to erection but then allows the erection to subside. This is done several times in succession over a period of at least 30 minutes. This gives the man confidence that during coitus he will not lose his erection and fail to recover it.

When the therapists judge that the time to attempt vaginal entry has arrived, they instruct the woman to adopt the superior position and, after arousing the phallus manually, to guide its insertion. They stress very emphatically, however, that the woman must not let her partner sense any sexual demand on her part at this stage. She is told to move slowly backward and forward and if the erection is lost to bring it back manually and continue. The exercise is an extension of the pleasuring exercise, and the purpose is not to bring either partner to orgasm. If orgasm occurs, that's fine,

but it is never programed or planned, and the therapists never specifically instruct a couple to try to achieve orgasm. Masters and Johnson had a 59.4 percent success rate with primarily impotent males using this method of treatment, and 73.8 percent success with secondarily impotent patients. This, they claim, is a very much better rate than psychotherapy ever achieved.

The Masters and Johnson techniques of sex therapy have come in for a lot of criticism. It has been objected that they dehumanize sex; that they regard it too much in terms of mechanical stimulus-response processes and ignore the psychological elements in sexual experience; or that they set too much importance on the female orgasm. Their supporters respond by pointing to the statistics showing positive results as a vindication of the techniques. But objections also arise regarding the type of patients with whom these results were obtained. The very fact that they sought professional help may indicate an exceptional and atypical degree of desperation about their sexual problems. However, the principle is nonetheless valid that when sexual dysfunctions manifest themselves in one partner of a marriage, the only way to solve the problem is through both partners working at it together with all the understanding and love they can muster.

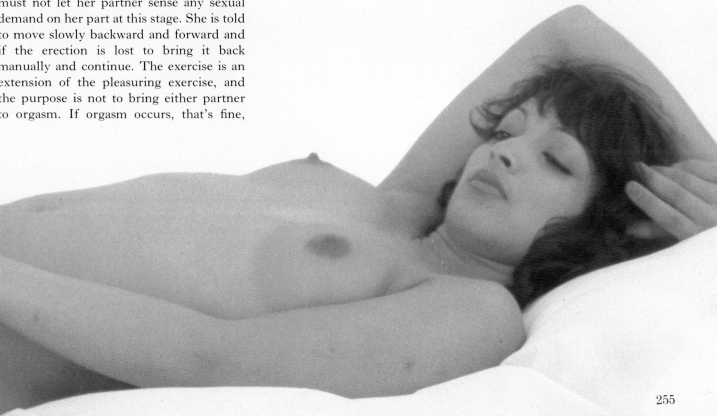

255

*Frigidity is such a common
problem that it is often
assumed by many, including
the victims themselves, to be
innate. The acceptance of
female sexuality has exploded
this myth and encouraged
many women to rediscover
their sensuality and at last
to enjoy sex.*

Frigidity

One of the most interesting points made in *Human Sexual Inadequacy* is that because women are biophysically "sexier" than men they are more susceptible to psychological and social influences in the prevailing culture that can block the expression of their sexuality. Masters and Johnson conclude that a balance is thus established between the sexes – in other words, women, particularly in our culture, are more frequently sexually dysfunctional than men, with the result that men are encouraged to retain an illusion of sexual superiority.

As previously noted, the idea that women do not particularly enjoy sex and only engage in it to satisfy their men has only quite recently been discredited and still survives among some people. It is easy to understand how a young wife, told reproachfully when she responded with enthusiasm to her husband's first love-making advances that "Ladies don't move," might subsequently become sexually dysfunctional – unable to achieve orgasm.

The word "frigid" is so often misapplied and has such emotional connotations that many sexologists prefer not to use it. A man may label a woman frigid simply because she does not appear to be interested in sex with him or if, when she does engage in it, the experience is not particularly rewarding for her. Some married women's attitude is that they "can take it or leave it," and they cater to their husbands' need for occasional ejaculatory release without enthusiasm, purely as a matter of marital duty. The attitudes behind this behavior are acquired, not inherent, and these women might find that more attention paid to their own sexual needs and enjoyments on the part of both partners, along with the mutual realization that women's sexuality is more complex than a man's, may lead to a more fulfilling sex life for both of them.

There are physical reasons why a woman may not enjoy sex. Some find intercourse painful because of an exceptionally thick hymen that has remained intact, or for a variety of other reasons. These conditions can usually be corrected surgically. The most common physical cause has nothing to do with frigidity; it is general fatigue, poor health, feeling low, or simply lacking in vitality. If a woman's life is an unrelieved routine of domestic drudgery and child-rearing she may often and quite understandably find that she has no energy left for sex.

In most cases of alleged female sexual inadequacy, however, the cause is psychological, and probably the most common such causes are fears. A woman may be so afraid of becoming pregnant that she cannot completely surrender herself to the feelings of the sexual act. She may block her responses because she fears disapproval – of a forbidding parental figure, perhaps, or of ingrained cultural morality. Frequently there has been an earlier disappointing or extremely unpleasant experience, so that a woman may fear being hurt or physically exploited. A loving partner may be able to allay such fears eventually, but first they must be identified, and often professional help is required to bring them up from the unconscious. Obviously, many women cannot count on the generosity or understanding of their men, which means their problem may be confirmed by custom and habit over a long period of time.

It should be plain, therefore, that ignorance on the part of their male partners is the primary reason for many women's supposed frigidity. Today, when information about sexual techniques and human sexuality is more widely available than at almost any other time in history, a surprisingly large number of men still do not know such basic facts as the existence and location of the clitoris or that a woman's full sexual satisfaction usually depends on a different technique and a longer period of arousal than a man's, and that individual women find different approaches stimulating. In some cases it is only through a person other than her husband, someone (male or female) more sexually sophisticated, sympathetic, and knowledgeable, that a woman finally discovers how mythical a condition her "frigidity" was.

Overcoming Frigidity

For the first 12 years of their marriage a couple, referred to as Mr and Mrs Smith, had a normal sex life. Mrs Smith regularly had orgasms, sometimes multiple, when they made love. But in the twelfth year Mr Smith lost his job and was unable to find another for some 18 months. He became depressed, began to drink heavily, and he became involved in an affair with another woman which his wife soon found out about. When she did she insisted that they sleep in separate rooms. Mr Smith then made efforts to rescue his marriage. He found a job, stopped drinking, and terminated the affair. After six months during which she had no sexual contact with her husband, Mrs Smith eventually returned to the conjugal bed, but she found herself no longer sexually responsive and did not experience orgasm. The situation remained like this for 10 years, at which time the couple were referred to Masters and Johnson for treatment.

This case was one of 342 that Masters and Johnson treated for female orgasmic dysfunction, and of this number they were able to help a total of 276, i.e. four out of five. Of the total number, 193 of the women suffered from primary orgasmic dysfunction, meaning that they had never experienced orgasm, and the remaining 149 had either stopped having orgasms altogether, such as Mrs Smith, or could only have them through some means other than intercourse, such as manual or oral stimulation.

The same principles and general tech-

niques apply in the Masters and Johnson treatment of female sexual inadequacy as in their treatment of the male. The two co-therapists emphasize the fact that it is the relationship between the couple that is the "patient," and they use "sensate focus" sessions as a means of recreating intimacy and for practicing the giving and receiving of physical pleasure. The psychotherapeutic aspect of the treatment is generally very important, and often the therapists establish themselves as authority figures who accept the woman's sexuality and, as it were, give her permission to enjoy it. This may help her to get rid of the inhibitions, ingrained beliefs, and misconceptions which block her spontaneous sexual response.

As the circumstances of each case of orgasmic dysfunction are different and the causes are extremely varied, each course of therapy must be individually planned and structured. The therapists try first of all to create between the couple a mood in which eroticism is possible, which often means bringing to light dislikes or resentments that they may have harbored for a long time. Then the woman is shown ways of achieving orgasm, while her husband is instructed in techniques of loveplay.

Genital play is considered by some nonorgasmic women as wicked, naughty, or infantile, and for such women the permission given by the therapists for her enjoyment of it plays an important factor in the treatment. The position recommended for the first sensate focus sessions has the man sitting against pillows at the head of the bed while the woman leans back against him and sits between his legs, with her legs crossing over his. This is a comfortable position in which the husband has easy access to his wife's primary erogenous zones and can also give her the feeling of being securely held. As the object is for the woman to concentrate on her arousal and sexual feelings, the husband is instructed to be quite undemanding at this stage and not to attempt intercourse. Usually after a few such sessions the woman does experience arousal, and when this has become a regular occurrence she is then encouraged to reciprocate the genital play and to regard her husband's phallus as an enjoyable plaything. The couple then naturally proceed to vaginal entry, but the man is expressly instructed not to make any thrusting movements. His wife adopts the superior position in which she can control the movements, and provided the psychotherapy has cleared away the mental blockages to pleasure, she can soon learn how to move and use her husband's organ to bring herself to orgasm.

As in the treatment of male dysfunctions, the normally functioning partner must control his or her own impulses in the interests of the therapy. In this case the husband must control his own ejaculation, so the treatment often includes training in ejaculatory control.

Sexual Incompatibility

Asked why their marriages broke down, many divorced people would claim sexual incompatibility. This term covers a multitude of ills, but very rarely indeed is such incompatibility of a physical or biological nature. The male and female sex organs are quite remarkably compatible in the sense that their respective size does not vary in relation to body size as much as the size of other parts of the body does. A small woman usually will have no difficulty accommodating the phallus of a large man if she is properly aroused. A heavy or obese man coupling with a small or frail woman in the "missionary position" can obviously hurt her or make it difficult for her to breathe, but knowledge of basic sexual techniques and the different coital positions can overcome most such problems.

What most people mean when they speak of sexual incompatibility is either a disparity in sex drive or frequency of the need for sex between the partners or else a marked difference in the kinds of sexual activity each person prefers. These incompatibilities may not be apparent in the early stages of a relationship. Before marriage a young couple's opportunities for intercourse may be nonexistent (through choice or otherwise) or limited. Nor do couples in the early stages of involvement necessarily engage in a full range of sexual activities. Often both partners are satisfied with fairly straightforward sexual encounters. The time when sexual incompatibilities are likely to surface comes after two or three years of marriage, which is perhaps one reason why 40 percent of the marriages that end in divorce do so in the first five years.

It cannot be denied that there are differences in sex drive and sex frequency needs between individuals, but to call someone "undersexed" or "oversexed" is irrelevant. Someone may seem undersexed if he or she is not "turned on" sexually at a particular time by a particular person, while someone else may seem oversexed because he or she

cannot find profound sexual satisfaction with any one partner. Differences exist between people in relation to their physiological functioning, in that some secrete sex hormones more abundantly than others and in some men the production of seminal fluid is faster or slower than average, but these processes are not sufficiently constant in any individual for them to be used to measure sex drive. The mean rate of hormone production is highly unstable and is subject to psychological factors.

According to Geoffrey Gorer's 1970 study of sexual attitudes in Britain, nearly half the women and one-third of the men believed that women's sexual desires were more "spiritual" and less "animal" than men's. Precisely what they meant by this is not clear, but it is true that males are more susceptible than females to psychological stimuli. Thus in a social environment where this type of sexual stimuli are abundant, men are more constantly on the brink of arousal than are women. Often the trouble is that after a certain time the man no longer gives his partner the necessary stimulation and preparation to help her sex drive to match his own.

The second type of incompatibility arises when one partner wants to engage in a type of sexual activity for which the other feels reluctant. This problem may have either cultural, aesthetic, or psychological causes, and it is important that both partners understand which cause is involved. As Kinsey showed, different codes of sexual practice prevail at different social levels; people of lower educational and socio-economic levels are far more likely to consider certain sexual activities "wrong" or "dirty" than those who belong to higher levels, and the latter are more disposed to elaborate sexual foreplay and variations of coital position than are the former. Such incompatibilities are particularly likely to arise in relationships where the partners are socially dissimilar, and usually accommodations are made in which the more inhibited partner becomes more sexually educated. Education, too, can go a long way toward dispelling aesthetic or psychological "hang-ups" about certain sexual practices, and when such incompatibilities are discussed within a context of love, forbearance. and humor the problem they pose can often be amicably resolved.

Problems after Pregnancy

Some aspects of sexual activity during pregnancy were discussed in chapter 6, but here will be considered the sometimes serious difficulties that can arise when a woman becomes a mother, with all that this change involves, both physically and psychologically.

Maureen Green, author of *The Sexual Side of Love*, recounts the experience of a young married couple named Jane and Peter. When Jane became pregnant they were both delighted at the prospect of their first baby. Jane had a difficult labor, after which she needed stitches, but she safely produced a daughter in whom both parents took great joy. On account of the stitches and because he understood that the new

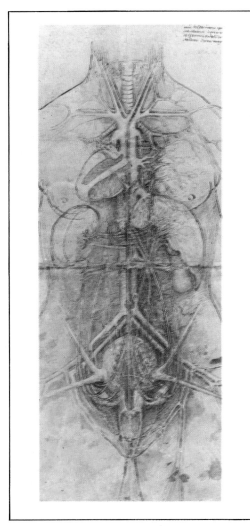

Left : ignorance about the female body has contributed to many myths about a woman's sexuality and fertility. The Italian artist Leonardo da Vinci made some of the first anatomical drawings of a woman's body, but his discoveries went unheeded for many centuries.

chores and responsibilities of baby care might be a bit overwhelming for Jane during the first weeks, Peter did not put his wife under any pressure to resume their normal sex life. However, when their daughter was six months old and Jane was still reluctant to make love, they both realized that something was seriously wrong. Jane visited her doctor at this time and hesitantly mentioned that she was puzzled about why she seemed to have lost interest in sex. The doctor questioned her about her attitudes to sex, marriage, and motherhood, and eventually it turned out that, although she had greatly enjoyed making love as a carefree young wife, she felt deep down that it was inappropriate for a mother to do so. She felt that as a mother she ought to have a more serious approach to life and that sex was frivolous and perhaps a bit undignified. She tended to identify with her own mother, who she suspected had never really approved of sex. When these underlying attitudes had been brought to light, her doctor was able to "give Jane permission" to combine the roles of mother and lover.

Peter and Jane were fortunate both in having a sympathetic doctor to consult and in realizing that their lack of sexual contact was making them both unhappy. Some couples do not see any connection between the anxieties and anticipation of pregnancy and subsequent problems that may appear in their marriage. John and Carol had had a satisfying sex life for the first two years of their marriage, although John had suffered occasional episodes of premature ejaculation. Carol was patient and understanding, and John had eventually become a confident lover. But watching the birth of their daughter Sarah was both an exhilarating and anxious experience for him. He may have felt, as some men do, that the mystery of his wife's body had been removed or that he now had to share her sexuality with the baby. More often the husband, having seen his wife suffer the pain of labor, is subconsciously afraid of hurting her during intercourse. In any case, when Carol and John resumed their lovemaking a few weeks after the birth, his old problem of being unable to sustain an erection returned.

For months they did not have sexual relations. But they did have arguments – about the baby, mothers-in-law, cooking, entertaining, jobs, money – everything but sex. Finally they sought marriage guidance

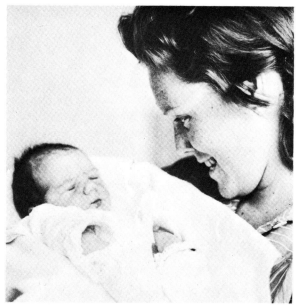

counseling, during which they both realized the source of the problem. "Looking back on it now, I suppose I just didn't have any patience this time," confessed Carol. "I was very involved in the baby and getting the housework done – being both a super-mother and a superhousewife. The sex part of it just wasn't important to me and in all my involvement with the baby I had forgotten how important it was to John." They received help from a sex therapist who taught them techniques which, with the sympathetic aid of his wife, would help John time his orgasm.

Sexual problems after the birth of a child are very common, and usually the reasons are very mundane indeed. "In most cases tiredness is the trigger," according to a doctor at the British Institute of Psycho-Sexual Medicine. "The new baby takes over, and quite apart from the sheer physical exhaustion of looking after the child there is the question of coping with a new lifestyle. Usually within the first two or three months the couple readjust emotionally and physically, and the sexual problems, if there were any, naturally disappear."

But for a great many people the readjustment is not so easy. "Some women become very anxious about motherhood, and this anxiety completely takes over," the same doctor warned. "Her husband may not understand. He may feel that motherhood should come as naturally to her as it seemed to come to their friends or relatives. He may not realize that for his wife motherhood involves learning new skills, adapting to

new responsibilities, every bit as much as any new job. He feels neglected and cast aside in favor of the new baby, and of course this resentment will be expressed in one way or another."

Another problem can arise when the husband suffers from an unconscious guilt arising from the time, harking back to young boyhood, when he was sexually interested in his own mother. An emotionally immature man may even see his wife as a substitute mother figure and thus encourage her to accept a purely maternal role toward both him and their baby. A particularly common situation results from the fact that, after a happy, relatively irresponsible period of living together, a man must suddenly share his wife's attention and love with another person – he is jealous, and this jealousy will be reflected in the couple's sexual relationship.

Finally, a woman goes through a variety of frequently unpredictable changes of mood and emotion during pregnancy and immediately after birth, due in large part to the complex interactions of hormones which take place at this time. Her whole self-image is in the process of alteration as well, and either of these major transformations may lead to sexual problems. The best advice for almost all new parents is to be as sympathetic, gentle, and caring as possible toward each other, both sexually and in other ways. In the few cases in which more serious or long-term difficulties arise, sexual therapy or psychiatric treatment directed at the particular problem will usually prove effective.

Approaching Middle Age

Of all the misconceptions exploded by modern sex research, those that affect the most people probably had to do with sex and age. It was once commonly thought that sex was a joy reserved for youth – that with advancing years the sexual appetite naturally waned and that for the elderly to seek sexual pleasure was somehow improper. Indeed, these beliefs are by no means rare today. It is not uncommon for a man in his 50s or 60s, consulting a doctor or psychiatrist because he is worried about apparent impotence, to be told that this happens at his age and he must reconcile himself to the fact. The impotence he experiences is more likely to be due to his worrying about the onset of age and possible erective or orgastic failure than it is to actual physical inability.

Modern findings suggest that sexual experience changes with age but that, given normal good health, people can remain sexually active into their 80s or even 90s, particularly if a spouse is still alive. Such activity can have a strongly positive effect on their general health and well-being. Young people, who may set great store by

Below : medical evidence has confirmed that men and women can continue to enjoy sex well beyond middle age. In fact a regular and interesting sexual relationship is extremely beneficial and healthy.

physical beauty, may find the very idea of sex among the elderly repugnant, but these opinions should not be a cause of worry to aging people who still need a regular sexual outlet, for such needs are entirely natural and healthy.

Another important influence on traditional thinking about sex and age was a misconception of menopause, which is often referred to as "the change of life." Confusion has been compounded by the belief that both men and women experience menopause, for this implies that the menopause meant the cessation of sexual functioning in addition to reproductive functioning. The two systems which include the human sexual organs – the reproductive system, that insures the continuance of the species, and the sexual system, which involves the mental health and psychological development of the individual, are in fact entirely independent, and the curtailment of the former does not physically impair the functioning of the latter. If sexual functioning appears impaired at or after menopause, the reason is almost certainly the person's belief that sex was meant for procreation and is inappropriate or improper when the age of possible childbearing has passed. But there is no inevitable diminution of libido with menopause, as evidenced by the fact that many postmenopausal women have a stronger sex drive than they have ever had before, possibly because they are now relieved of the worry of becoming pregnant.

Dr Robert Chartham has quoted a selection of letters highlighting some of the sexual problems of the elderly. One 74-year-old widower writes that he still feels a strong need for sexual release once or twice a week, but that if he makes a tentative suggestion to a woman he is invariably repulsed and accused of being a "dirty old man." He has neither the money nor the inclination to frequent prostitutes, so he is reduced to masturbation, which he finds unsatisfying. In another letter a 69-year-old widow confesses that she masturbates about once a week because sometimes she is so physically tense that she must do something, though she feels it is not a "decent" thing to do. A 64-year-old woman whose conjugal sex life had ceased seven years before wrote of a surprising and delightful resumption of sexual activity with a younger lover, with whom she does things she had never done in her life before. She enjoys this but at the

Right : with the major pressures of family and business life behind them, a couple approaching middle age can begin to rediscover the value of each other's company.

same time feels ashamed, because although it would be "all right for a young and passionate couple, for a woman of my age they seem unseemly, prurient, and nasty." Again, a 74-year-old woman wrote expressing her distress upon discovering that, though her husband makes love to her much less frequently than he once did and less often than she would like, he still masturbates two or three times a week.

These sexual problems can be multiplied throughout the population. In a Scandinavian university city, students are reported to have set up a sexual servicing organization for the benefit of elderly single people, but this is not likely to establish a precedent in countries with a less open attitude to sex. The sociosexual problems of the elderly are certainly very difficult to solve, but those that are basically psychological or stem from misconceptions about the sexual aspects of aging can often be alleviated by the reassurance provided in the findings of modern research.

Never Too Old!

Kinsey was the first sexologist to make a specific study of the elderly, and although his sample of 87 white males and 39 black males was too small to allow statistical analysis, the study did turn up some facts that seemed to go against prevailing ideas of the aging process in relation to sex.

Kinsey's most important observation was that sexual activity does not suddenly stop at any particular age and that the process of gradually diminishing activity, which begins in a man's early 20s, carries on into old age. Only 5 percent of his sample had become sexually inactive by the age of 60; by the age of 70 the figure was 30 percent, but there were tremendous individual variations – one 70-year-old was still averaging more than seven ejaculations a week, and one couple, aged 88 and 90, were still having intercourse ranging from once a week to once a month.

Masters and Johnson used their laboratory techniques to ascertain precisely what happens physiologically as people get older. They were able to point out certain advantages of the later years of sexual activity, provided that people understood and allowed for the changes that inevitably occurred in their sexual response cycles.

The first phase of sexual response, the excitement or arousal phase, generally takes longer in middle age than in youth. An older man will find that his erection comes more slowly and that it is not as hard as it was when he was young, but, as Masters stressed, "his potential for erection remains unchanged." Given time and appropriate stimulation he will become as erect as ever. Too many men worry themselves impotent, whereas if they accept the slow-down as natural (like the fact that they cannot run around the block as fast as they once could), they should have no trouble.

It is in the plateau phase that the older male may enjoy advantages over the younger, for he is generally able to achieve much better control of his ejaculation. As his urge to ejaculate is less intense, he can remain in a state of pleasurable erection and stimulation for a longer time. But in the orgasmic phase there are perhaps less welcome changes in the response pattern. The "inevitability stage," when a man feels his orgasm coming and can no longer hold it back, may last for only half as long as before (two to four seconds), and the "expulsion stage," when the semen is ejaculated, may involve fewer spasms or, as is frequently the case in the man over 50, only one spasm. After orgasm the older man's resolution phase is generally much shorter than a younger man's. He loses his erection much sooner, and the subsequent refractory phase, before he can have another erection, may take hours.

Masters has said that if he were asked to single out the most important statement in *Human Sexual Inadequacy*, he would choose the point that "the factor of reduced ejaculatory demand for the aging male is the entire basis for effective prolongation of sexual functioning in the aging population." In other words, the older man has less need to ejaculate, so that if he does so when he really needs to and does not feel a failure if on some occasions he has intercourse without ejaculation, he will be able to keep his erective potency.

In the female, too, the stages of sexual response change their characteristics in the later years. A young woman usually produces vaginal lubrication within 15 to 30 seconds of arousal, whereas a postmenopausal woman may require four or five minutes; but as the older male takes longer over arousal this need be no disadvantage. In the plateau phase the older woman does not manifest the changes in skin color that a younger woman does, nor does her vaginal canal increase in size. The experience of orgasm is generally shorter for the older woman, consisting perhaps of four or five vaginal contractions instead of eight to twelve. As in men, the postorgasmic resolution phase becomes more rapid with age.

When these differences between sexual response in the young and old are understood, many of the worries that a large number of people have about their sexual functioning as they get older can be dispelled. Sexual capacity does change with age, but it need never terminate, and the quality of its satisfactions in a loving and mature relationship can more than compensate for the quantity and frequency of outlets enjoyed in youth. Continuance of sexual activity helps keeps the entire physical organism vigorous and in tone and contributes to general good health.

Right : sexual capacity does change with age, but any decline in physical intensity is more than compensated for by the love, understanding, and mutual growth that develops in a longstanding relationship.

Sex and Your Health

The occurrence of sexual dysfunction as a concomitant of age is much less likely than that of dysfunction of the heart, liver, kidneys, nervous system, or other body organs and processes, and the probability of its incidence can similarly be greatly reduced by the adoption of an appropriate lifestyle, diet, and mental attitude. But what of other organic dysfunctions that age is prone to and their effect on sexual life?

In the case of heart disease, three heart specialists conducted a study in 1964 of the sexual activity of men who had had heart attacks. Two-thirds of these men had been given no advice on the matter by their doctors, and the rest had only been given vague cautionary advice. Of the total, 10 percent had become completely impotent and only some 30 percent had resumed their normal pattern of sexual activity. The figures indicate that ignorance and fear had resulted in the reduction of their sexual activities, and the specialists maintained that such a reduction was not only unnecessary but would probably have an adverse effect on the general health of the patients. Furthermore, they found no correlation at all between the severity of the heart attack or the age of the patient and the pattern of sexual activity following the attack.

It is obvious that during the sexual act there is a great increase in a person's heart rate, breathing, and blood circulation, and it is natural that people who have had heart attacks should be concerned lest they put excessive strain on their hearts and precipitate a relapse. But they can engage in totally satisfying sexual activity without overstraining the heart. It is probable, in any case, that during daily living they strain their heart more than they would by engaging in sex. When medical researchers monitored the hearts of 14 patients who had had attacks, they found that over a period of 48 hours the electrocardiograph showed a higher heart rate than during sexual activity on several occasions, for instance when driving a car in heavy traffic, engaging in heated discussion, and playing

Right : in the past, yearly pregnancies from marriage to middle age – this couple has 20 children – were common, particularly in times of high infant mortality. The exhausting round of child-bearing and child rearing took a heavy toll on a woman's health, and many women died in childbirth. Today the psychological interrelation-ships between sex and health are more likely to cause problems.

Below : sexual activity is a form of exercise : it increases the heart rate and is therefore beneficial for the body. Physical overreaction is unlikely to occur, so the risk of a heart attack is minimal unless other factors such as the stress of an illicit affair are present.

ball with a child. These researchers came to the conclusion that if a heart patient can climb a flight of stairs or walk briskly for a few minutes, he can equally well engage in intercourse.

Studies made of the incidence of "coital coronaries," i.e., cases of heart attacks occurring during intercourse, have made the interesting finding that a majority of these occur during extramarital coitus.

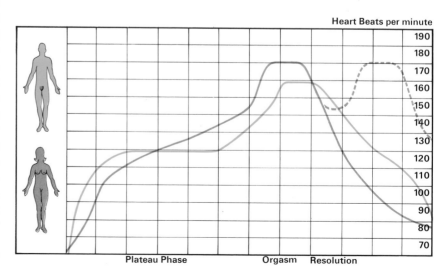

	Heart Beats per minute
	190
	180
	170
	160
	150
	140
	130
	120
	110
	100
	90
	80
	70

Plateau Phase   Orgasm   Resolution

Medical researchers have suggested that among the reasons for this may be excessive consumption of rich foods and intake of alcohol, as well as the fact that extramarital circumstances might have produced increased emotional tension in the form of excitement, feelings of guilt, and fears of discovery.

Although alcoholism is not, strictly speaking, an organic dysfunction, it is an ill the aging may suffer which drastically affects sexual functioning. Several factors tend to increase the consumption of alcohol in later years. Regular use may have built up a tolerance, and some may find in its effects a welcome diversion from worrisome preoccupations. Such increased consumption can easily become alcoholism, i.e., absolute physical dependence on a regular and heavy intake of alcohol, but even in less extreme cases it can severely impair sexual activity. Although it is true that after one or two drinks a person may experience a relaxation of tension; and that the lifting of anxiety and inhibitions may result in a temporary improvement in sexual functioning, the borderline beyond which alcohol consumption desensitizes the nervous system and leads to sexual failure is impossible to ascertain with any precision. This is so even in any one individual, because reactions differ depending on variables such as mood, time of day, and general physical condition. Although the alcoholic state may seem conducive to the enjoyment of sex at the time someone is intoxicated, the enjoyment, particularly in later years, may prove elusive, and the physical capacity for having an erection may well disappear.

Surgical Operations

Left : many operations require a period of convalescence to get the body back to normal strength.

Right : a person who has undergone an operation involving the sexual organs can feel extremely vulnerable. There is an assumption that part of one's sexuality has been removed. During the period of recovery it is crucial that the patient's partner is sympathetic and supportive.

When surgery is performed on parts of the sexual system, the question of the post-operative functioning of that system is naturally of profound concern to the patient; too often doctors fail to allay the worries a patient may have but is too embarrassed to express. The most common of such operations are hysterectomy (removal of the female's uterus) and prostatectomy (removal of the male's prostate gland).

Normally a hysterectomy is performed because of the growth of a fibroid, or noncancerous, tumor in the womb; less frequently it may be to remove a cancerous growth. Sometimes the cervix, and occasionally one or both ovaries, must be removed as well, but normally the vagina and external genitalia are unaffected. Therefore a hysterectomy need not affect a woman's subsequent sex life; physically she remains as capable of arousal, excitement, and orgasm as before. If she has lost one or both of her ovaries she may feel a lessening of sex drive due to a diminished production of sex hormones, but simple hormone treatment can correct this.

If a woman finds that her sexual desires have declined after hysterectomy, and it is ascertained that the cause is not hormone deficiency, the reason is very likely to be psychological. Many women feel that, lacking a womb, they are somehow less feminine. If the operation is performed after the onset of menopause, this feeling may be alleviated somewhat by the knowledge that the womb had already become nonfunctional. But the fear of losing the womb may be as profound and deep-seated as the male's fear of castration and therefore equally unsusceptible to reason. In such circumstances the reassurance that a husband can give, by showing that he still regards his wife as sexually appealing, is probably the best means of restoring an interest in sexual functioning.

Prostatectomy becomes necessary if a man develops cancer of the prostate or if the gland enlarges to such a degree as to interfere with the flow of urine. As the prostate gland produces seminal fluids, the nonappearance of these in subsequent sexual intercourse can cause a man great concern. No emission occurs at orgasm because the sperm, which are produced in the testes (not the prostate), flow back into the bladder. This is because after prostatectomy the neck of the bladder remains open when

be; some patients have reported that their subsequent orgasms were actually of increased intensity. A recent study of 280 men who had had prostatectomies revealed that 81.4 percent of them were still sexually active. The rest said they were impotent, but as one of the researchers who conducted

a man is sexually aroused. If someone is worried about the absence of semen because he thinks it signifies he is infertile, it may be helpful to follow a tip given by the sex counselor Robert Chartham, who has himself had a prostatectomy, to urinate into a glass after orgasm in order to see the semen floating in the urine.

The sensations of orgasm after prostatectomy are often different from before, and a man who undergoes surgery must be prepared for his orgasms to be less intense, although they need not necessarily

the study remarked: "It is by no means clear that those males who reported having lost their potency following surgery of the prostate did so because of the operation *per se* rather than because of other contributing factors." The other factors referred to are primarily psychological, chiefly worries about potency and performance. Ideally, both men and women who undergo sex-organ surgery should understand clearly beforehand the groundlessness of most of their natural fears about subsequent loss of sexual appetite and function.

Sex Aids

The fact that in recent years "sex shops" have sprung up in many large cities indicates a booming market in sexual aids and apparatus. Whether this boom is symptomatic of the spread of sexual liberation and the democratization of sophisticated sexuality, or of a malaise in which an elusive satisfaction is sought through novelty and gimmickry, is a debatable point and outside the scope of this book. Here only the variety and value of such sexual aids will be discussed. These aids may be grouped into categories of artificial genitalia, sexual deficiency compensators, and special effects stimulators.

The artificial genitalia are known as dildoes (penis substitutes) and merkins (vagina substitutes). Dildoes simulating the texture and shape of an erect penis are sometimes used by lesbian lovers, and double ones with belts which enable both women to experience penetration simultaneously are obtainable. Some heterosexual lovers have recourse to the dildo as a means of bringing the woman close to orgasm, particularly if the man suffers from hairtrigger trouble. There are dildoes that warm up, others that vibrate, and some are provided with a hollow tube in which an appropriate fluid can be put and squeezed out to simulate ejaculation.

The use of penis-shaped vibrators is apparently fairly common today, and Masters and Johnson recommend their use for women in training their own sexual response. Vibrators are generally marketed as general massagers and body stimulators, but their chief uses are masturbatory and in playful sex.

It is less easy to simulate the vagina, and merkins made of rubber or plastic and containing a warm liquid cannot afford anything like the sensations that a man obtains from vaginal penetration. They too are available with vibratory capacity or as part of the "anatomy" of life-sized inflatable dolls, but such refinements seem to have little appeal except for those few who are desperately sexually deprived. Their availability, however, probably lessens the incidence of injury that could result from the use of inappropriate sexual aids such as vacuum cleaners.

Aids that compensate for sexual deficiencies are generally designed for the use of males with erection problems. Some time ago we received unsolicited through the mail an offer of a product charmingly named "Magnaphall," a cream which allegedly increases the dimensions and firmness of the male organ. Though we did not feel the need to avail ourselves of the offer, it probably worked, if at all, on the principle of a genital irritant, like the supposed aphrodisiac known as "Spanish fly." Such products cannot compensate for a lack of erective potency, which generally has a psychological rather than a physical cause, and if occasionally a genital irritant

Sex aids make no claims to cure sexual dysfunctions but they provide amusement and a change of sensation.

272

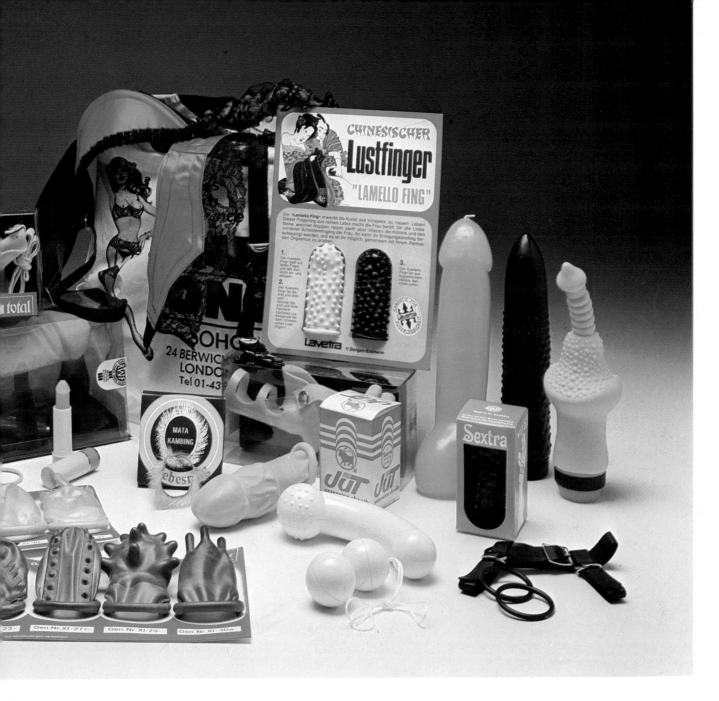

is wanted in order to produce a novel sensation, a dab of perfume or toilet water will do just as well.

Various frames and splints are available to help the flaccid penis attain phallus pretensions (if not dimensions), but their efficacy is dubious and their aesthetic appeal to most women is nil. The most successful erective aid, in fact, is a ribbon, band, or a ring tied or fixed fairly tightly around the base of the penis. This constricts the flow of blood out of the organ but not into it and thus allows an erection to build up gradually and be sustained. This device, easy to improvise and quite harmless, is often recommended by doctors for the erective problems of older men.

Aids designed to stimulate special effects are generally produced for the use of the woman. There are "Chinese bells," which are hollow plastic, ivory, or metal spheres, some empty and some containing mercury, which when worn intravaginally give a woman stimulating sensations as she moves. There are also condoms with all kinds of weird and wonderful protuberances that are supposed to enhance a woman's sensations during coitus by continually stimulating her clitoris or cervix.

While many sex therapists do not deplore the use of sexual aids and apparatus if a couple finds them effective in facilitating or heightening sexual pleasure, most incline to the view that mechanical, chemical or imagination-stimulating sex aids are all subject to the law of diminishing returns, and that the most reliable aphrodisiac is love.

Chapter 10
Homosexuality

In June 1970, 15 to 20 thousand homosexuals gathered for a "Gay Liberation" march through New York City, many wearing buttons inscribed "I'm Gay and I'm Proud!" After the 1960s demonstrations by blacks, students, and women, this latest protest was regarded by some as either a stunt or a comedy, but in fact it was an assertion on the part of homosexuals that they were no longer going to be secretive, guilty, or apologetic about their sexual orientation, but were going to accept themselves and demand that others accept them as they were. Psychologists as well as the general public held many inaccurate ideas as to why people were homosexual and what their activities were, and one of the tasks of Gay Liberation was to educate people out of these negative and insulting misconceptions. That task has by no means been accomplished yet – homosexuality is still surrounded by ignorance and prejudice, and many homosexuals suffer because of their sexual orientation. But some headway has been made since 1970, and today a more accepting and understanding attitude toward homosexuality is becoming more and more widespread.

The Gay Liberation Movement has enabled many homosexuals to come out and unite against the discrimination which society has subjected them to throughout the ages.

Root Causes and Reasons

Homosexuality is a complex phenomenon. The forms it takes are as various as the forms of heterosexual attraction and relationship, and to attempt to formulate an umbrella theory to cover all cases in which people are attracted to members of their own sex would be a vain endeavor; some of the theories can nonetheless be explored.

When the existence of the sex hormones was discovered in the 1930s and biochemists learned how to synthesize them, many experiments were carried out to determine what effects injections of sex hormones would have upon animals and human beings. It was observed that when doses of testosterone were administered to spayed animals, or to men who had suffered damage of the testicles, they seemed to manifest stronger masculine characteristics and a notable increase in sexual desire. Naturally a number of researchers then began to wonder whether homosexuality was attributable to a deficiency of the male hormone. Many tests were carried out, but their results did not support the theory. When homosexuals were given testosterone they did indeed show a heightened degree of sexual energy and interest, but they showed no more interest in females than they had before.

There are other theories for physical causes of homosexuality. Some neurophysiologists have suggested that homosexual behavior may be due to brain lesions or malfunctions, and it is true that sexual behavior disorders sometimes follow brain damage. Attempts to change homosexuals into heterosexuals by means of electrosurgery on the brain have, however, produced inconsistent results.

Another theory is that homosexuality is congenital and due to some inherited defect. Evidence given in support is that people born to elderly mothers are more likely to be homosexual, and it is known that genetic disorders are more commonly transmitted by older parents. But there may be many other factors, psychological or environmental, which both influence sexual behavior and occur with higher frequency

Left : the image of the homosexual has been culturally fixed as a direct opposite to the stereotyped masculine heterosexual male – hirsute, muscular, aggressive.

Right : the castration complex, classically illustrated by Delilah cutting Samson's hair and depriving him of his virility, has been often cited as a reason for a man becoming a homosexual.

when a child's parents are elderly. So theories which claim purely physical reasons for homosexuality are all dubious in one way or another. Homosexuals, it seems, are not born, but made – environmental influences and experiences in early life seem to be the prime determinants for the direction of sexual impulses.

The tremendously influential theories of Sigmund Freud did no more good for the status of homosexuals than they did for women. Freud and other psychiatrists of his school proposed a number of psychological explanations of homosexuality, all of which implied discredit to the homosexual. Many of these are still influential today both among psychiatrists and the general public.

According to these theories the archetypal male homosexual, as a child, identified too closely with his mother or was smothered by her love. He may avoid women of his own age in order to stay true to her; or because he identifies all women with his mother and feels that to have sex with any of them would be sinful; or he may subconsciously wish to have sex with his mother; or he may identify with his mother to the extent of wanting to take her place with his father, thereby either to win the love or appease the hostility of the dominant male in his life. If the father was a severe and unaffectionate man, the boy might have lacked a sympathetic model of masculinity

with which to identify and may have reacted against the model his father represented. He would therefore have tended to identify more with his mother and thus to become effeminate. He may, on the other hand, have a "castration complex" and subconsciously fear that he will lose his penis through intercourse with a partner who lacks this prized anatomical property. Such men will supposedly choose to have sex with other males for safety's sake.

The foregoing are some of the "theoretical" causes of homosexuality put forward by traditional psychiatrists. However sympathetically someone may be diagnosed in a particular case, the inescapable conclusion that these theories imply is that the homosexual male is inadequate or deviate. As a result of both the Gay Liberation movement and additional scientific research, these "traditional" theories have been rejected by most professionals.

Sexual Segregation

Homosexual practice is not peculiar to man, as is sometimes thought, but is found throughout the animal world. Even fish engage in it, as the British zoologist Desmond Morris demonstrated in a well-known experiment, reported in a paper entitled "Homosexuality in the Ten-Spined Stickleback." He found that when females were excluded from the aquarium, groups of male sticklebacks establish among themselves a hierarchy in which some are dominant and others submissive, and that the members of this hierarchy manifest male and female sexual behavior respectively. When those behaving in a "female way" are put into a separate aquarium, a new hierarchy emerges – some become masculine and dominant.

The experiment neatly illustrates two important points about homosexuality. First, that the sexual impulse itself is so strong that animals will direct it toward members of their own sex when those of the opposite sex are not available; and second, that social position within a group can have an influence on sexual behavior, and homosexual practices can be a means of establishing and maintaining a dominance-submission hierarchy.

These observations apply to human as well as animal societies. In situations where males are separated from females for prolonged periods homosexuality is common practice. The dominant parties in such relationships may not consider themselves homosexual at all. Indeed, many would, under changed circumstances, establish a relationship with a female instead, but others continue throughout their lives to eschew female contacts in favor of submissive males.

It is useful to make a distinction between the homosexual act and the homosexual personality. A large proportion of people have been involved in at least one homosexual act at some time in their lives, but the homosexual personality is relatively rare. It is widely believed that such a

Below : while sexual segregation may encourage homosexual relationships, it is not in itself a cause of such traits. At least 50 percent of men admit to at least one homosexual relationship, many at school, but it is only a small proportion who continue when they enter a mixed society.

personality can be recognized by characteristics of effeminacy (in the male) or masculinity (in the female homosexual), and that true homosexuals invert their gender role in the sexual act.

However, this view is not only wrong but illogical. A male whose primary sexual outlet is sodomizing other males is no less homosexual than those he sodomizes, but both the law and public opinion in general seem to consider his behavior less reprehensible than that of the stereotypical effeminate and submissive homosexual, whose conduct is often condemned as being "against nature."

Those homosexuals who persuade themselves that because they take the male-dominant role they are not really homosexual probably feel a basic dislike or fear of females. This may be due to early experiences with a mother or sister or because their first sexual encounter with a female was unpleasant or traumatic, as is sometimes the case when a boy goes to a prostitute. The dislike and fear may also be based upon ignorance of or misconceptions about the female. Dislike and fear can sometimes be overcome, however. Homo-

sexuals who seek psychotherapy sometimes respond to treatment which involves making them aware of the origins of their feelings about women and encouraging them to take a different view. But in individuals on whom such therapy does not work, the homosexual behavior may be due to sexual imprinting, which, as noted in the discussion of fetishism, is very difficult to eradicate. If a person's first experience of orgasm is with a homosexual contact, the orgasm reflex may be triggered subsequently only by such contacts.

Many homosexuals are high achievers and very successful in their professions, a fact which makes it difficult to accept the psychiatric view that their sexual practices are symptomatic of immaturity and general feelings of inadequacy.

Taking into account some of the sociological as distinct from the psychological causes of homosexuality makes for a broader view of the phenomenon more consistent with observable facts. One implication of this view is the rather surprising idea that in human beings sex is a learned behavior, which shall be considered in the next section.

279

Left : many societies have recognized that homosexuality is not incompatible with traditionally ascribed behavior. One of the most common themes in Renaissance art was that of the beautiful youth David who slew the giant Goliath. This version is by Verrocchio.

A Behaviorist View

Sex is, in fact, a learned behavior in all of the more highly evolved mammals. Male monkeys brought up in isolation, never witnessing sexual intercourse, and introduced when mature to a female have no idea what to do with her. They experience genital sensations and erections, but until they are shown how, or discover at length by trial and error, they do not know how to copulate. The reason is that the more highly evolved an animal is, the more of its functions are controlled by the cerebral cortex, that part of the brain in which the processes of thought, imagination, memory, and learning take place.

In fact, human beings have three brains superimposed one upon the other – the old reptilian or limbic brain, the cortex, and the neocortex or "thinking cap." The old brain controls instinctual behavior and physiological processes, but in more evolved species these fall increasingly under cortical control. There is sometimes conflict between the two control centers, as when people feel sexual attraction toward each other and suppress it for some reason, or when a man suffers with the problem of "the unconvinced phallus." But it is the cortical involvement in human sexuality that makes sex a far more exciting and rewarding experience for us than it is for the lower animals, which couple only when they are in season or rut. The cortical influence also makes it necessary for us to learn to express sexual feeling.

Learned behavior obviously varies very much more than instinctual, depending on how it is learned, from whom, and under what circumstances. Wide differences exist between the sexual manners and mores of people of different races, nations, or backgrounds precisely because sex is a learned behavior. As nature does not determine sexual behavior, no such behavior can be "against nature." All it can be against is the prevailing code of a particular society. The code of our society favors heterosexual monogamy and disapproves in varying degree of any sexual behavior that falls outside this strict norm. The process of learning socially approved behavior begins early in life and is assisted by influences from many quarters. There are, as shown elsewhere in this book, many points to be made in favor of our prevailing norm, but observations of sexual lifestyles in other societies invalidate claims that it is a norm for human beings generally.

It is well known that homosexuality was practiced by the classical Greeks and was considered in no way incompatible with their high achievements and ideals. Sanctified sodomy and fellatio are part of the initiation rites of many tribal societies, and the practice was common among early Hebrews. For some South American tribes today homosexuality is the rule, and heterosexual couplings occur only on two or three annual ceremonial occasions when the males get drunk in order to be able to perform. Young males of some North American Indian tribes were trained especially for the sexual pleasure of other males. In some tribes dominant males were permitted a male "wife," sometimes in addition to one or more female wives. A "wife" might then himself take a mistress, in relation to whom his behavior would be entirely masculine.

Taking all its cultural manifestations into account, then, it is obviously preposterous to suggest either that homosexuality is unnatural or pathological or to attribute it to an Oedipus or castration complex. Although powerful influences in our society push people to conform to the norm of heterosexual monogamy, some individuals are subject to other strong influences just at the stage in life when sexual behavior is learned, and these influences can determine their lifelong sexual predilections.

Above : social norms and expectations play as important a role in determining sexual behavior and inclinations as do basic instincts. Even the effects of initial experiences are very much dependent on cultural upbringing.

281

Male Institutions

In their study *Patterns of Sexual Behaviour*, published in Britain in 1965, the psychologists C S Ford and F A Beach demonstrated that human beings are capable of responding to a wider variety of sexual stimuli than they normally do, but that part of the process of learning sexual behavior is learning to suppress responses to stimuli considered inappropriate. Freud, too, observed that in young children sexual patterns are polymorphous, that is, they are a combination of male and female patterns. It appears that, before human beings start learning the type of sexual behavior considered right by their particular society,

they are by nature bisexual.

Some people remain bisexual into adult life and are capable of enjoying sex with either a male or female partner. This is in a sense quite a remarkable achievement. After sexual tastes have become ingrained people normally acquire an aversion to the "opposite" of what arouses them. Most men who have learned to respond sexually to the

Above right : in laying down rules for celibacy in clerics, early Christian doctrine only considered temptation from members of the opposite sex.

Above : Freemasons' initiation ceremony. Sexually exclusive societies have always appealed strongly to men.

roundness, smoothness, and softness of the female form feel an aversion to the idea of sexual contact with an angular, hairy, hard male body. The bisexual's achievement is the capability of harboring two quite different and normally exclusive sets of tastes and criteria, and in any particular sexual situation to be able to shut off the one that is inappropriate and switch on the one that is appropriate. This is analogous to the achievement of the person who is bilingual and thus capable of switching from one language to another – which means from one mode of thinking to another – with ease. And bisexuality, like bilinguality, is generally learned early in life. If a person had early sexual experiences of an enjoyable and positive kind with members of both sexes, he or she may have learned associations for particular characteristics of each sex so positive as to prevent the formation of aversions.

A person may become bisexual in adult life, usually by "unlearning" averse reactions toward the sexual characteristics of his or her own sex. For instance, in circumstances of great distress a person may be comforted by a friend; the comforting may lead to sexual contact. Adult lesbian relationships, particularly, are inclined to begin in this way, because in our culture affectionate physical contact between females is considered acceptable up to a point – and that point is easily surpassed.

Because adult males are not, under ordinary circumstances, allowed much physical contact with each other, they have a tendency to create special institutions and circumstances under which such contact is permitted and/or from which females are excluded. Anthropologists have attributed the phenomenon they call "the male bond" to our primate ancestry and to the fact that in our dim past the males of the species would bond together for the purposes of hunting or fighting. They believe that the tendency to form such bonds is inherent in males of all ages, as evidenced both by boyhood gangs, exclusive men's clubs, and such august institutions as the College of Cardinals. There are countless other examples such as the Freemasons, the Rotarians, college fraternities, and officers' clubs, as well as clubs and teams devoted to spectator sports.

Anthropologists and psychologists suggest that male bonding today is not so much an atavistic behavior based on the experience of early man's hunting and fighting parties, as rather a means of channeling off the homosexual elements of men's basic bisexuality. Some male-bond institutions and practices show what may be considered sexual elements – for instance, communal nude showers after football games, the stag parties held before a man gets married, and the initiation practices of college fraternities.

Frequently male-bond institutions have no purpose other than to enable men to be together, although they may ostensibly

gather to transact business, for serious discussion, or for planning and executing charitable works. The feeling of male togetherness and the exclusion of women are the real attractions of such male-bond societies. If the members were told that they were actually engaged in expressing their latent homosexuality in a socially acceptable manner, most of them would probably be affronted and angry, but nonetheless research suggests that this is what they are doing.

Above : the male bond manifests itself in the preference for spending one's time socially in the company of other men.

Left : anthropologists and psychologists see exclusively male team work as a common and socially acceptable expression of latent homosexuality.

Facts and Figures

Of the many disclosures regarding human sexual behaviour made by the Kinsey Reports, none aroused such vehement reaction as their facts and figures relating to the incidence of homosexuality. For something that was often considered unnatural, esthetically and morally heinous, and in most places was illegal, according to the Kinsey findings homosexuality was remarkably common. As the first report vividly put it, "One male in three of the persons that one may meet as he passes along a city street" has had some homosexual experience. The researchers admitted that when they began their investigations they had not anticipated such incidence data, and had repeatedly wondered whether their samples might be untypical, but each independent study, whether undertaken in a large city or a rural area, in a church school or a state university, produced remarkably consistent data.

Of course, the Kinsey finding was not that one man in three was a homosexual, but simply that one in three at some time in his life had had a sexual experience with another male which led to orgasm. Kinsey pointed out that if his statistics had not been based on the experience of orgasm but had included males who had engaged in homosexual practices that stopped short of orgasm, the figure would have been over 60 percent. Furthermore, "An additional group of adult males . . . avoid overt contacts but . . . are quite aware of their potentialities for reacting to other males." It is not surprising that these unemotional statements of fact, which in the climate of the time were considered to impugn the masculinity and morality of the males in the population, should have called forth a reaction of rejection and vilification of those who made them.

Between the extremes – the male whose only sexual outlet is with other males, and the male who has a single homosexual experience – are infinite degrees both of frequency of homosexual activity and of its relative place in people's sex lives. In his sample Kinsey found correlations between the incidence of homosexuality and the factors of educational level, age, and marital status. By the age of 15, the incidence of active homosexuality among males was 27 percent; by the late teens it had risen to 33 percent; it fell significantly between the ages of 21 and 25, and then rose steadily among males who remained unmarried to reach 39 percent of those between 36 and 40 years of age. The fall in "active" incidence in the early 20s Kinsey attributed to the fact that a majority of men got married at this age. He also speculated that this was when males of basically homosexual orientation attempted to make the heterosexual adjustments which society demanded – an attempt which some would abandon without success when they had reached their mid-20s, when they would reconcile themselves to the fact that they were homosexual.

The foregoing figures were the mean averages for males irrespective of educational level. When this factor was taken into account, the figures showed far more homosexual activity among the middle stratum of males, which included those who had been educated to high school level but not beyond, than among the less or more educated. In this group 32 percent were actively homosexual in their early adolescent years; of those who remained unmarried 54 percent were actively homosexual by the age of 30. This contrasted with the figures of 21 percent and 40 percent respectively among males with a college education. Furthermore, after marriage, between 9 and 13 percent of the middle group of males (with a high school education) continued to have homosexual relations, while only 2 or 3 percent of college-educated males admitted to doing so. Kinsey warned, however, that married, college-educated males were the most disposed to deny and cover up their homosexuality.

The question of how many homosexuals there are in a population is thus very difficult to answer because of the various definitions of what constitutes a homosexual at any particular age. If the question is taken to mean what proportion of the male population has no sexual contact with females but obtains all its outlets, except masturbation, through other males, then the Kinsey findings suggest that the answer at the time of his study was 7.4 percent at age 15, 4.9 percent at age 20, 2.9 percent at 25, 2.6 percent between 25 and 35, but only 1.8 percent by the age of 45. The incidence of homosexuality today is probably at least as great as it was 30 years ago and might even be greater, considering the increasing level of public tolerance.

The Lesbian Relationship

The fact that females tend to demonstrate affection toward one another more than males, that they often embrace, kiss, and hold hands in public, is sometimes cited by men to support the claim that lesbianism is more common than male homosexuality. Kinsey's study showed, however, that this was a fallacy. He suggested that men misinterpreted such female behavior by thinking of it in terms of male psychology. In fact, most female physical contact is a demonstration of friendship and affection, and nothing more, and the incidence of homosexual practice among women is far less than among men.

Whereas about 50 percent of the males in the Kinsey sample admitted some degree of homosexual response, only 28 percent of the females did; 37 percent of the males had had contact to the point of orgasm, while only 13 percent of the females had. The discrepancies between male and female homosexual response during adolescence and the late teens were particularly striking. Although schoolgirls may often have "crushes" on one another or on their teachers, only 4 percent of the females had reached orgasm in homosexual contacts by the age of 20 (compared with 33 percent of males). When educational level was taken into account, another noticeable difference emerged – the more highly educated females were far more prone to lesbianism than those at either of the lower educational levels. Among the females who had had only a high school education, 18 percent said they had been erotically aroused by other females and 5 percent had experienced orgasm through such contacts; among the college-educated group the respective figures were 25 percent and 10 percent, and among a smaller group of female graduates the figures were 33 percent and 14 percent. Kinsey suggested that at higher social levels, from which most of the better educated females came, greater moral restraint might have been put upon pre-marital heterosexual activity, thus causing the women to put more emphasis on finding homosexual outlets. Another and perhaps

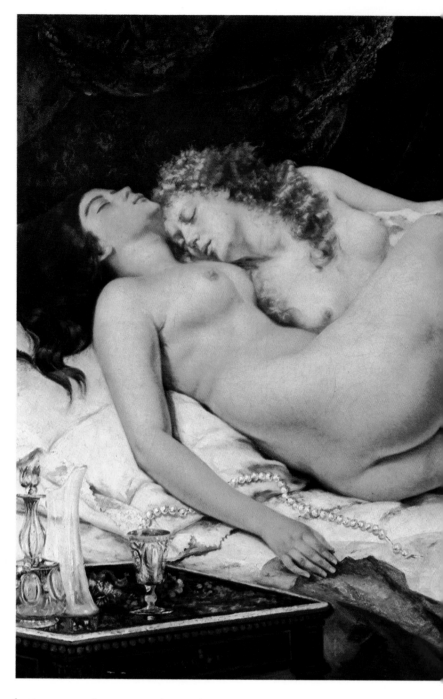

better reason he proposed was that a more enlightened and accepting view of homosexuality might be more prevalent at the higher educational levels; a further reason, especially in the light of the more recent Hite Report, could be that the better-educated females were more likely to be critical of and dissatisfied with male sexual performance.

Females were found to be less promiscuous than males in their homosexual relations. Of those who had had homosexual experience, 51 percent had had only one partner (compared with 35 percent of males); only 3 percent had had more than

Homosexuality is less common in women than men, and contrary to popular belief, most examples of demonstrative behavior between women have their basis in friendship, not sexual attraction.

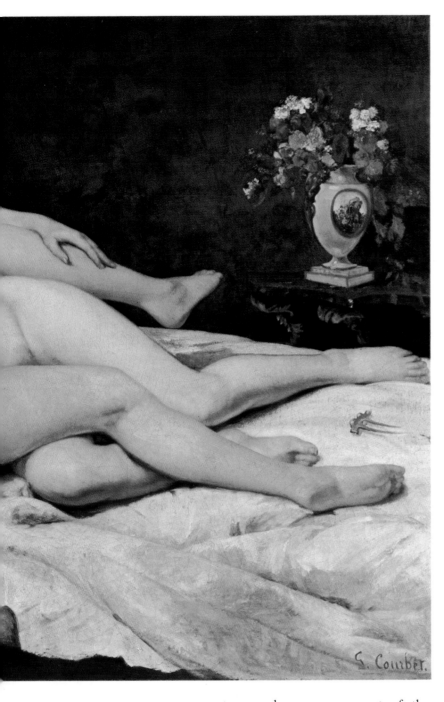

was that homosexuality was a continuing way of life for far fewer females than males.

Dr Richard Green, formerly of the University of California Gender Identity Research Treatment Program, has suggested that in our age there may now be an increase in lesbianism and/or bisexuality "partly for political reasons" – as a way that women can "disassociate themselves from the extraordinary dependency they've had on men all these years." One of the most striking points about the answers to Shere Hite's questionnaires, she observed, "was how frequently, *even though it was not specifically asked,* women brought up the fact that they might be interested in having sexual relations with another woman." In response to the questions, "What would you like to try that you never have?", a considerable number of women mentioned lesbian contact. Following are some quotations:

"I've never had a physical relationship with a woman but I feel it would be more satisfying than with a male."

"I have been brought up to believe women are more attractive and more beautiful and I am beginning to believe it."

"I'd love to massage a woman I liked and was turned on to, and then gradually arouse her sexually through massage and then slowly make love to her and then stop and talk, then love again, then sleep together. I'd like with her to know myself better. But I'd never have the nerve!"

"I would like to have sex with women. I think I am a lesbian, which is not too helpful since I'm married, and don't feel capable of a divorce at this point, and living on my own, etc. However, someday it'll probably get to be too much, and I'll have to."

"I want a woman lover – or more. I generally want *closer* relationships with women; I want to do all the things only *men* are supposed to do! I want to explore!"

It is not clear to what extent current lesbian practice and the lesbian longings that the above quotations express are motivated by a rejection of men, either for sexual political reasons or because of their supposed incompetence as lovers compared with women, but undoubtedly both factors play a part. In concluding her discussion of lesbianism the author of *The Hite Report* points out: "It is important for women to recognize their own potential for having sexual feelings for other women . . . with the possibility of sexual intimacy."

10 partners, whereas 22 percent of the homosexual males had. Only slightly over 1 percent had been involved in homosexual activities that led to orgasm after they had married. Furthermore, the tendency was for female homosexual experience to be confined to a brief, limited period. In 47 percent of the cases activity had been confined to a year or part of a year – a frequent pattern was one of intense and repeated experiences over a period of weeks or even days followed by a complete cessation or long lapse of activity. In only a quarter of the cases had the activity continued for more than three years. The implication

Consummating the Homosexual Relationship

The "straight" view of homosexuality may incline to overemphasize the phallic element. People may simply envisage males sodomizing each other or females using dildoes on each other, and perhaps it is because of these images that many regard homosexual practice as perverse, bestial, or entirely carnal. Often people fail to appreciate that in most homosexual relationships there is just as much tenderness and affection as in many heterosexual relationships.

As males and females have different physiological and psychological triggers for sexual arousal, it is possible in certain cases that two people of the same sex may know better how to give sexual pleasure to each other than partners of the opposite sex (unless they are very experienced and sympathetic lovers). This could be one reason why some people who have had both types of experience say that those they had with a partner of the same sex were more exciting

Below : the condemnation of gays by a heterosexual society is partly based on the many misunderstandings of homosexuals' relationships and their sexual activity.

and satisfying than those they had with a partner of the opposite sex. Partners of the same sex also tend to employ a wider variety of sexual techniques, partly because the physical pattern of such intercourse is not as stereotyped as that of heterosexual intercourse, with its focus on penis-vagina penetration, and also because the psychological roles of the partners are not as defined and limited by tradition.

Male homosexuality in adolescence does not generally go further than mutual masturbation. As in heterosexual relationships, it takes some time for the full range of potential sexual activity to be explored, and the circumstances of such adolescent contacts tend to limit them to short duration. This is particularly true when the partners are both inexperienced, though if one is older and more experienced then more sophisticated techniques may be employed.

The next technique to be tried is usually mouth-genital contact, leading ultimately to the performance of fellatio to the point of orgasm. Men with a strong demanding fellatio libido sometimes engage in homosexual acts simply because they cannot find a woman sufficiently uninhibited, knowledgeable, and similarly inclined to gratify them. They mentally focus on the oral-

genital contact and screen out the other characteristics of their sexual partners.

The act of penetration can be simulated in femoral intercourse, when the penis is stimulated to the point of orgasm between the partner's thighs. Many homosexuals do not go further than this, but some do consummate their lovemaking with anal penetration and coitus.

The taboo upon anal intercourse is so strong that its practice between men and women is frequently associated with latent homosexual desires, although it does occur in heterosexual intercourse. According to Kinsey, about 50 percent of married couples practice anal penetration with finger or phallus at least once. Anal intercourse may seem inconceivable due to the action of the anal sphincters, two rings of muscles at the opening of and inside the anus, which normally keep the passage tightly closed. But these muscles can be deliberately relaxed – the outer one without much difficulty and the inner one with practice, in circumstances where a person is at ease with and aroused by a sexual partner. Often a lubricant is used to facilitate pene-

tration, for the passage does not naturally secrete lubrication with arousal as the vagina does. When penetration has been effected the phallus enters the rectum, the broad passage from the bowel which is normally free of feces. For the passive male partner the experience of such deep penetration can be one of peculiarly intense pleasure because it results in stimulation of the prostate gland, which can produce an intense and prolonged orgasm. The orgasm reflex involves strong contractions of the anal sphincter, which also intensify the excitement of the active partner.

The anecdotal evidence available suggests that anal intercourse is fairly rare except among men whose orientation is exclusively homosexual, and even for these men the phallic element is not necessarily of such preeminence as heterosexuals sometimes imagine, unless the participants are engaging in sex for a nonsexual motive such as the assertion of personal dominance. Homosexual consummation is generally preceded by just as passionate demonstrations of affection and tenderness as that shown by heterosexual lovers.

Sex without the Phallus

Most lesbian couples do not consist of a mannish dominant woman and her submissive, ultrafeminine partner. In fact many lesbian couples would be indistinguishable from a pair of female friends.

According to the Kinsey researchers' data, only 40 percent of heterosexual females experienced orgasm during intercourse nine times out of ten after five years of marriage, whereas 68 percent of females who had had homosexual relations for about the same number of years were brought to orgasm by 90 percent or more of their contacts. The implication that on the whole lesbians have more satisfying sex lives than heterosexual women is not very flattering to men, and that may be why it was one of the most contentious points raised by the second Kinsey Report.

The point made in the previous section that homosexual sex techniques are less stereotyped and more varied than the techniques normally practiced by heterosexuals applies to females as well as to males. It is also true that the stereotypical lesbian relationship – comprising one "butch" or masculine dominant female who dresses in mannish clothes and a very "womanly" or feminine one who is submissive to the other – is actually quite rare. Lesbian relationships and affairs tend to be between two equally feminine women and to be based, just as heterosexual love is, on intense emotional involvement which is expressed quite naturally through sexuality.

Many people wonder what lesbians do together, or imagine that they must rely on artificial phalluses. But in fact they do together many things that an experienced and considerate male lover can do for a woman, and many of them do not use a substitute for the male organ. Some frank descriptions of what they do, given by lesbians who answered Shere Hite's questionnaires, are as follows:

"As far as how we relate to each other physically – we hug a lot and kiss and caress each other. As for 'technique,' we masturbate each other with our hands and fingers and orally, as well as combining both. Also mutually masturbate, with other parts of our bodies. Basically, the same things a man and woman can do without a penis, and *usually don't*!"

"Sex with a woman includes: touching, kissing, smiling, looking serious, embracing, talking, digital intercourse, caressing, looking, cunnilingus, undressing, remembering later, making sounds, sometimes gently biting, sometimes crying, and breathing and sighing together."

"Sex with a woman for me has involved kissing, feeling one another completely . . . pressing mound of Venus against mound of Venus or each other's leg. Also cunnilingus and manual and even anal lingus!"

Another contributor to *The Hite Report* gave a lucid itemized account of why she preferred homosexual to heterosexual love: "My best sex experiences were with my woman friend, not because I was orgasmic, because I generally wasn't, but because (1) she was a woman and it's much easier for me to give myself emotionally to a woman, to surrender my ego; (2) her skin was so soft and smooth, the vulnerability sent me; (3) the opportunity to act the aggressor and the lover was wonderful; (4) lovemaking was so mutual, endless, unhurried, she didn't quickly tighten up into a ball of sweat and demand the old in and out; (5) I didn't worry about coming, there was no program; (6) I didn't worry about my body, whether it was 'adequate;' and (7) I didn't worry about her sexual-moral judgment, where I was going to be placed on the spectrum of female frailties (angel or whore?)."

This woman's point that sex with another woman is less hurried, longer, and less programed than with a man was made by many women. "It's like a circle, it goes on and on," one wrote, and another said, "It isn't all automatically 'over' because somebody orgasms."

For most lesbian lovers the actual experience of orgasm is less important than the emotional closeness, warmth, gentle sensuality, tenderness, understanding, and consideration they experience. In fact, both men and women heterosexuals could probably not find better instruction on how to improve their own sex lives than by reading the chapter on lesbianism in *The Hite Report*.

Homosexual Commitments

Heterosexuals who hold homosexuals in contempt often rationalize their feelings by saying that they are promiscuous, incapable of lasting relationships, and interested only in sex. They quote newspaper reports of homosexuals charged with accosting strangers in public toilets to show that their opinion is well founded. It is true that a small minority of homosexuals are as promiscuous as any heterosexual Casanova, and are so constantly on the lookout for new partners that it seems they have no other object in life. These "cottagers" (frequenters of public toilets) and "cruisers" (who pick up one-off partners in known gay establishments) are often regarded with contempt as well by fellow homosexuals. Considering the risks they take – plainclothes police often visit these places for the specific purpose of catching people importuning – these men might be considered either to be sexually desperate or to get an extraordinary degree of erotic satisfaction from hurried sex with a stranger. However, the psychologist Dr C A Tripp, a former associate of Kinsey who has made a special study of homosexuality, discovered two points relating to the "brief encounter" contact that do not fit the image of superficial promiscuity and incapacity for an enduring rela-

tionship. He found that more than half of the continuing relationships he studied had begun with such contacts, and that most promiscuous males had had serious relationships at some time.

Serious continuing relationships between homosexuals may not be as conspicuous to some as the phenomenon of homosexual

Above : Radclyffe Hall (left) the author of The Well of Loneliness, *seen here with her partner Una, Lady Troubridge. They lived together for 27 years.*

Far left : some countries, such as Denmark, take a progressive and enlightened view toward homosexuality, and partners can live together openly without being discriminated against.

Left : marriage ceremony between two Danish lesbians who had lived together for five years.

promiscuity, but both males and females often form partnerships that last for years or decades. Such relationships have certain characteristics and problems quite distinct from those of heterosexual relationships. It is not only the lack of ties, such as a legal contract or commitments to children, though these factors do tend to make for a looser homosexual bond than operates in many heterosexual partnerships. There are also problems of rapport, role-playing, and sex. According to Dr Tripp, "The heterosexual blend tends to be rich in stimulating contrasts and short on rapport . . . By comparison, homosexual relationships are over-close, fatigue-prone, and are often adjusted to such narrow, trigger-sensitive tolerances that a mere whisper of disrapport can jolt the partners into making repairs, or into conflict."

Homosexual couples may tend to be oversensitive to each other, to be quick to take offense and flare up in anger, and Tripp explodes a popular misconception in attributing this characteristic to a high degree of rapport rather than to neurotic instability.

Problems of role-playing are not as important in homosexual relationships as some heterosexuals imagine. Often neither partner adopts a completely opposite gender role to form a parallel to the husband-wife relationship. Instead the two individuals settle on a workable division of labor and decision-making, based upon their respective abilities, and in this sense there is probably less problem with role-playing than in many heterosexual relationships. Conflicts may arise during these early stages, of course, and relationships sometimes break under the stress of them, but once each partner's distinct functions and roles have been established the day-to-day matters of living together can usually be managed quite smoothly.

Sex causes more difficulty. "Sexual interest between homosexual partners," Tripp wrote, "tends to decline more sharply than in heterosexuality." He claimed that this was particularly true of lesbian partners, suggesting that the problem stemmed not only from close rapport and familiarity but also, possibly, "from the relatively low libido of many women." He pointed out, however, that many lesbian relationships continue after keen sexual interest has waned, which to him suggested "that women have certain 'nest-building' proclivities

which permit them to extract more non-sexual rewards from a close relationship than men can." Male homosexuals sometimes agree to have "outside" sexual contacts with other partners to make up for a decline of erotic interest in each other, and one advantage of the close rapport between them is that such arrangements often work better than they do in heterosexual relationships.

Above : a high degree of rapport between homosexual partners may be the reason for their apparent extreme oversensitivity to one another.

Homosexuals are People Too

The problems that homosexuals experience derive mainly from social condemnation of their sexual orientation. These may involve discrimination in their careers or personal conflicts concerning their own feelings and personalities.

Despite the efforts of the Gay Liberation movement, many homosexuals are still disinclined to profess openly their sexual proclivities and prefer to be discreet, if not actually secretive, about their contacts. Male homosexuals in government employment are particularly vulnerable to occasional "clean-up" campaigns, and the ac-

Below : every year many US cities celebrate the founding of the Gay Liberation Movement with a "Gay Pride" parade.

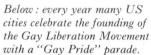

companying disrepute renders them vulnerable also to blackmail and various forms of coercion. This is why there is always a public outcry when someone highly placed in government or diplomacy is "exposed" as a homosexual. Although the homosexual outlook and orientation may be a positive advantage in some professions, diplomacy included, someone in the public eye must be careful if his or her sexual orientation toward the same sex is not to be used to destroy his or her prospects. At the other end of the occupational ladder discretion is advisable, too, for ill-educated people may tend to be even more intolerant of what they regard as sexual perversion.

Tripp found that more than 90 percent of the homosexuals he interviewed reported that they did not regret their sexual orientation, but that about the same percentage said they would not recommend it for others. This seeming contradiction implies that they were doubtful whether others would find the rewards commensurate with the costs, and they probably considered themselves fortunate to have come through the attendant tribulations to a positive attitude toward their own homosexuality.

Many homosexuals go through agonies of conscience and self-appraisal before accepting that they are what they are, and so insidious are the conventional views that some are convinced that they must be perverted, sick, or sinful. If they are less resilient in stressful situations than hetero-

Left : a popular misconception is that the "drag queen" caters to homosexual tastes and is often one himself. In fact drag is more a parody of women.

Right : homosexuals have been portrayed by gross and absurd characterizations, which are an insult and an effrontery to their dignity, although occasionally, as here on the sixth anniversary march of the Gay Liberation Movement, New York, 1975 a small minority of their number pander to an exaggerated image of this kind.

sexuals are, and more likely to break down or concede defeat, this is not due to any inherent weakness of character but because they have always had a less firm foundation on which to build their ego and sense of personal worth. One of the first things the Gay Liberation movement will hopefully accomplish is the liberation of its members from the crippling sense of isolation, abnormality, and inadequacy under which many homosexuals labor, particularly in youth when the sense of self is especially unstable and vulnerable.

Some people, unable to reconcile themselves to their homosexuality, try to combat it by marrying a member of the opposite sex. A few only discover after a period of marriage that their sexual orientation is in fact toward their own sex. Yet others use the institution of marriage as a cover for their homosexuality.

Robert Chartham relates the case of a patient named Martin, who had discovered his homosexual orientation at the age of 15 when he had an affair with a teacher at his school. Afterward he had a series of affairs but no stable relationship, and a number of his experiences were unpleasant. He was even blackmailed, and so at the age of 25 he

sought security in marriage to a woman a year older than himself. His wife did not suspect that he was homosexual, and occasionally he managed to make love to her (although he found it repugnant). However, he refused to have children with her, always for plausible reasons but really because he feared that his child would inherit what he felt was his "abnormality."

After some years of marriage, during which he had several furtive homosexual affairs, Martin admitted to his wife at the height of a quarrel the real reason for his refusal to have children. Her reaction surprised him. She became silent, calm, and thoughtful. The following day she told him what she had decided. If he would father her child and remain with them to give the child a semblance of a normal home life, she would make no sexual demands on him and he would be free to have as many homosexual affairs as he wished, though she would be less accepting if she ever discovered that he was sleeping with another woman. Martin agreed and the arrangement worked. For these two people a livable compromise solution had been found to the problems created by one partner's homosexuality.

Homosexual "Cures"

As homosexuality is neither an illness nor generally speaking a symptom of psychopathology, the question of whether it can be "cured" is essentially misconceived. However, it is true that some homosexuals, particularly males, suffer such distress on account of their sexual orientation that they do seek help and would be grateful if a way could be found to transform them into heterosexuals.

Kinsey set up a research project to find out whether any treatment had been successful in effecting the reorientation of homosexual desire. Many psychiatrists claimed to have found such a method, but when the Kinsey researchers investigated they found that the "cures" were very dubious indeed. Kinsey recounted the story of a man who had once phoned him and said that he was a former homosexual who had been cured. When Kinsey interviewed him, the man said, "I have now cut out all of that [homosexual behavior] and don't even think of men – except when I masturbate."

The trouble with psychiatric treatment is that it is based on Freudian concepts of homosexuality, which consider it as pathological and a consequence of childhood trauma. Many a homosexual who has sought the help of a psychiatrist has had reason to regret doing so, for he or she has been told that as a condition of recovery he must first accept that he is ill, and, as Tripp says, the therapy has left him with "even less self-acceptance than he started with."

Psychiatric treatment involves making a male homosexual patient remember and bring to his awareness the childhood fixation or experience that made him afraid of physical contact with women, and then urging him to overcome this and deliberately to seek such contact. But no matter how deeply the analyst probes, he may fail to find a history that fits the phobia theory. The very axioms of Freudian analysis have been called into question by modern research, which has shown, as Tripp reports, "that dominant mothers and weak fathers correlate with nothing at all except each other, that ... a boy's closeness to his mother has a higher correlation with heterosexual than with homosexual outcomes ... that a young boy's awkwardness with (and disparagement of) females is among the highest prognostications of his later attraction to them ... and so on and on to the utter embarrassment of every formal psychiatric theory without exception."

It could be said that homosexuality has had as bad an effect on psychiatry as psychiatry has had upon homosexuality, because it has proved recalcitrant to treatment by accepted psychiatric methods. Nevertheless, there are still diehards who follow the strict Freudian line and impute all a person's problems to his or her homosexuality and try to reorient the person sexually, even though that was not the object of the patient seeking therapy.

Harm can be done, too, by the use of behavioral therapy. As sex is a learned behavior, some psychologists believe that its behavior patterns can be unlearned and new ones developed to replace them. The treatment is known as operant conditioning, and it involves a process of reward and punishment. The punishment is known as aversion therapy, and consists, for instance, of showing a male homosexual pictures of nude men and simultaneously giving him an electric shock or inducing in him by drugs a feeling of nausea, in the expectation that he will develop unpleasant associations with homosexual feelings. Conversely, pictures of nude women might be shown to him while he was under the influence of a sexual stimulant. Such methods of treatment raise the serious moral question of whether such gross interference – which implies that a person is a thing to be modeled rather than a human being with complex emotions – can ever be justified, even if the person requests it.

Fortunately, today an increasing number of psychotherapists take the view that their task is not to adjust their patients to a so-called "norm" but to assist their self-development and self-fulfillment. Their treatment of someone with problems attributable to his or her homosexuality is aimed at making the person accept that the orientation is homosexual and ridding him or her of any feelings of guilt or shame because of it. Increasingly people are recognizing the fact that homosexuality is in many cases something to be accepted and lived with rather than cured.

Artists, the Acceptable Homosexuals

Society has been more indulgent to the homosexual artist than to those in other walks of life.

Many outstanding writers and artists have been homosexuals. The Dutch Renaissance scholar and theologian Erasmus (above right) and the 19th-century French novelist Marcel Proust (1871–1922) (right) are two notable examples.

Below : Michelangelo's "David." Michelangelo brought the representation of the male nude to its pinnacle, and he even used male models for statues of females.

The Gay Manifesto declares, "Homosexuality is *not* a lot of things. It is not a makeshift in the absence of the opposite sex; it is not hatred or rejection of the opposite sex; it is not genetic; it is not the result of broken homes, except inasmuch as we could see the sham of . . . marriage. *Homosexuality is the capacity to love someone of the same sex*."

The positive phrases and nonapologetic tone of this definition express the changing attitude to homosexuality in our time. This change is taking place not only among homosexuals themselves but extends to open-minded people everywhere. What Oscar Wilde called "the love that dare not speak its name" is today increasingly declaring itself as a healthy and normal expression of sexuality. Some people see the change as a symptom of cultural decadence, but others take the view that it is symptomatic rather of an expansion of understanding, sympathy, and emancipation from a restrictive and negative morality based primarily on fear and ignorance.

Many people are beginning to consider whether there might not be some positive benefits to society in the existence of homosexuality. Although homosexuals are to be found in all professions and walks of life, they seem to some to be more prevalent in certain professions, particularly in the theater and the arts. There are two possible explanations of this: first, that theatrical and artistic people assume and are allowed more freedom to be nonconformist than people in other professions; and second, that there is some correlation between their homosexuality and their artistic talent. The first point is undoubtedly true – theatrical people particularly have always been rather set apart from the rest of society, whether because of their unsettled way of life, their tendency to be extrovert and demonstrative, or their glamour, is debatable. The second point is more difficult to ascertain, but it is also more interesting. If it could be shown that certain acknowledged achievements in the arts correlated with the homosexual orientation of their creators, the positive value of homosexuality would be obvious.

It is difficult to establish such correlations, for creativity is a complex process that involves much more than sex. However, some outstanding examples of homosexual passion find clear expression in art. Michaelangelo's paintings and sculptures, for instance, enable us to see the male nude transformed by the artist's passion in a way unfamiliar to most of us. In the literary arts homosexuality often coexists with a certain delicacy of sensibility and "negative capability," or nonjudgmental openness to impressions and feelings, that Keats said was the main quality of the poet – although of course, heterosexual writers can possess these qualities, too.

So it must be concluded that, though there may be positive benefits to society in homosexuality, it is basically an impertinence to require a minority of the human race to justify its sexual tendencies by its professional achievements. Homosexuality simply exists as a fact of life, and it does not need to be explained away or justified.

Questions and Answers

In the course of a single week one doctor was consulted by four women about sexual problems. The first was pregnant and was worried about making love with her husband because she feared it might injure the baby. The second found intercourse painful and was afraid that she was "built too small" to enjoy a normal sex life. The third was miserable because she did not have an orgasm each time she had intercourse and was afraid that she was frigid. The fourth was surprised to find herself pregnant because she had thought she could not get pregnant during her period. Despite today's openness about the subject of sex and the wide availability of information, many people remain ignorant of basic facts and worry unduly about problems which could be alleviated by simple knowledge. Most of the relevant facts have been objectively presented in the preceding chapters, and in conclusion some questions will be posed and answered which either summarize the most important points already made or treat subjects of general concern which have not yet specifically arisen.

Common Questions and Misconceptions

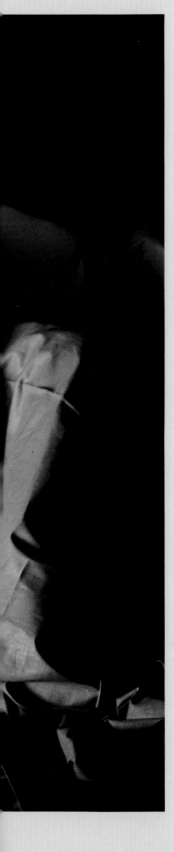

Can masturbation spoil heterosexual response?

In extreme cases it can, but it can also, in certain circumstances, improve heterosexual response. By definition heterosexual response is response to another person (of the opposite sex), and it involves emotion and commitment. If masturbation is used as a means of avoiding involvement, emotion, and commitment over a long period of time, it can result in the person becoming so fixed in a self-regulated mode of sexual release that he or she is incapable of a full heterosexual response. The ability to surrender completely to one's partner and to sexual feelings is essential to a full response; the practice of masturbation does not train this ability but, on the contrary, enables control of the flow of sexual feeling. But this reservation applies only when masturbation is the primary or sole mode of sexual release. Kinsey found that females who had practiced masturbation experienced orgasm in the first years of marital sex more frequently than those who had not, and Masters and Johnson have found that some problems of impotence can be overcome by training sexual response through the use of masturbation.

Is it in any way harmful to go without sex for a long period?

It depends on the age and circumstances of the person concerned. In a sense, no one goes without sexual outlets of *some* kind for long periods, but if we are talking about the pros and cons of celibacy, this does no harm provided the sexual energy does not get pent up into frustration but finds expression through physical or creative effort. People who can thus channel their sexual energy for a long period are rare, however. It has often been observed that regular sexual activity is conducive to longevity and physical vigor in later life, and that the sexual function tends to decline and the physiological processes concerned atrophy somewhat if they are not exercised. So to go without sex for a long period in later life can be harmful in the sense that

the body may no longer produce and release sufficient quantities of the hormones that promote youthfulness as well as sexuality.

Should sexual intercourse between lovers result in simultaneous orgasm?

The fact that the female's vaginal muscular contractions at orgasm occur at the same intervals as do the male's genital contractions suggests that simultaneous orgasm is nature's supreme reward for successful sexual performance, but in fact these synchronous contractions are meant primarily to help the sperm along their way to the womb. In other words, physiologically the simultaneous orgasm serves a reproductive function as distinct from a sexual function. Psychologically it may enhance a couple's sense of union if they "come together," but on the other hand there is much to be said for the nonsynchronous occurrence of orgasm. Provided that the interval is not too long, the joys of giving and of receiving the consummation of love can be enjoyed as two distinct experiences. Certainly, "success" in making love does not depend on the achievement of simultaneous orgasm, and failure to achieve it does not signify any inadequacy in either partner or in their relationship.

Do people have the best chance of a lasting sexual relationship if they are basically similar or if they are basically opposite?

The reason heterosexual couples are supposed to remain erotically interested in each other longer and more intensely than homosexual couples has been assumed to have something to do with the attraction of opposites. Profound sexual gratification proceeds from the release of built-up tensions, and it is a fundamental principle of life that tensions build up through the interaction of opposites. Couples who interact strongly, and who remain independent and unpredictable individuals, are more somewhat likely to build up a sexual "charge" repeatedly over a period of time than couples who are basically similar. But on the other hand, relationships do not usually endure on the strength of the sexual bond alone, and a basis of rapport and shared interests and values is generally a precondition of lasting sexual attraction.

Does a woman produce genital fluids or "love juices" as pornographic writers call them, at the moment of orgasm?

No, but her vaginal walls produce lubricating fluids throughout the arousal phase of sexual response, and these can be quite copious. Also, it is not as rare for women as it is for men to urinate when sexually aroused, and sometimes though not normally, a woman experiences such a strong orgasm that the resulting feelings of abandonment and relaxation can cause the muscle that keeps the bladder closed to relax a little so that some urine is contributed to the orgasmic flow.

Do homosexual men dislike women?

Negating the theory that homosexuality is based on the fear or dislike of the opposite sex, homosexual men tend to like women more than many heterosexual men do. Kinsey found that some two-thirds of the heterosexuals in his sample did not really like women. Homosexual males with a tendency toward effeminacy may be less likely to be irritated by supposedly "characteristic" feminine traits and foibles than heterosexual males. Also, women often find homosexuals more likable, sympathetic, and better company than men they might enter into a sexual relation with, and it is by no means unknown for a woman to live with or even marry a homosexual for the sake of the understanding and companionship he can give her.

Does sexual desire vary at different times of the month?

Yes, it does, in men as well as women, although of course women have in the menstrual cycle a clear point of reference for their monthly variations in sexual feeling. No pattern is constant for everyone, however. Many women find that their sexual desire is intensified just before, during, or just after a period. In others, premenstrual tension may lessen sexual desire. Some women are more sexually responsive in the middle of their cycles, particularly at the time of ovulation. Men are not usually aware of any periodicity in their sexual feelings and most are susceptible to arousal at any time, but modern studies of biorhythms have revealed that men have a 23-day physical energy cycle and a 28-day emotional cycle, and both of these effect their sexual feelings and readiness for arousal at any particular time. In long-term relationships the biological rhythms of a couple come to interact and mesh.

Can sex help you lose weight?

Sexual intercourse is a form of exercise requiring at least a minimum degree of exertion, so for that reason it can help a person to lose weight. It has been estimated that on average, making love uses up only about 150 calories, which is a loss about equal to that of 30 minutes' jogging, which is not enough to make much difference on its own.

What Men Want to Know

Can a man tell if a woman has had an orgasm?

There is no female sign of orgasm so obvious as the rapid detumescence of the male phallus, but there are other signs such as deep, rapid breathing and muscular spasms throughout the body, so that when a woman has a strong orgasm the man may know. But not all orgasms are so intense as to produce these signs, and a woman may experience orgasmic satisfaction without giving any clear demonstration of the fact. Sometimes women pretend orgasm or pretend that their feelings are more intense than they actually are, and these pretenses are difficult for a man to detect. Some nonorgasmic women pretend for years without their partners or lovers ever suspecting, and although they probably consider that they do this for the best of reasons, in fact they may be doing irreparable damage to the relationship by subordinating their own need for a sexual outlet. If a woman often experiences orgasm, her husband may possibly know when she does not by the feeling of unresolved tension and restlessness in her body, and if he is no longer able to complete the process for her phallically he can still do so manually.

What differences between male and female sexual response should a man be aware of when making love?

He should be aware that, generally speaking, a woman's sexual arousal builds up more slowly than a man's. He should be aware, too, that all of a woman's body is responsive to stimulation, and that general body caresses should precede genital touching. He should also bear in mind that any break in the process of arousal, any interruptions that may occur, can mitigate the effect of the stimulation achieved up to that point. He should further remember that sex has a dual purpose – reproduction and pleasure – and that while penis-vagina penetration is essential to reproduction, it is only one mode of pleasuring and should not be engaged in to the neglect of others.

What does it signify if a woman cries after intercourse?

It may signify that she has had an orgasm, which as an experience of flooding release, of really letting go, can mean a variety of pent-up emotions are expressed. In his studies of the physiology of orgasm, Wilhelm Reich noted that because it involves the relaxation and spasm of muscles all over the body, if certain muscles are locked they can block the flow of sexual energy and prevent orgasm from occurring. Muscles become locked when emotions are suppressed, and when the muscular tension is released the emotion may be released, too. The emotion of sadness becomes locked in the small muscles of the face, and the tide of sexual feeling as it flows toward orgasm may thus release pent-up sadness, even if the emotion has nothing to do with the situation or the relationship. Another reason a woman may cry is that she may have found some of the preceding sexual activity extremely painful, or it may even mean that she has not achieved orgasm but cries as an alternative form of release for the sexual tension thus built up.

What is the difference between ejaculation and orgasm, and can one occur without the other?

Ejaculation and orgasm are two different body processes, and although it is desirable that they should occur simultaneously, often they do not. Semen can exude from a man's penis after a period of stimulation without his feeling anything in particular, and the experience of orgasm can be felt without any ejaculation – for instance, in preadolescence, after removal of the prostate gland, or when a man has made love so many times in succession that his reservoir of semen is exhausted. When orgasm occurs without ejaculation in such circumstances there is nothing to be concerned about, but when ejaculation occurs without orgasm the person should seek the help of his sexual partner, in the hope that they be able to alleviate this problem together by the methods described in Chapter 9.

Is there such a thing as the male menopause?

Some men go through major changes in middle age, but it is not strictly correct to speak of these as a menopause, which means the termination of menstruation and capacity for reproduction in a woman. Psychological effects often accompany the physical occurrence of menopause, and these include worries about aging or losing sexual appeal. The male climacteric is a similar psychological crisis, during which a man often reviews the life he has lived so far and assesses his future. The reproductive function does not cease in the male, but he may feel that with age his sexual capacity is diminishing; indeed, it is, but only slowly and slightly. If he suffers a great diminution of sex drive the cause is more likely to be worry, ill health, or lack of erotic stimuli, but some males in middle age react in the opposite manner and pursue a "last fling" and galvanize their supposedly waning energies by seeking an affair with a younger woman. There is no physical reason, however, why potency should wane in a healthy male as he ages, any more than there is any physical reason why a female should not remain sexually active after her reproductive function has ended.

What Women Want to Know

How often does the average woman experience orgasm?

Taking the Kinsey sample as an indication, one answer is that she experiences orgasm through intercourse six times out of ten when she is a young woman and nine times out of ten when she is older and more experienced. The female orgasm, however, often occurs through the sexual stimulation that precedes or follows phallus-vagina contact. If by "how often" is meant how many times a week, the Kinsey finding was that in married women the incidence of orgasm was 2.2 times per week at age 20 declining to 0.8 times per week at age 50; in unmarried women the average incidence remained about 0.5 times a week between the ages of 20 and 50. *The Hite Report* suggests that of women who experienced orgasm and who masturbated, 96 percent experienced orgasm "regularly" during masturbation.

Is there anything wrong with having sexual intercourse while menstruating?

There is no medical reason why intercourse should not take place while a woman is menstruating, but if she suffers severe period pains a woman will probably not desire sex at this time. Also, many couples find the blood produced unesthetic, and prefer to wait until the period is over before resuming sexual activity. There are circumstances, however, in which other considerations may override this — for instance, if a couple is reunited after a long time. In fact, the flow of menstrual blood tends to slow down during intercourse, though an increase in the flow may occur afterward. A diaphragm may be used to hold back the flow, and if this is the woman's normal method of contraception she should continue to use it, for although it is unlikely for a woman to become pregnant during her period, it is not impossible.

How can a woman who has never had an orgasm learn how to do so?

One way is for her to enlist the aid of a sexually knowledgeable, sensitive, and understanding man, but perhaps the best method is for a woman to develop her orgasm reflex herself. At first it may take up to 45 minutes of clitoral stimulation to trigger the reflex, but a woman can soon learn to speed up the escalation. Breathing exercises can help: breathe deeply and exhale completely, making sure that there is no muscular tension in the pelvis, buttocks, or groin at the end of the exhalation. Practice building tension with the intake of breath and completely relaxing it with the exhalation. Another exercise that helps the orgasm reflex is to practice contracting and relaxing the vaginal muscles. Sexual fantasizing can help, too. Don't forget that what makes human sex special is the creative power of the human imagination. As the philosopher Ortega y Gasset wrote in his essay *On Love*: "Nine-tenths of that which is attributed to sexuality is the work of our magnificent ability to imagine."

What differences between male and female sexual response should a woman be aware of when making love?

Many women still feel inhibited about taking an active part in lovemaking, but the stereotype of the male-dominant, female-submissive type of sex does not usually afford either party the maximum satisfaction. For both, the triggering of the orgasm reflex depends on a complete surrender, so each must provide the other with something to which to surrender. As arousal escalates in the man, sensation becomes genitally focused, and continued and varied genital stimulation carries him toward his climax. Although a man can reach orgasm within two to five minutes, generally a woman takes much longer, and she should make him aware of her own rate of arousal so that he does not reach his climax too soon and leave her unsatisfied. It is essential to the success of an erotic relationship that both partners help each other to attain full orgasmic satisfaction and that neither settles for less.

Is it normal to have sexual feelings when breast-feeding a baby?

Some women feel guilty being erotically stimulated when suckling, and some stop breast-feeding because they feel the sensations are inappropriate. Masters and Johnson found four cases of women who actually had orgasms when breast-feeding, and several other women experienced a copious flow of milk from their breasts when they had an orgasm. The fact that suckling helps the womb shrink after childbirth indicates that there is a physiological connection between the two areas. Thus sexual sensations accompanying breast-feeding are quite normal and not anything of which a woman need feel guilty or ashamed.

If a woman discovers that her husband has a taste for pornography – that he buys "girlie" magazines or goes to sex movies – what should her reaction be?

This problem often causes wives distress and frequently appears in advice columns. Often a wife's immediate reaction is a sense of betrayal, as though her husband's having sexual fantasies in which she personally does not figure is a kind of infidelity. Another common reaction is a feeling of inadequacy, of having failed, in that she has not been able to give her husband enough love and sexual fulfillment to satisfy him. Sometimes the discovery has proved so distressing to a woman that she breaks off sexual relations and may even seek a divorce. But these are overreactions, for a man's interest in pornography does not necessarily imply that his relationship with his sexual partner is inadequate or unfulfilling. It is simply a fact that sexual response is quite easily triggered by psychological and visual stimuli, and that men often enjoy the pleasure of mild sexual arousal which does not lead to an immediate outlet. In many cases, they carry over the arousal from the fantasy situation into their actual sex lives. In other cases, however, there may be an element of wishful thinking in the fantasizing, and both partners may wish to use these to make their sex life more exciting.

Teenage Problems

How young is too young for love and sex?

Between those who frown upon any form of premarital intercourse and those who see nothing wrong with it no matter how young the couple there is a vast range of variously qualified opinion. As people mature they become capable of different kinds of love, and the question becomes one of which kind is appropriate to express through sexuality and at what age this kind of love becomes manifest. The first feelings of love develop toward parents and members of one's immediate family, and in most cultures the sexual expression of these feelings is considered inappropriate. In childhood and adolescence people often feel attracted to members of both sexes, and this attraction generally tends toward romantic and sexual expression, although in girls genital sexuality is usually a considerably later development than in boys. If we believe that sexual intercourse should take place only between people who both really desire it, who understand what they are doing, and who are prepared for the consequences of the act, then few adolescent couples would meet these conditions. By consequences we do not refer only to the possibility of pregnancy, but also to creating a strong emotional bond with another person. Both sexes usually develop physical sexuality before becoming emotionally sexual, so perhaps "too young" is any age before sex and emotion become integrated; however, this standard would disqualify some people for a very long time.

Aren't the joys of sex exaggerated?

Young people often ask this question in one way or another. A 19-year-old girl wrote that she had been sleeping with her fiancé for a year and was distressed because "although I'm terribly fond of him, I don't feel anything when we make love." A 16-year-old boy wrote after having sex with a girl for the first time: "It was alright, but I don't know why all the fuss is made of it. I feel more when I do it to myself." Many young people today are disillusioned by their first experiences of sex, and the reason may be partly that the great emphasis put on sex in our culture makes them expect too much. But mainly it is their failure to understand that it takes time to develop sexually just as it does to develop in any other way. The joys of sex are not exaggerated, but they may be elusive at first, and a person may have to wait for and work at achieving the greatest satisfactions and joys that sex can give. But if the joys of sex were instantly available, at the flick of a switch as it were, then we would probably become sated with them, whereas in fact new feelings and experiences can be explored through sex over many years.

Can the genitals be damaged by masturbation?

This is one of many worries that young people have about the practice of masturbation, and it cannot be emphasized too strongly that masturbation can do no physical damage at all, provided that no unsuitable mechanical means or implements are used. A woman about to be married wrote to the sex counselor, Robert Chartham, stating that she had been masturbating two or three times a week for 10 years, and asked, "Will I have deformed myself in any way so that he will know by looking at me?" A young man wrote to the Swedish sex counselors, the Hegelers: "My penis is wonky, presumably because I have masturbated so much. I'll never dare to show myself to a girl naked." In both cases the counselors assured the correspondents that their apprehensions were groundless. There are variations between the genitals of individual males and females, but these are very rarely malformations, and they are never produced as a result of masturbation.

How can we understand what love and sex are really all about when we see and hear so many widely differing ideas and attitudes?

This question has no simple answer because of the complexity of the subject. Not only do love and sex have entirely different

meanings for different people, but sex can mean something entirely different to one person at different times. It can express itself as a longing to love someone and be loved; it can be a daydream of physical intimacy with some remote ideal; and it can even manifest itself in intense feelings toward beauty in nature or art.

Adults often seem hypocritical in their views on love and sex. Some churchmen insist that sex is a sin except for the purpose of procreation, whereas others say that sex is a God-given gift to be enjoyed. Parents speak at different times of sex as an exalted form of love and conversely as a potentially dangerous trap resulting in unsuitable relationships or unwanted pregnancies. Love songs, poems, and romantic stories portray sex as a glory and a joy, whereas "dirty" jokes and stories are slyly sniggered at. But real sexual love as part of a deep and permanent relationship can no more be defined or analyzed than can moving art or music.

Is sex simply a matter of glands?

It is for animals, who in the mating season will couple with the opposite sex of their own species almost indiscriminately. But young human adolescents' sexual drives are not focused on the achievement of intercourse with whichever member of the opposite sex is convenient. On the contrary, boys and girls on the verge of adulthood tend to be *romantically* rather than *sexually* attracted, by physical and personality characteristics that appeal to them as individuals, and most young human beings feel that, before their relationships become sexual, it is necessary for them to be or believe themselves to be "in love."

If marriage is so wonderful, why are so many married people miserable and why are there so many divorces?

The romantic, fairy tale idea of "they married and lived happily ever after" is entirely false and dangerously misleading. Marriage is not the key to a magic garden in which everything will be as perfect and blissful as it was during the first stages of courtship. Human beings are constantly changing and growing, widening their experiences and knowledge of life and of the world. If the "being in love" phase does not develop into a deep, loving partnership based on friendship, mutual respect, and shared interests, with both partners making allowances for and adjustments to the other, a couple will sooner or later find that they have become two strangers living together. When this happens it is sad and disappointing. But the failures probably stand out more than the successes. It is important for young people to realize that the majority of married people do succeed in maintaining good partnerships, and they cope together with the inevitable problems and difficulties of life.

For Parents about Children

At what age do children normally begin to have sexual feelings?

It is normal and natural for children to have sexual feelings from birth, but their feelings are not as strong as in adults nor are they necessarily focused on the genital organs. It is, however, common for baby boys to have erections, and both boys and girls quickly discover, by accident, that they get pleasant sensations from touching their genitals or rubbing them against something. This early kind of masturbation is a natural part of a child's development.

What should parents do if their children masturbate?

Absolutely nothing. Masturbation is a normal part of a child's behavior. It is important that the child not be made to feel that it is wrong or shameful. Any expression of disgust or disapproval on the part of a parent must be carefully avoided, and the best way to deal with it is to ignore the matter. If a child masturbates or "plays with" him or herself in public or in front of other people, a parent should not show alarm or embarrassment but should simply distract the child's attention to something else.

Can the way a child is toilet-trained influence his or her later sex life?

According to some child psychologists it can. Unnecessarily strict or harsh toilet training may cause sexual problems and inhibitions later because the organs of sex and excretion are closely connected physically, and a child may easily link the two functions. The majority of very young children are interested in, even fascinated by, urination and excretion because of the pleasurable sense of release both these functions can give. If a parent reacts with anger or disgust at an occasional (and inevitable) "accident" or loss of control, the child may grow to feel that the whole of that part of his or her body is dirty or unpleasant. Some children quickly become toilet trained and should be encouraged to feel proud of their achievement, but others are slower to learn and need patience and gentle persuasion, never scolding or punishment of any kind.

When and how should a child be told the "facts of life"?

It is probably preferable that parents tell their children about sex first rather than leaving it to teachers, for the parents alone are able to put the subject in the appropriate context of family life. The right time to explain is when a child asks or shows curiosity, and the right manner is a perfectly natural one. It is not helpful, however, to overburden the child with information. It should not be necessary to set aside a special occasion for an extended talk on the topic, since a parent alert to the child's requests for knowledge will normally find plenty of opportunities to impart as much as is required. If a girl starts menstruating or a boy has his first "wet dream" (nocturnal seminal emission) without understanding what is happening, this signifies a failure on the part of the parents to fulfill their responsibilities. It might be necessary at some stage for parents to broach these topics and explain in simple terms what happens and why. As some girls have their first menstrual period as early as age 10, they should be made well aware of these facts before this age.

What level of language should parents use when talking about sex?

This can be quite a problem, because usually the parent wishes to avoid conveying either an overly clinical or unnecessarily crude attitude to sex. The simplest and most direct words can carry crude associations through being used as expletives or insults, and medical words are, as Eric Berne (author of *The Games People Play*) said, "dry words for wet feelings." For the sexual activity "lovemaking" is perhaps the best term, and for the sexual organs themselves "genitals," "penis," "vagina," and "clitoris" are suitable, though the more colloquial terms may be used instead. Ejaculation can be referred to as "coming," and

in talking to a boy about masturbation certain more vernacular words may be considered both inoffensive and graphic, if both the boy and his parents are more comfortable with them, though some parents may prefer the term "self-stimulation." The main point is that a parent should use the type of language that he or she can use unself-consciously and unpatronizingly, avoiding coyness at all costs.

Is it a good idea for children to see their parents naked?

It is, provided that the parents and the children feel natural and unembarrassed about it, and particularly if the practice of being naked together starts early in life. The visible sexual differences between mother and father will inevitably give rise to questions, enabling the parents to begin sex instruction early and in a natural and casual way. Nakedness, however, should not be imposed on an unwilling child – if an adolescent develops inhibitions about it the parents should have regard for these feelings. Of course, nakedness and sexual intercourse are two different things. Parents who carry their belief in frankness and openness to the point of wanting their children to watch their lovemaking are surely misguided, for children are unable to understand the emotional side of sex, and without that understanding the sexual act can appear disturbingly violent, painful, and even ugly.

Children are sometimes subject to the attentions of exhibitionists. How should parents or children react when someone either exposes himself or masturbates in front of them?

This situation can be alarming, particularly for parents whose young children experience such encounters, but a point to bear in mind is that for exhibitionists this behavior is their means of obtaining sexual outlet, and they very rarely attack anyone. Children are more inclined to be amused than alarmed by the experience, and this is probably an appropriate reaction.

Worries about Pregnancy

Is there any danger in smoking cigarettes during pregnancy?

Many women smokers find tobacco nauseating very soon after becoming pregnant. This is a natural bodily defense against the intake of a substance which could possibly harm the embryo. A number of statistical studies have shown that women who smoke tend to produce babies who weigh less than those of women who do not; smokers also suffer more miscarriages, stillbirths, and neonatal (newborn) deaths. A slightly higher incidence of congenital heart disease (0.73 percent compared with 0.47 percent) has also been found among babies born to smokers. The harmful effects of a mother's smoking during pregnancy appear to persist into the childhood of her offspring: a study comparing the abilities of 11-year-old children showed that those born to mothers who had smoked more than 10 cigarettes a day during pregnancy were from five to seven months behind those of nonsmoking mothers.

Is it dangerous to drink alcohol during pregnancy?

There is no danger if the intake of alcohol is moderate, but if it is heavy the chances of the child's survival are greatly diminished and the hazards of its early life greatly increased. A recent American study showed that 17 percent of babies born to mothers who were alcoholics died within the first week after birth, whereas the mortality rate among babies born to nonalcoholic mothers was only 2 percent. In addition, 32 percent of the children of alcoholics were underweight at birth, and by the age of seven 44 percent of them scored poorly (70 or under) on IQ tests.

How can drugs help a woman to become pregnant?

If a woman finds that she cannot conceive, the cause may be a failure to ovulate, in which case a drug known as Clomiphene may be effective. It enables about 30 percent of women who are prescribed it to conceive, though precisely how it works

it produces results in a matter of minutes. In this test the sample of urine is mixed with other substances which show up the presence or absence of HCG.

Either the biological or chemical test can detect pregnancy as early as three weeks after conception – usually about a week after the first missed period. Although the tests are 95 percent accurate, errors can occur if there is not enough HCG in the urine at the time of the test or if a mistake of some kind is made in the laboratory. So although one negative result is not always completely reliable, a single confirmed positive result is usually all that is needed to establish pregnancy.

Is it possible to tell the sex of a child before it is born?

Yes, it is possible to determine the sex of a child before it is born. At present there is only one method of doing so – taking a sample of the amniotic fluid surrounding the baby in the womb, which contains some of its cast-off cells. In 90 percent of cases, when the chromosomes of these cells are examined under a microscope they will reveal the baby's sex. The sample of fluid can be obtained through the wall of the mother's abdomen, and only a local anesthetic is necessary. But simple though the test is, and slight though the risk is to the mother, doctors do not usually use this surgical method unless it is medically necessary – for instance, if a serious hereditary sex-linked disease is suspected. An X-ray cannot reveal the sex of a child in the womb because it only shows the bones and fetal position of the baby.

If her first pregnancy ends in a miscarriage is a woman likely to lose her second baby, too?

This question worries many women whose first pregnancy has ended in a miscarriage, but the fact is that the chances of giving birth to a normal healthy baby the next time are as good as if the woman had never had a miscarriage. About 15 percent of pregnancies end in miscarriage, but the

is not clearly understood. Women who experience multiple births as a result of taking a fertility drug have usually been given Pergonal, an extract of hormones obtained from menopausal women. It stimulates the ovaries to produce eggs as well as the hormones that prepare the womb for pregnancy. The drug must be administered with great care under hospital conditions, for if the dosage is miscalculated an excessive number of eggs may be produced. When infertility in the woman is due to a failure of the pituitary gland to produce the hormones FSH and LH (follicle-stimulating hormone and luteinizing hormone), synthetic hypothalmic releasing drugs may solve the problem.

How do pregnancy tests work?

Pregnancy tests are conducted to detect the presence of the hormone HCG (human chorionic gonadotropin), which appears in the urine of a pregnant woman. In the biological test a sample of urine is injected into a laboratory animal such as a toad. If the result is positive – that is, if the urine does contain HCG – the animal will ovulate. This test takes several days to produce results. The second type of test, a chemical test, is now much more widely used because majority of women who lose a baby in this way never do so again. And although it is distressing when it happens, it usually occurs because something is wrong with the baby or it is not developing properly. If a woman has three or more successive miscarriages, extensive tests are usually advised to try to find the reason, but even after two or three miscarriages the chances of a woman giving birth to a healthy baby are still extremely good.

How long after a miscarriage should a woman wait before becoming pregnant again?

Many doctors advise that such a woman wait for about six months, but there is no medical reason to wait so long if she is anxious to become pregnant again as soon as possible and is in good health. The most usual reason for delaying another pregnancy

is the depression that often follows a miscarriage, and some women temporarily lose interest in sexual intercourse or even develop a fear of it. This is a perfectly understandable reaction which should gradually pass. Discussing the problem with her partner and sympathetic friends may be of considerable help, but if the feelings of depression or aversion to intercourse have still not faded after a long period a doctor should be consulted.

What is the safest age to have children?

Research carried out in many different countries indicates that women between the ages of 18 and 25 have the highest chances of problem-free pregnancies and of delivering healthy, normal babies. Women under 18 or over 30 run a slightly higher risk of complications during pregnancy and should seek prenatal care as early as possible. However, other factors than age determine the effects of each and every pregnancy; so there is really no particularly "safe" age to have a baby – each case is entirely individual.

Is it true that a woman is less likely to conceive after the age of 30?

Fertility does gradually decline with age in women as well as in men, but up until the age of about 38 or 40, when a woman tends to ovulate less regularly, a couple's chances of having a baby are still good if they are both in good health and have intercourse fairly frequently.

Can a woman become pregnant if a man ejaculates outside her vagina?

Coitus interruptus as a method of birth control is inadvisable precisely because pregnancy *can* occur even if a man withdraws and ejaculates outside a woman's vagina. A few drops of semen may leak into the vagina before the man withdraws, and even if this does not happen there is still a risk of pregnancy: semen can pass through an opening in the porous hymen even if it is unbroken.

Index

Numbers in italics refer to page numbers of illustrations

A

abnormalities, 87
  congenital, 90
  Ellis's work, 13
  see also deviation
abortion, 11, 219, 240
  American law, 241
  early attempts to obtain, 221
  in sex education, 244
  legal reasons for, 241
  possibility with menstrual extraction, 240
  suction, 241
  time limits, 241
abortionists, "backstreet," 240
abstinence
  during and after pregnancy, 185
  leading to infertility, 85
  rare situation, 205
  see also celibacy; chastity
acceptance of the individual, 58
active elements, 28
admiration, 58
adolescence, 196-7
  see also young people
adoration, 58
adultery, *see* extramarital relationships
advertising, use of sexuality in, 30, *30*
affection
  in home life, 202
  in homosexual relationships, 288
  necessity in marriage, 190
affirmation of personality, 58
agape (type of love), 41
age
  effects on sexual experience, 264
  of consent, 196
  see also elderly people
Akhenaton, *90*
alcohol
  drinking during pregnancy, 317
  possible cause of impotence, 84, 254
  to release inhibitions, 49, *49*
alcoholism
  effect on sexual functioning, *268*, 269
American Psychiatric Association, 206
American Psychological Association, 31
amniotic fluid
  used to determine sex of fetus, 318
Amsterdam, sex shops in, *21*
anal intercourse, 289
  condemned by Stopes, 13
  portrayed in *Last Tango in Paris*, 19
  unlawful in some countries, 86
anal penetration, 289
androgens, 48
animal contacts
  in fantasies, 120

with females, 121
Anteros (Greek god of passion), 55
anxiety
  basis of premature ejaculation, 250-1
aphrodisiacs, 49
Aphrodite, 55
areolae, 101
arousal, 78
  female, 105
    overtures to, 127
  periodicity in men, 304
  psychological, 73-6
  relative slowness in women, 306
  technique, 130-1
  visual stimuli, 118
art
  attempts to convey sexual experience, 27
arts
  homosexuality in, 299
attraction
  chemistry of, 48-9
  eyes, 52
  factors influencing susceptibility, 40
  homosexual, 276
  of like for like, and of opposites, 38
    in marriage, 168
  points of, 43
  personality, *53*
  rational choice, 43
  romantic, 313
  signals, 51
  visual, *42*
attractiveness, 38
attribution theory of love, 40
Augustine, Saint, 30-1
autoerotic stimulation, 70-1
  see also masturbation
aversion therapy, 298
Avery, Paul, 215

B

B-love (Maslow's definition), 60, 62-3
babies
  birth as possible crisis point in marriage, 170
  nursing as peak experience, 62
  resentment of, 263
  sex determination during pregnancy, 318
  see also breast feeding; children; family
A Bacchanalian Revel Before a Team of Pan (Poussin), *205*
Bara, Theda, *18*
Barbarella (director: Vadim), 54, *54*
Bartholin glands, 122
Beach, F A, 282
Beatrice, 47

behavioral therapy
  in homosexuality, 298
Belle de Jour (director: Buñuel), 18, *18*
Beospir, 231
Bergman, Ingmar, 18
Bernard, Jessie, 31, 100
Berne, Eric, 24, 81, 169
Bernini, Gianlorenzo, *110*
Berscheid, Ellen, 43
bestiality, *see* animal contacts
Bettleheim, Bruno, 22
Binnet, Alfred, 88
biochemical reactions, 48-9
biological drives, 30
  see also sex drives
biorhythms, 182-3, 304
birth control, 11, 188
  clinics, 221
    burned down in early days, 20
    first in Amsterdam, *228*
    first opened, *12*, 13
  effect on premarital sex, 194
  effect on society, 242
  in Soviet Union, *15*
  methods
    Greek, *220*
    mechanical, male, 226-7
    natural, 222-3
    coitus interruptus, 224-5, 238-9, 319
    coitus reservatus, 224
    rhythm method, 222-3
    temperature method, 223
  necessary limit to freedom to procreate, 242
  no longer man's sole responsibility, 187
  prescriptions from doctors, 221
  religious prejudice against, 220
    Roman Catholic teaching, 223
  sterilization, 236-8
  see also contraceptives; Stopes, Marie
bisexuality, 282
Bitching (Marion Meade), 100, 212
biting, 129
block pessary, *226*
blood pressure, 45, 79, 105
Blues singers, 16
boarding schools, homosexuality in, 278-9
bondage, *86*, 87, 179
boot fetish, *86*
brain
  control of basic functions, 281
  dysfunction theory of homosexuality, 276
  pleasure centers, 54
  structure, 281
Brando, Marlon, 19, *19*
brassieres, 101
breast-feeding
  stimulation from, 309
  see also babies

breasts, 101
  development at puberty, 101
  erogenous zone, 127
  plastic surgery, 101
  psychological importance, 101
  response during arousal, 105
  rolling phallus between, 131
  sexual stimulant, 52
  sizes, 101
  stimulating to produce orgasm, 110
British Columbia University, 40
British Institute of Psychosexual
  Medicine, 263
Britton, Harry, 20
Broken Vows (Calderon), *217*
brothels, 201
  see also prostitution
Buñuel, Louis, 18
buttocks, sexual stimulant, 52
Byron, George Gordon, Lord, 99

C

Calderon, Philip Hermogenes, *217*
California University: Gender Identity
  Research Treatment Program, 287
Call the Doctor (Turner), 220
Cameron, Hugh, *29*
Campbell, Mrs Patrick, 183
cancer
  of the cervix, 234
  of the prostate, 91, 270
  of the uterus, 270
candidiasis, 122
The Canterbury Tales (Chaucer), *200*
Carefree Love (Delvin), 221
caring, 60
Casanova, Giacomo, 126, *198*
Cassolette, 49
castration complex, *277*, *277*
Catholic Theological Society, 24
celibacy, *282*
  not harmful *per se*, 302
  see also abstinence; chastity
censorship, 16
  abolished in Denmark, 19
  of films, 18
Cerne Abbas giant, *66*
cervical cap, *228*
cervix
  cancer of, 234
  clear secretion from, 122
    changed by pill, 233
  physiology, 103
  removal during hysterectomy, 270
Chaldean legal code, 198
chancres, 93
chaperonage, *195*

Charles II, behavior during the reign of,
  10
Chartham, Robert, 176
  on married homosexuals, 295
  on sexual problems of old age, 265
chastisement, 120–1
chastity
  early reasons for, 194
  in medieval France, *194*
  still relevant, 195
  see also chaperonage; virginity
chastity belt, *194*
Chaucer, Geoffrey, *200*
chauvinism, 199
chemistry, 48–9
  incompatibility, 93
  see also biochemical reactions
childbearing, 11
childbirth
  not a "passive" function, 28
  see also babies
children
  commitments to, 60
  father's participation in upbringing, 11
  father's role in caring for, *171*
  illegitimate, 21
  looked after by paid helpers, *172*
  masturbating, 314
  restricting freedom of parents, 172
  sexual feelings, 314
  sexual patterns, 282
  shared care, 172
  see also babies; family
China
  sexual practices, 78
  "Chinese bells," 273
chivalry, 46–7, 58
choice, freedom of, 98
Christian church
  view of sexuality, 193
  see also religions
chromosomal abnormalities, 90
cigarette smoking during pregnancy, 317
circumcision, 68
  to correct phimosis, 91
The City of Women (Pisan), *29*
"clap" (gonorrhea), 92
Cleopatra, 36
clitoral orgasn, 112
clitoral stimulation, 99
  during masturbation, 117
clitoris, 102
  hypersensitization during plateau phase,
    105
  response to stimuli, 105
  stimulation during foreplay, 129
Clomiphene, 317
clothing
  corsetry, 101, *101*
  erotic significance, 51

"unisex," 28
  see also fashion
Club of Rome, 242
codpieces, *66*
cohabitation
  survey on attitudes to, 21
coil, *see* intrauterine devices
coitus interruptus, 224–5
  possibility of pregnancy, 319
  tabular explanation, 238–9
coitus reservatus, 224
  see also Karezza
Columbus, Christopher, *92*
Comfort, Dr Alex, 25, 49, 70, 126
Coming of Age in Samoa (Mead), 206
commitment, 60
  essential to good lovemaking, 126
  in marriage, 168, 169
communal living, 166
  in 1960s, *203*
  reasons for breakup, 206
  to compensate for lack of family
    affection, 202
communication
  importance in marriage, *189*, 190
  improvement following therapy, 249
compatibility, 41, 190
  essential for good lovemaking, 126
condoms, 226–7, *226*, *227*
  advantages, 227
  disadvantages, 227
  reliability, 227
  tabular explanation, 238–9
  types sold as sex aids, 273
confidence
  essential to good lovemaking, 126
congenital defects, 90
  theory of homosexuality, 276
continence, 204
  consequent spare energy, 204–5
contraception, *see* birth control
contraceptives
  availability, 221
    to school-age children, 196
  change of emphasis, 187
  in sex education, 244, *245*
  use to overcome inability to ejaculate,
    252
  see also condoms; diaphragms;
    intrauterine devices; pill
Copper-7, 231, *231*
Copper-T, 231, *231*
coquettish behavior, 130
corona, 68
  swelling during plateau phase, 79
corpus luteum, *232*
corsetry, 101, *101*
"cottagers," 292
courtesy of male to female, 47
courtship rituals, 46–7

Cowper's glands, 69, 78
"crabs" (lice), 92
creativity
    possible correlation with homosexuality,
        299
Crowley, Alisteir, 21
"cruisers," 292
"crushes" among schoolgirls, 36, 286
Cuber, John, 205
cuissade, 148-9
cultural role division, 28
cunnilingus
    in lesbian relationships, 291
cystitis, 123

D-love (Maslow's definition), 60, 63
Dalkon Shield, *231*
dancing
    as courtship ritual, 17
    sexuality of, 17
danger
    effect on attraction, 40
Dante Alleghieri, 47, *209*
David, *280*
The Death of Sardanapalus (Delacroix), 77
Deep Throat, 19
Delacroix, Eugène, 77
Delvin, David, 221, 224
Deneuve, Catherine, 18, *18*
Denmark
    abolition of censorship, 19
    enlightened attitudes toward
        homosexuality, *292*
depression
    after miscarriage, 319
    postnatal, *263*
Deri Jagadamba, Temple of, *204*
destiny, 43
deviation, 86, 88-9
    female, 120-1
    in sex education, 244
diaphragms, 228-9, *228, 229*
    disadvantages, 228
    introduced from France, 13
    tabular explanation, 238-9
digital penetration, 129
dilatation and curettage (D and C), 241
dildoes, 272
Divine Comedy (Dante), 47
divorce
    during first five years of marriage, 170
    following permissive marriages, 216
    quick, in Mexico, *173*
    through incompatibility, 172
    through infidelity, 210
domination

in fantasies, 120
    in sex games, 179
Don't Look Now (director: Roeg), 19
douche, tabular explanation, 238-9
dress, *see* clothing; fashion
"drop-outs," 202
drugs
    possible cause of impotence, 84
    to aid fertility, 317-18
Dryden, John, 36
Duke University, 251
Dumas cap, *228*
"dutch cap," 220, 228, *228*
    see also diaphragms
dyspareunia, 123

"earth mother" figure, *98*
economic indepencence of women, 11
The Ecstasy of St Theresa (Bernini), *110*
ectopic pregnancy, 231
education
    of women, *100*
    see also sex edhcation
effeminacy in males, 279
Egg, Augustus, *210*
Ehrlich, Paul, *95*
ejaculate, 69
ejaculation
    arresting, 131
    controlled by squeezing, 251
    differentiated from orgasm, 307
    during coitus interruptus, 224
    effect of prostate gland removal, 81
    external ejaculation and possible
        pregnancy, 319
    failure, 252
    "hairtrigger trouble," 250-1
    normal sperm count, 225
    problems with a psychological cause,
        253
    signs of onset, 81
elderly people
    compensation for reduced capacity, *266*
    sexual activity, 266
    sexùal problems, 265
Ellis, Albert, 55
    on sex without love, 206
Ellis, Havelock, 13, *13*
    on male deviations, 86-7
    criticisms of, 220
emetics
    effect on reliability of pill, 234
Emmanuelle (director: Jaeckin), 19, *289*
emotional needs
    fulfillment in marriage, 170

emotions
    integrating with sexual feelings, 310
    not synonymous with sensations, 60,
        188
energy
    related to sexual continence, 204-5
"English hat," 226
Ennui (Sickert), *61*
environmental influences
    tending to homosexuality, 276
erection
    during arousal phase, 78
    in baby boys, 314
    period of time maintained, 78
    physiology, 67
    priapism, 91, *91*
erective failure, 84, 254
    in middle age, 264
    linked to alcoholism, *268*, 269
    use of ribbon or band to overcome, 273
erogenous zones, 127
Eros (Greek god of love), 55
eros (type of love), 41
estrogen, 48, 233
    secretions, *232*
exhibitionism, 89
    female, 121
    reaction of children to, 315
extramarital relationships
    attitudes to, 208-11
    by mutual agreement, 55, 209
    correlation with cultural development,
        204
    correlation with social class, 208
    fear of discovery, *211*
    heart attacks more likely than within
        marriage, 268-9
    infatuations, *174*
    in saving a marriage, 217
    mutual affairs, 215
    problems of, 216-17
    reawakening passions, *211*
    value of discretion, 216-17
    with colleagues, 212
    see also prostitution
eyes
    attractiveness related to size, 52
    expression, 52-3

facial characteristics
    in women, 52
Faed, Thomas, *167*
Fallopian tubes
    sterilization by tying, 237
    sterilization using laparascope, 238
Fallopius, Gabriel, *227*

family
  effect of "permissive society," 16
  effect of sexual revolution, 10
  optimum size, *236*
  size, related to social matters, 11
  threatened by adultery, 208
  see also babies; children
family planning clinics, *see* birth control:
  clinics
fantasies
  female, 118–20
    orgasms achieved by, 110
    recurrent themes, 119–20
  in sex games, 179
  male, 73–7
    "girlie" magazines, 118
  to obtain orgasm, 309
fashion, in clothes, 17
  codpieces, *66*
  see also clothing
fatalism, 43
father
  participation in child's upbringing, 11,
    171
  possible effect in homosexuality, 276–7
fatherhood
  psychological adjustment to, 188
Faults on Both Sides (Faed), *167*
feelings
  distinguished from emotions, 60
fellatio, 131, 182
  as part of initiation rites, 281
  in *Deep Throat*, 19
  in homosexual relationships, 288
female suffrage, 11
females
  blending of role with male, 28–9
  idealization of males, 199
  Leonardo's discoveries, *262*
  masculinity in, 279
  physical contact between, 282
    not necessarily sexual, 286
  role changes in society, 10
  role training in infancy, 28
  sexual response, 104–11, 309
  see also sexuality: female; wives;
    women
feminity, 28, 29
feminists
  protests against sexual triviality, 20, *20*
  see also Women's Liberation Movement
femoral intercourse, 289
Ferenczi, Sandor, 81
fertility
  after 30th birthday, 319
  drugs to aid, 317–18
  effect of pill, 235
  not affected by intrauterine devices, 230
fertilization, *243*
fetishism, 49, 86–7, 88

distinguished from sex games, 179
  psychological basis, 88
fibroids, 270
fidelity
  definition among prostitutes, 121
  see also extramarital relationships
financial problems in marriage, 172
flanquette, 150–1
Flesh (director: Warhol), 19
Follicle Stimulating Hormone (FSH), *232*
follicles, *232*
Fonda, Jane, 54
foot fetishes, 88
Ford, C S, 282
foreplay, 126–9
foreskin, 68
  warts, 91
Forum magazine, 88
Fragonard, Jean-Honoré, *55*
freedom of choice, 98
Freeman, Gillian, 87
Freemasons' initiation ceremony, *282*
"French letter," 226
Freud, Sigmund, 13, *13*
  argument for restraint, 204
  children's sexual pattern, 282
  concept of homosexuality, 298
  differentiation between clitoral and
    vaginal orgasm, 112
  explanation of homosexuality, 276
Friday, Nancy, 119, 121
friendships, 190
fright
  effect in attraction, 40
frigidity, 256–7, *256*
  causes of, 257
  fear of, 26
  therapy sessions, 259
fulfillment
  refusal to accept lack of, 33
The Function of the Orgasm (Reich), 13

Galen, 82
Gay Liberation, 275
  limited success of movement, 294
Gay Manifesto, 299
gender concepts, 28
  see also females; femininity; males;
    masculinity
genital diseases
  causing impotence, 84
genital irritants, 272–3
genitals
  artificial, 272
  fear of damage by masturbation, 311
  female, 102, *102*, 304

male, 68–9, *69*
  of intermediate gender, 90
  size compatibility, 260
  surgical operations, 270–1
"girlie" magazines, 118
give-and-take relationships, 56
Gladstone, Catherine, *169*
Gladstone, William, *169*
glans penis, 68
  anesthetizing, 251
gonorrhea, 92
Gorer, Geoffrey, 166, 174, 261
  on double standard in premarital sex,
    198
  on extramarital relations, 210
  on marital breakup, 170
  on shared interests in marriage, 190
  on virginity at marriage, 195
granuloma inguinale, 94
Greece, homosexuality in, 281
Green, Maureen, 202, 262
Green, Richard, 287
group sex, 215

hair length, 28
"hairtrigger trouble," 250–1
Halleck, Seymour, 206
harems
  homosexual relationships in, 279
Haroff, Peggy, 205
Hawaiian attitude to sex, 206
health
  sexual contribution to, 26, 268–9
heart
  as seat of emotions, 45
heart disease
  and sexual activity, 268
  in babies of smoking mothers, 317
heartbeat, rate of, *see* pulse rate
hermaphroditism, *91*
Hefner, Hugh, 17
Hegelers, 120–1, 181, 215
Der heimliche Liebhaber (le Prince), 175
hemophilis vaginalis, 122
hermaphrodites, in science fiction, 29
heterogamous marriages, 168
heterosexual response
  effect of masturbation, 302
  see also sexual response
heterosexuality
  as cultural norm, 281
Hirschfeld, Magnus, 88
Hite, Shere, 20, 26, 113
The Hite Report, 20, 26, 98, 113, 188
  on female masturbation, 116
  on female orgasm, 112, 114

The Hite Report cont :
  on lesbian techniques, 291
  on obtaining orgasm through
    masturbation, 308
  on reasons for lesbianism, 286
  on wish for lesbian contacts, 287
Hogarth, William, 54, *168*, *208*
holiday affairs, 40, *41*
homogamous marriages, 168
homosexuality, 21, 275–99
  as one of several response patterns, 298
  commitment, 292–3
  consummating the relationship, 286–7
  continuing relationships, 292
  decline of interest between partners, 293
  distinction between act and personality,
    279
  Freudian concept, 298
  in animal kingdom, 278
  in arts and the theater, 299
  in sex education, 244
  incidence, 284
  incidence of promiscuity, 286
  latent, expressed in male institutions,
    283
  liking for women, 304
  marriage to heterosexuals, 295
  portrayed in movies, 18–19
  positive definition, 299
  possible correlation with creativity, 299
  practiced by Greeks, 281
  prevalence in some professions, 299
  psychotherapy, 279, 298
  quality of relationship, *285*
  regular practice in some cultures, 281
  related to social factors, 284
  relationships among men, *278*
  rise of dominance, 278
  role playing, 293
  root causes, 276–7
  self-assessment, 294–5
  sense of isolation and inadequacy, 295
  social condemnation, *288*, 294
  tendency to oversensitivity, 293
  use of behavioral therapy, 298
  vulnerability to blackmail, 294
*Homosexuality in the Ten-spined
  Stickleback* (Morris), 278
hormonal changes, 45
hormones, 48
  action of pill on secretions, *232*
  deficiency theory of homosexuality, 276
  disorders causing impotence, 84
  failure of glands to secrete, 90
  in the pill, 233
  release as result of sexual activity, 303
  therapy, 270
  variations in secretions, 261
"Horse of Hector" position, 142–3
Hughes, Howard, 18

human chorionic gonadotropin (HCG),
  318
Human Sexual Inadequacy (Masters and
  Johnson), 15, 247
Human Sexual Responses (Masters and
  Johnson), 15
Hurana, C, 78
husbands
  early property rights, 198
  excessive devotion to work, 172, *173*
  important qualities, 166–7
  traditional role, 166
hymen, 103
  as unsatisfactory barrier to sperm, 319
  problems of thickness, 257
hysterectomy, 270

Ideal Marriage (van de Velde), 184
  condemnation anticipated by author,
    220
ill health
  leading to infertility, 85
  possible cause of impotence, 84
  see also medical problems
illegitimate children
  survey on attitudes to, 21
impotence, 84–5, 253
  due to worry in old age, 266
  reported following prostatectomy, 271
  primary and secondary types, 254
  treatment for, 253
imprinting, 49
  as basis of homosexuality, 279
In Praise of Older Women (Vizinczey), 200
incest
  in fantasies, 120
incompatibility, 43, 260–1
  as cause of divorce, 172
indecent exposure, *see* exhibitionism
independence, 63
  economic, 11
  women's, 98
India
  birth control schemes, 242
  early birth control methods, *220*
  erotic techniques cultivated, *204*
inexperience, sexual, 200–1
infantilism, attributed to sex games, *179*
infatuation, *174*
infertility, 15
  caused by trichomoniasis, 122
  causing problems in marriage, 170
  due to abstinence, 85
  male, definition of, 85
infidelity
  among women, 208

  as cause of marriage breakdown, 167
  reasons for, 209
  survey on attitudes, 21
inhibitions, 56
  contributory cause of impotence, 84
  see also religious inhibitions
insecurity resulting in possessive
  behavior, 216
instinctive behavior, 281
intercourse
  age at first experience, 100
  anal, 13, 19, 86, 289
  as form of exercise, *268*, 304
  as meditation technique, 225
  crying following, 307
  during menstruation, 308
  during pregnancy, 184–5
  emotional development, 201
  femoral, 289
  four phases, 78–9
  frequency, 175
  in marriage, for procreation, 220–1
  monotony, 176–7
  need to learn techniques, 187
  painful, 123
  positions, 132–63
    cuissade, 148–9
    different levels, 138–9
    flanquette, 150–1
    "Horse of Hector," 142–3
    kneeling, 156–7
    "Lyons stagecoach," 144–5
    missionary, and variations, 132–7
    rear entry, 152–5
    side by side, 146–7
    sitting, 162–3
    standing, 158–61
    woman above, 140–1
  reasons for act, 22
  see also sex
interests shared in marriage, 190
intrauterine devices, 230–1, *230, 231*
  advantages, 230
  disadvantages, 231
  morning-after coil, 240
  possible modes of action, 231
  tabular explanations, 238–9
Ivan IV ("The Terrible"), 94

Jacobs, Aletta, *228*
Jagger, Mick, 17
Jahan, Shah, 204
jealousy, 58, 206
  of extra-marital relations, 216
Jewish legal code, 198
Johnson, Samuel, 36

Johnson, Virginia E, *14*, 15
  for further details of research work *see*
    Masters, William H and Johnson,
    Virginia E: research
The Joy of Sex (ed. Comfort), 25, 49, 70,
  126
Joyce, James, 118
Julius Caesar, 36

K

Kama Sutra, 49, 125, 126
Kant, Immanuel, 22
Karezza, 91, 224
Keats, John, 299
The Killing of the Earl (Hogarth), *208*
Kinsey, Alfred C, 14-15, *14*
  distinguishing human from animal
    sexuality, 177
  on differing codes of sexual practice, 261
  on double standard on premarital sex,
    198
  on erotic fantasies, 73
  on extramarital relations, 208
  on female fantasies, 118
  on female masturbation, 116
  on female orgasm, 110
    frequency, 308
    multiple, 113
  on incidence of homosexuality, 284
  on lesbianism, 286, 291
  on orgasm, 82
  on premarital sex, 195
    related to education, 206
  on reorientation of homosexual
    tendencies, 298
  on sex within marriage, 174
  on teenage sex, 196
  on use of masturbation by women, 302
  reasons for male deviations, 86
  study of elderly people, 266
Kinsey Institute, 15
Kinsey reports, 14
kneeling positions, 156-7

L

labia
  changes during arousal, 105
  majora, 102
  minora, 102
  stimulation during masturbation, 117
laboratory techniques, 15
laparoscopic sterilization, 238
Last Tango in Paris (director: Bertolucci),
  19, *19*

Lawrence, D H, 18
  influence on attitudes to sex, 31
laxatives, effect on pill, 234
leather fetish, *86*
Lee, John, 41
The Left Hand of Darkness (Le Guin), 29
Legman, G, 126
Le Guin, Ursula, 29
Leo, John, 215
Leonardo da Vinci, *262*
Le Prince, Jean-Baptiste, *175*
lesbianism, 286-7
  emotional involvement, 291
  portrayed in films, 19
  related to educational level, 286
  relationships outliving sexual interest,
    293
  research into satisfaction, 291
  springing from comfort in distress, 282
  stereotype, 291
  use of dildoes, 272
libido
  dependent on testosterone levels, 48
  differences of age, 200
  Freud's work, 13
  not lessened by menopause, 265
lice, 92
license, 204-5
  acting against responsibility and
    maturity, 206
  problems incurred, 206
light industry, employment of women, 11
Limits to Growth (Club of Rome), 242
Lippes loop, 231, *231*
Lolita (Nabokov), 86
loops, *see* intrauterine devices
Lorenz, Konrad, 49
love
  different kinds distinguished, 35
  falling in, 36-7
  in home environment, 202
  meaning of, 56-7
  not synonymous with sexual expertise,
    126
  relationship with sex, 311
  romantic, 38-9, 58
  stability, 45
  types, 40-1
Love and Orgasm (Lowen), 112, 115
Love and Will (May), 15
Love without Guilt (Ellis), 55
Lovelace, Linda, 19
Lowen, Alexander, 26, 81, 112, 115
  on limited orgastic response, 253
Lu, W, 78
Ludus (type of love), 41
Lushington, Edmund, 60
Luteinizing Hormone (LH), 232
lymphogranuloma venereum, 94-5
"Lyons stagecoach" position, 144-5

M

Mace, David, 31
"Magnaphall," 272
"maidenhead" (hymen), 103
Makavejev, Dušan, 19
"male bond," 283
male institutions, 282-3
"male menopause," 307
males
  as dominant sex, 10
  biorhythms, 183
  blending of role with female, 28-9
  contact through institutions, 283
  effeminacy, 279
  more prone to sexual deviation, 86
  role training in infancy, 28
  sexual response, 309
  stereotype, *276*
  see also husbands; men; sexuality: male
mammoplasty, 101
Man and Woman (Ellis), 13
Manhattan, 215
mania (type of love), 41
Mark Antony, 36
marriage, 165
  arranged, *168*
  as only outlet for sexuality, 193
  between career-dominated people, 205
  by formal contract, *166*
  changes in partners' relationship, *168*
  commitment in, 168, 169
  components for stability, 190
  decline in frequency of intercourse, 175
  effect of abstinence during pregnancy,
    185
  effect of extramarital activities, 215
  effect on incidence of homosexuality,
    284
  effecting change in personality, *174*
  emotional security, 183
  expression of commitment, 60
  financial stresses, 172
  full acceptance of partner, 190
  homosexual, 294, 304
  importance of communication, *189*, 190
  importance of mutual growth, 190
  importance of rituals, *165*
  need for basic zest, 190
  need for liking, 190
  need for privacy, 172, *172*
  possible causes of breakdown, 170
  private reasons for, 166
  questioning of traditional views, 166
  reasons for breakdown, 167
  responsibilities, 188
  sexually dysfunctional, 247
  shared interests, 190
  success and failure, 313

marriage *cont :*
threat of monotony, 176–7
types, 168–9
Berne's classification, 169, *169*
unsatisfactory, cause of infidelity, 209
vows, 168
Marriage Contract (Hogarth), 168
marriage guidance counseling, 263
Married Love (Stopes), 12
masculinity, 28, 29, 65
in females, 279
Maslow, Abraham, 60, 63
on sex games, 179
masochism, 87
female, 120–1
in fantasies, 120
Masters, William H, *14*, 15, 60
Masters, William H, and Johnson,
Virginia E, research, 247
female orgasm, 112
four phases of sex act, 78
multiple female orgasm, 113
phases of female sexual response, 104
physiological changes with age, 266
psychological causes of impotence, 85
recommends masturbation, 70
sex during pregnancy, 185
sex therapy clinics, 248
successive orgasms, 83
use of masturbation to overcome
impotence, 302
use of partner surrogates, 254
masturbation, 70–2
comparison of male and female
incidence, 116
connection with prostitis, 91
effect on sexual response, 302
fear of damaging genitals, 311
female, 116–17
correlation with educational level, 116
premarital, 117
social acceptability, 116
techniques, 117
use to achieve orgasm, 110
fixation problems, 71–2
in children, 314
in front of children, 315
in sex education, 244
mutual, *223*, 288
by lesbians, 291
obtaining orgasm, *111*, 308
out-dated attitudes, 70, 72
percentage of married sexual activity,
174
portrayed on film, 18
use of vibrators, 272
see also autoerotic stimulation
matriarchical societies, 28
maturity
diminished by sexual license, 206

factor in good lovemaking, 126
in marriage, 170
related to sexual experience, 196
May, Rollo, 15, 58
Mead, Margaret, 206
Meade, Marion, 100, 116, 212
medical problems
congenital defects, 90
female, 122–3
see also ill health
Meir, Golda, 100
men
attributes attractive to women, 43, 52–3
double standard of sexual behavior,
198–9
rejection as lovers by women, 287
romanticism, 38
threatened by the sexual revolution, *20*
view of women's sexual needs, 261
vulnerable to criticism, 65
see also sexuality, male
menopause, 265
"male," 307
no effect on libido, 265
Mensinga, W P J, *228*
menstrual cycle, 183
affecting sexual desire
"safe" period, 222
varying testosterone levels, 48
menstrual extraction, 240
menstruation, 122, *232*
explaining to daughters, 315
intercourse during, 308
mercury treatment for syphilis, *92*
merkins, 272
Michelangelo, 299, *299*
middle age, 264–5
"male menopause," 307
Midsummer Night's Dream (Shakespeare),
36
Millett, Kate, 47, 56
mini-skirts, 17
Minnesota University, 43
Minuetto in Villa (Tiepolo), 47
miscarriages, 185
possibility of consecutive, 318
time lapse before subsequent pregnancy
319
Miss World contest, protest against, *20*
missionary position, 132–3
variations, 134–5
mistresses, 212
monogamy, 13
as cultural norm, 281
as evidence of security, 203
conducive to creativity, 205
favored by Western society, 281
portrayed as a trap, *206*
serial, 166, 169
mons veneris, 102

mood changes, 263
morality, sexual, 13
confusion among the young, 22
cultural differences, 281
double standard, 21
effect of "permissive society," 16
"Old" and "New," 20–1
Moravia, Alberto, 66
morning-after coil, 240
morning-after pill, 239–40
Morris, Desmond, 278
motherhood, inhibiting enjoyment of sex,
262
mothers
dubious significance in homosexuality,
298
overidentification of homosexual child,
276
unmarried, *199*
motion pictures, 18–19
motivations for sex, 22–3
Mount of Venus, 102
Mowrer, Herbert, 206
multiple births, 318
mumps, cause of infertility, 85
muscular contractions
during arousal, 105
during female orgasm, 106
during plateau phase, 79
in male orgasm, 81
relaxed in postcoital state, 82
synchronous in orgasm, 303
muscularity, in men, 53
music
erotic significance, 51
indicator of popular trends, 16
mutual affairs, 214–15
*My Secret Garden : women's sexual
fantasies* (Friday), 119
Mythological Couple in Embrace (Titian),
27

Nabokov, Vladimir, 86
Naples disease, *see* syphilis
Nash, Ethel M, 44–5
naval life, homosexuality in, 278
needs, hierarchy of, 60
negative reactions, 181
Neill, A S, 196
New York City Museum
Venereal Diseases Exhibition, *95*
New Zealand female suffrage, 11
nipples, 101
erection of, in males, 78
in foreplay, 129
stimulation during masturbation, 117

non-specific urethritis (NSU), 93
non-specific vaginitis (NSV), 122
Noyes, John Humphrey, *224*
nudity, 58, *59*
   acceptability of mixed bathing, 21
   female, 21
   in films, 18
   in photography, 17
      as means of sexual arousal, *76*
   male, 21
   parental, 315
nymphomania, 121

O

office parties, 212
On Love (Ortega y Gasset), 309
Oneida community, *224*, *225*
operant conditioning, 298
Oppenheimer, Dr W, *230*
opposites, attraction of
   in marriages, 168
oragenital stimulation
   in foreplay, 129
Oragenitalism (Legman), 126
oral sex, *87*, 223
   condemned by Stopes, 13
   portrayed in *Deep Throat*, 19
   unlawful in some countries, 86
orgasm
   as "rebirth," 81
   importance of considerations, 188
   effect of coitus interruptus, 224
   emphasis placed on achievement, 33
   failure in middle age, 264
   faking, 33
   female, 106, 110-15
      changing social attitudes, 110
      clitoral, 112
      correlation with premarital sex, 111
      dysfunction, 258
      frequency, 308
      heterosexual as opposed to lesbian, 291
      in older women, 266
      learning reflex, 308-9
      manifestations, 306
      means of achieving, 110
      multiple, 113
      sequential, 113
      variations in intensity, 110
      see also vaginal orgasm
   impotence, 114-15
   inability to achieve, 84
   incidence of fetishism, 88
   lower importance to lesbians, 291
   male, 81
      achieving second, 83

   after prostatectomy, 271
   differentiated from ejaculation, 307
   impotence, 253
   physiology, 81
   may precipitate labour in late
      pregnancy, 185
   not expected in sex therapy sessions, 255
   psychological effect, 81
   simultaneous, 303
   synchronous contractions, 303
The Orgy (Hogarth), 54
Origins of the Sexual Impulse (Wilson), 87
Ortega y Gasset, Jose, 58, 309
Ota rings, *230*
Ota, Tenrei, *230*
Ottesen-Jensen, Elise, *244*
The Outcast (Redgrave), *199*
The Outlaw (director: Howard Hughes), 18
ovaries
   removal of, 270
   stimulation by drugs, 318
ovulation in menstrual cycle, *232*
oysters, 49

P

Packard, Vance, 22, 23, 30, 205
pain
   in fantasies, 120
pair bonding, 43
Pakistan
   family planning campaign, *242*
Palmer, Raoul, 238
Paolo and Francesca, *209*
papillons d'amour (lice), 92
parental nudity, 315
parenthood
   responsible, 242
parents
   problems of giving moral guidance, 22
"partner surrogates" in therapy, 254
Pascal, Blaise, 45
passion, 55
passive elements, 28
Past and Present (Egg), *210*
Patterns of Sexual Behaviour (Ford and
   Beach), 282
patriarchal societies, *10*, 28
Paul, Saint, 193
peak experiences, 62, 63
pedophilia, 86
pelvic movements, 79
penetration
   anal, 289
   digital, 129
   varied by different positions, *132*

penis
   malformations, 91
   physiology, 68-9
   size, 53
      importance to men, 66-7
      Masters and Johnson's research, 67
      relative to body size, 67
      substitutes (dildoes), 272
   ulcers and warts, 91
   see also castration complex; glans;
      penis; phallus
Pepys, Samuel, 210
Perfumed Garden, 126
perfumes, 48
   erotic significance, 51
Pergonal, 318
permissive society
   compared with ancient Roman society, 204
   effect on family, 16
   results, 17
personal relationships, 22
   acceptance of the individual, 58
   give-and-take, 56
pessaries, 229
   block, *226*
   mass production, *228*
phallus
   arousal techniques, 130
   obsessions, 66-7
   usual angle of elevation, 78
   see also castration complex; penis
pheromones, 48, *48*
phimosis, 91
photography
   female nudes, 17
   pinups, *101*
physical attributes, 52-3
   attractiveness, 43
   pill, 232-5
   advantages, 234
   biochemical action, *232*
   contraindications, 234
   deleterious side effects, 234
   effect of laxatives and emetics, 234
   effect on future pregnancies, 235
   health considerations, *235*
   mass propaganda, *234*
   "morning-after," 239-40
   precautions during first cycle, 233
   types available, 233
Pincus, Gregor, *233*
Pinter, Harold, 179
pinups, *101*
Pisan, Christine de, *29*
Planned Parenthood, 20
plastic surgery on breasts, *101*
plateau phase, 79
   in female, 105
   in old age, 266

Plato, 37

Plato's Retreat ("swingers" club), 215

Playboy, magazines and clubs, *16*, *17*

The Pleasure Bond (Masters and Johnson), 15, 60

pleasure centers in the brain, 54

pleasuring sessions, 255

political ruin from sexual affairs, 212

polygamy, 166, 203

Pomeroy, Wardell, 14

pop music, 16

population explosion, 242

pornography, 16
  government action required, 21
  in movies, 18
  wife's reaction, 309

Porter, Cole, 16

possessiveness, 58, 206
  result of extramarital activities, 216
  varying forms of, 216

postcoital state, 82–3

postnatal problems, 262–3
  depression, 263

Poussin, Nicolas, *205*

"pox" (syphilis), 93–4

pragma (type of love), 41

pregnancy
  abstinence during and after, 185
  after taking pill, 235
  cigarette smoking during, 317
  determining sex of fetus, 318
  drinking during, 317
  due to condom failure, 227
  ectopic, 231
  effect of unsuccessful morning-after pill, 240
  fear of, 221
    causing frigidity, 257
    causing inability to ejaculate, 252
    in premarital sex, 199
  following miscarriage, 319
  husband's responsibilities during, 188
  in women over 30, 319
  intercourse during, 184–5
  optimum age band, 319
  possible crisis in marriage, 170
  problems following, 262–3
  result of external ejaculation, 319
  safety of intercourse, 15
  tests, 318
  unlimited, consequences, *221*
  unwanted, 15, 219, 239
  importance of sex education, *244*
  wanted, *240*

premarital sex, 194–5
  advantages, 200–1
  among 18–19 year olds, 196
  correlation with educational level, 195, 206
  correlation with female orgasm, 111

cultural differences of attitude, 194
  double standard, 198
  no later regret by women, 199
  survey on attitudes, 21

premature ejaculation, 250–1
  treatment, 251

Premature Ejaculation: a New Approach (Semans), 251

Presley, Elvis, 16

priapism, 91, *91*

Priapus (Roman god of Gardens), *91*

prisons
  homosexual relationships in, 279

privacy
  in marriage, 172, *172*
  role in intercourse, 177

procreative purpose of sex, 30, *31*

professions
  acceptance of women in, 11

progesterone, *232*, *233*

progestogens, 48

promiscuity, 13, 121, 202–3
  among psychiatric patients, 206
  in homosexual relationships, 286
  male, reasons for, 202–3
  not related to availability of contraceptives, 221

property rights, 198

prophylactics 226, *226*

prostate gland, 69, 81, 237
  effect of removal, 81
  medical problems, 91

prostatectomy, 270

prostatic cancer, 91

prostitis, 91

prostitution
  in fantasies, 120
  limitations, 212
  Marie Stopes accused of encouraging, 12
  reasons for preference by some men, 212
  to provide for deviant requirements, 120
  without love or commitment, *202*
  see also brothels

prudishness, 10

psychiatric treatment
  of homosexuals, 298

psychological factors
  advantages of the pill, 234
  affecting hormone production, 261
  belief in importance of sexuality, 31
  causes of frigidity, 257
  in fetishism, 88
  in causes of impotence, 85
  in causes of promiscuity, 203
  problems of role blending, 28
  sexual aspects, 13

psychotherapy
  for homosexuals, 279, 298

puerperal infection, 185

pulse rate, 45, 79, 105

pupils (of the eyes)
  enlarged during arousal, 52

puritanism, 10

radiation
  possible cause of infertility, 85

rape, *55*, *119*
  in sex games, 179
  portrayed in films, 18

rear entry positions, 152–3
  turning away, 154–5

Redgrave, Richard, *199*

refractory period, 83

Reich, Wilhelm, 13, 56, 63
  film on his work, 19
  on effect of muscular locking, 307
  on effect of orgasm, 81
  on frustration, 201
  on promiscuity, 203

religions
  affecting birth control programs, 242, *245*
  imposing celibacy, *282*
  prejudice against birth control, 220
  teaching love instead of war, 63
  view of sensuality, 193

religious ecstasy, *110*

religious inhibitions
  as root cause of impotence, 254

reputation, moral, 198

resentment of new baby, 263

La Résistance Inutile (Fragonard), *55*

resolution phase, 82–3
  in female, 106, 109
  in older people, 266

respect for the individual, 58

respiration rate, 79

Responsibility (Cameron), *29*

responsibility
  diminished by sexual license, 206
  for the partner's commitment, 22
  inherent in sexual experience, 196
  marital, 188
  women's, in marriage, 186–7

Restoration period in English history, 10

restraint, in relationships, 204–5

"rhythm method," 222–3
  tabular explanation, 238–9

ritual behavior, 46

Rock, John, *233*

rock culture, 16

Roeg, Nicholas, 19

role playing, 293

role training in infancy, 28

Rolling Stones (pop group), 16, *17*
Roman Catholic Church
    attitude to birth control, 223, *245*
Roman society, 204
    collapse of moral standards, *205*
romance
    personal view of, 46
Romeo and Juliet (Shakespeare), *36*
Rosarium Philosopharium, *37*
Royden, Maud
    strong criticism of, 220
"rubber," 226
Russell, Jane, 18
Russell, Ken, 18

S

sadism, 87
Saf-T-Coil, 231, *231*
"safe" period, *223*
St George and the Dragon (Ucello), *46*
St Paul, Minnesota, 20
Salvarsan 606, *95*
Samoan attitude to sex, 206
Samson and Delilah, *277*
Sanger, Margaret
    strong criticism of, 220
satyrs, *66*
scientific investigation of sexual problems,
    38
Schneider, Maria, 19, *19*
scratching, 129
scrotum, 68
    varicocele, 90
Seaman, Barbara, 20, 21
security
    in home environment, 202
    in marriage, 183
    lack of, in promiscuity, 203
seduction, 187
segregation of sexes, 278-9
selfishness, 170
Semans, James, 251
semen
    propulsion, 81
    see also ejaculation
seminal fluid, 69
seminal vesicles, 81, 237
Seneca, 45
Senejem, *166*
sensibility
    essential to good lovemaking, *126*
    to partner's tastes and distastes, *181*
sensory awareness, 249
The Sensuous Woman, 68
Seventeen magazine, 196
sex
    as learned behavior, 279, 281

change of attitudes following sexual
    revolution, 24
cultural differences in behavior, 281
disillusionment of young people, 310-11
effect of biorhythms, 182-3
enjoyment of, promoted by Stopes, 12-
    13
ethics of, 24
expectations, 33
for pleasure, 30, 31
freedom from compulsion necessary,
    26-7
group, 215
health aspects, 26, 268-9
ignorance of facts, 12, 14
    leading to unwanted conception, 219
in middle age, *264*
negative attitudes to, 24
possibility of variety, 125
related to love, 311
relationships between likes and
    opposites, 303
relative ages of partners, 200
Samoan attitudes to, 206
"spectator" role of one partner, 249
various definitions, 10
weight loss potential, 304
Western attitudes, 22
within marriage, *174-5*
without love, 54-5, 206
    see also intercourse
sex aids, 272-3
Sex as a Regenerative Force (Bernard), 31
sex drives, 54
    decline following hysterectomy, 270
    diminishing in middle age, 307
    finding alternative outlets, 302
    variation between partners, 260, 261
sex education, 99, 244-5
    adjunct of therapy, 248
    from parents, 315
    level of language used, 315
    quality of instructors, 244
    to relieve sexual "hangups," 261
    use of aids, *244*
"sex flush," 78, 105
sex games, 179
sex-linked diseases, 318
sex organs, *see* genitals
sex roles, 28-9
sex shops, 21, 272-3
sex therapy, 247
    benefits of, 248-9
    positive results, 255
    shortage of therapists, 248
    treatment for frigidity, 258-9
    treatment routine, 248
    use of "partner surrogates," 254
sexologists, 14-15
    validity of findings, 119

sexual activity
    quantity and quality, 26
Sexual Anomalies and Perversions
    (Hirschfeld), 88
sexual behavior
    correlation with social class, 174
    ethics, 22
    influence of social position, 278
    scientific analysis, 14
Sexual Behavior in the Human Female
    (Kinsey), 14
Sexual Behavior in the Human Male
    (Kinsey), 14
sexual defects, congenital, 90
sexual desire
    varying in intensity during the month,
    304
sexual experience
    double standards for men and women,
    198-9
    related to energy, 204-5
    related to maturity, 196
    see also inexperience, sexual
sexual liberation, 9
sexual license
    fear of over-extending, 20-1
    sixteenth-century view, *21*
sexual peaks, 200
    influence on infidelity, 209
Sexual Politics (Millet), 47
sexual problems
    basis, 248
    see also sex therapy
sexual responses, 78-9
    in sex education, 244
    in women, 104-11, 309
    male, 309
    male/female differences, 309
    phases, in old age, 266
sexual revolution, 10-11
    effect on views of marriage, 166
    rationalization period, 20
    seen as of little help to women, 98
The Sexual Revolution (Reich), 13
The Sexual Side of Love (Green), 202, 262
The Sexual Wilderness (Packard), 22, 23,
    205
sexuality
    abuse in advertising, 30, *30*
    acceptance of, 24
    as basic human drive, 13
    as psychological necessity, 31
    element of violence, 87
    emphasis on in 1960s, 26
    female, 97, *256*
        complete emotional involvement, 100
        Freud's errors, 13
        idealized by men, 199
    greater freedom to develop, 195
    human and animal distinguished, 177

sexuality *cont :*
  in sex education, 244
  involving the brain's cortex, 281
  male
    female attitudes to, 198
    fixations, 88
  of the child, 245
  peaks at different ages, 100
  sports car as a symbol of, *26*
  variation between the sexes, 77
  wealth of available information, 186
Sexuality – Regeneration and Self-
  Discovery, 31
Shakespeare, William, 36
  on orgasm, 82
shame, about extramarital relationships,
  216
sheath, 220
shoe fetishes, 88
Sickert, Walter Richard, 61
side-by-side positions, 146-7
The Silence (director: Bergman), 18
silence, in marriage, 190
sitting positions, 162-3
skin disorders, 91
slapping, 129
smear tests, 234
So What About Love? (Webb), 115
sodomy, 278, 279
  as part of initiation rites, 281
soft chancre, 94
Sorokin, Pitirim A, 18
Soviet Union
  birth control programs, *15*
"Spanish fly," 272
speech
  place in foreplay, 129
  see also communication
Spermatorrhea, 72
spermicidal agents, 227
  tabular explanation, 238-9
  used with diaphragms, 228
sperm, 68, *224*
  in urine after prostatectomy, 271
  low concentrations, 85
  number in average ejaculation, *225*
standing positions, 158-9
  poise and balance, 160-1
Steptoe, Patrick, 238
sterility, male
  definition of, 85
sterilization, 236-8
  of women, 237
  tabular explanation, 238-9
stilbestrol, 240
stimulation
  autoerotic, 70-1
  clitoral, 99
    during foreplay, 129
    during masturbation, 117

  response, 105
  from bodily secretions, 49
  genital
    in cure for premature ejaculation, 251
  of breast-feeding, 309
  of erogenous zones, 127
  of vulva, 102, *103*
  response capabilities, 282
  to achieve multiple female orgasm, 113
  to produce female orgasm, 110
  using the woman's whole body, 306
  see also visual stimulation
Stopes, Marie, 12-13, *12*
  condemnation of anal intercourse, 13
  strongly criticized, 220
storge (type of love), 41
strippers, *120-1, 121*
striptease, *73, 74*
Studies in the Psychology of Sex (Ellis), 13
submission
  in sex games, 179
  see also domination
suction abortion, 241
suffragettes, *see* female suffrage
superstition, in birth control, *222*
surgical operations, 270-1
surrender, 56-7
suspenders, 88
swapping partners, 215
sweating
  in postcoital state, 82
"swingers" clubs, 215
Symposium (Plato), 37
syphilis, 93-4
  congenital, *94*
  said to have been brought to Europe by
    Columbus' crew, *92*
  sores on mouth, 93, *93*
  symptoms, 94

teasing, 130
techniques, 125-63
  homosexual, variety in, 288, 291
  in context of lovemaking, 127
  manuals, 125
  need to learn, 187
  overcoming frigidity, 257, 258-9
  overemphasis, 26
  problems of routine, *177*
teenage sex, 196-7
  age questions, 310
  confusion on moral issues, 22
  survey on attitudes, 21
  see also young people
temperature method of birth control, 223
Terman, L M, 195

terror
  in fantasies, 120
testicles, 68
  enlarged by varicocele, 90
  overheating due to varicocele, 90
  overheating leading to infertility, 85
  position during arousal phase, 78
  position during plateau phase, 79
  undescended, 68, 90
testosterone, 48
  effect of injections, 276
  limited effect of supplements, 49
theater
  homosexuality in, 299
thrombosis
  among women on the pill, 234
Tiepolo, Giovanni Domenico, *47*
tiredness
  leading to sexual problems, 263
Titian, *27*
toilet training
  effect on adult sex life, 314
Tolstoy, Leo, 193, 221
topless dresses, 17
  on nightclub waitresses, 21
Toronto University, 41
Toulouse-Lautrec, Henri, *94*
Toynbee, Arnold, 205
transformation
  in fantasies, 120
transvestism, 88
Trash (director: Warhol), 19
tribal societies
  initiation rites and ceremonies, 22
trichomoniasis, 122
Tripp, C A, 292, 294
  on homosexual "therapy," 298
troilism, 215
Trojan wars, 36
Turner, E S, 220
The Two of Us (Moravia), 66

Ucello, Paolo, *46*
ulcers, affecting penis, 91
Ulysses (Joyce), 118
The Undergrowth of Literature (Freeman),
  87
unicorn legend, *194*
uniform fetish, *86*
"unisex" manifestations, 28-9
unmarried mothers, *199*
Unwin, J, 204-5
urethra, 69
  displaced outlet, 90
  semen discharged into, 81
urination during orgasm, 304

urine
   use in pregnancy tests, 318
uterus
   infections aggravated by intrauterine
      devices, 231
   lining changed by the pill, 233

vacuum curettage, 241
Vadim, Roger, 54
vagina
   change in position at puberty, 101
   changes during arousal, 105
   digital penetration, 129
      during masturbation, 117
   lubricating secretions, 304
   normally unaffected by hysterectomy,
      270
   orgasmic "platform," 106
   physiology, 103
      reason for lack of sensation, 112
   position in young baby, 101
   substitutes (merkins), 272
   symptoms of disorder, 122
vaginal cancer, 240
vaginal contractions
   timing synchronous with male orgasm,
      81
vaginal deodorants, 122
vaginal discharge, 122
vaginal orgasm, 99, 112
vaginal secretions, 105
vaginismus, 122-3
Van de Velde, T H, 184, 220
varicocele, 90
variety in sex, 125
vas deferens, 69, 236
vasectomy, 85, 236
   effects, 237
venereal diseases, 31, 92-5
   benefits of early treatment, 95, 95
   benefits of sex education, 244
   clinics, 122
Venus of Willendorf, 98
Verrocchio, 280
vibrators, 272
Victorian moral code, 199

"fallen woman" concept, 202
on adultery, 210
violence
   correlation between crime and movies,
      19
   element of sexuality, 87
Virgin Spring (director: Bergman), 18
virginity
   double standard, 198
   research statistics, 195
   see also chaperonage; chastity
"virgin's veil" (hymen), 103
visual stimulation, 130
   from pornography, 309
   of women, 186
   to affect arousal, 118
Vizinczey, Stephen, 200
voyeurism, 88, 89
vulva, 102
   symptoms of disorder, 122

waltz, 17, 17
Warhol, Andy, 19
warts, under foreskin, 91
Webb, Leonard, 115
weeping after intercourse, 307
"wet dreams," 315
wife-swapping, 215
Wilde, Oscar, 299, 299
Wilson, Colin, 87
wives
   as medieval chattels, 10
   as substitute mother-figures, 263
   important qualities, 166-7
   persuaded to sleep with business
      colleagues of husband, 215
   traditional role, 166
The Wives' Handbook, 220
women
   attitudes of heterosexual men, 304
   attributes attractive to men, 43, 52-3
   deviant behavior, 120-1
   double standard of sexual behavior,
      198-9
   effect of sexual revolution, 98
   employment in light industry, 11

facial characteristics, 52
fashions during 1960s, 17
medical problems, 122-3
more prone to sexual dysfunction, 256
problems of sexual liberation, 100
relationships with homosexuals, 304
roles as wives and mothers, 100
romanticism, 38
suffering in adulterous relationships,
   208
taking initiative in lovemaking, 187, 187
trivializing effect of permissive society,
   20
use of masturbation, 302
workforce during wars, 11, 11
see also females; sexuality, female
Women in Love (director: Russell), 18
Women's Liberation Movement, 11, 98,
   99
world population growth, 242
World Wars I and II, 11, 11
WR – Mysteries of the Orgasm (director:
   Makavejev), 19

"X position," 145

The Ying-Yang (Hurana and Lu), 78
yoga, 125, 225
young people
   availability of contraceptives, 221
   change in values, 22
   disappointment with sex, 310-11
   falling in love, 36-7
   gaining experience, 201
   sexual experience of, 194
   see also teenage sex

zest for life, 190

Picture Credits

Key to picture positions (T) top (C) center (B) bottom; and in combinations, e.g. (TR) top right (BL) bottom left.

Endpapers	Bill Carter © Aldus Books
2–3	Alec Murrey © Aldus Books
8–9	Bill Carter © Aldus Books
10(T)	Bibliothèque St. Genviere/Giraudon
10(B)	The Mansell Collection, London
11(T)	Imperial War Museum, London
11(BR)	Keystone
12(T)	The Mansell Collection, London
12(B)	International Planned Parenthood Federation
13(L)	Bavaria-Verlag
13(R)	The Mansell Collection, London
14(T)	William C. Dellenback, Institute for Sexual Research
14(B)	Popperfoto
15	International Planned Parenthood Federation
16	Syndication International Ltd.
17(R)	British Museum/Photo R. B. Fleming © Aldus Books
18(B)	National Film Archive
19(T)	Kobal Collection
19(B)	Contemporary Films Ltd.
20	Keystone
21(T)	Pictor International
21(B)	Basle Museum/Colorphoto Hinz
23	Pictor Ltd.
24–25	Bill Carter © Aldus Books
26	Zefa
27	Photo Edward Leigh, reproduced by permission of the Fitzwilliam Museum, Cambridge
28	Zefa
29(T)	Reproduced by permission of the Trustees of the British Museum
29(B)	Aberdeen Art Gallery
30	Syndication International Ltd.
31(T)	McCorkell Sidaway & Wright Limited, courtesy T. Elliott & Sons Ltd.
31(B)	Victoria & Albert Museum, London/Photo John Webb © Aldus Books
32, 34–35	Bill Carter © Aldus Books
36(L)	The Mansell Collection, London
37(TL)	Photo Mike Busselle © Aldus Books
37(TR)	Borelli Collection/Giovanna Moro
37(B)	British Library/Photo John Freeman/Robert Harding Associates
38	British Museum/Photo R. B. Fleming © Aldus Books
39(L)	Mel Calman
39(R)	Three Lions
40	*Radio Times* Hulton Picture Library
41(L)	Zefa
41(R)	FPG
42, 44	Bill Carter © Aldus Books
46	Musée du Louvre/Michael Holford Library photo
47	Fotografia Ferruzzi, Venezia
48(L)	Bodleian Library, Oxford (MS. Ashmole 399, f. 19)
48(R)	Syndication International Ltd.
49	Zefa
50–51	Bill Carter © Aldus Books
52(L)	The Mansell Collection, London
52(TR), 53	Bill Carter © Aldus Books
54(T)	Kobal Collection
54(B)	Reproduced by permission of the Trustees of Sir John Soane's Museum
55	Nationalmuseum, Stockholm
57, 59	Bill Carter © Aldus Books
61	The Tate Gallery, London
62	Hallinan/FPG
63	Reproduced by permission of the proprietors of *Punch*
64–65	Bill Carter © Aldus Books
66(T)	Picturepoint, London
66(BL)	Francis Bartlett Foundation, Museum of Fine Arts, Boston/Photo Thames and Hudson Ltd.
66(BR)	The Walker Art Gallery, Liverpool
67(L)	Trewin Copplestone Publishing Ltd.
67(R)	© Bamforth Company (Marketing) Ltd.
69	Alan Holingbery © Aldus Books
70–71	Bill Carter © Aldus Books
73	Syndication International Ltd.
74–76(L)	Bill Carter © Aldus Books
76(R)	Photo Mike Busselle © Aldus Books
77	Giraudon/Robert Harding Associates
79–85	Bill Carter © Aldus Books
86(T)	Keystone
86–87(B)	Bill Carter © Aldus Books
87(T)	Keystone
88	Syndication International Ltd.
89	Bill Carter © Aldus Books
90	Musée du Louvre/Giraudon
91(T)	Naples Museum/Eric de Maré
91(B)	Museo Nazionale, Rome/Anderson
92, 93(T)	Robert Harding Associates
93(B)	World Health Organization
94(L)	*Radio Times* Hulton Picture Library
94(R)	Novosti Press Agency
95(T)	The Mansell Collection, London
95(B)	Camera Press
96–97	Bill Carter © Aldus Books
98(L)	Foto Salmer, Barcelona
99(T)	Werner Wolff/Transworld
99(B)	Keystone
100(T)	Musée des Beaux-Arts, Rouen/Giraudon
100(B)	Keystone
101(T)	Bill Carter © Aldus Books
101(B)	The Mansell Collection, London
102–103	Alan Holingbery © Aldus Books
104–109	Bill Carter © Aldus Books
110	Scala
111(T)	Syndication International Ltd.
111(B)	Bill Carter © Aldus Books
114	*Observer*/Camera Press
115	Michael Boys/Susan Griggs Agency
116–121	Bill Carter © Aldus Books
122	Dr. R. D. Catterall
123	Photo Mike Busselle © Aldus Books
124–163	Patricia Ludlow © Aldus Books
164	Peter Thiele/Zefa

166	Pictor International
167	The Tate Gallery, London/Photo John Webb © Aldus Books
168(T)	Zefa
168(B)	National Gallery, London
169(T)	*Radio Times* Hulton Picture Library
169(B)	Glasgow Art Gallery
170	Hallinan/FPG
171	Eve Arnold/Magnum
172(T)	Capitoline Museum, Rome/C. M. Dixon
172(B)	© Marshall Cavendish Ltd.
173(T)	*Observer*/Transworld
173(BR)	Rene Burri/Magnum
174(T)	Robert McFarlane © Marshall Cavendish Ltd.
174(B)	Photo John Freeman © Aldus Books
175	Alte Pinakothek, courtesy Bayerische Staats-gemäldesammlungen, München/Joachim Blauel
176-183	Bill Carter © Aldus Books
184-185	Patricia Ludlow © Aldus Books
186(B)	Syndication International Ltd.
187	Monty Coles © Marshall Cavendish Ltd.
189-192	Bill Carter © Aldus Books
194(L)	Musée de Cluny/Giraudon
194(R)	Kalmar County Museum/Photo Rolf Lind
195	David Paramor Picture Collection, Newmarket
196	John Seymour © Marshall Cavendish Ltd.
197	*Parents Magazine*, Paris
198	Collection of the late Armando Preziosi/Photo George Rainbird Ltd./Robert Harding Associates
199	Royal Academy of Arts, London
200(L)	By permission of The Huntington Library, San Marino, California
201	Bibliothèque Nationale, Paris/Robert Harding Associates
202(L)	The Walters Art Gallery, Baltimore
203(T)	Adam Woolfitt/Susan Griggs Agency
203(B)	Erich Hartmann/Magnum
204(T)	Kumar Sangram Singh Collection/Photo Robert Skelton
204(B)	Raghubir Singh/John Hillelson Agency
205	National Gallery, London
206	Mel Calman
207	David Hamilton/Transworld
208	National Gallery, London
209	Angers Museum/Mauro Pucciarelli
210	The Tate Gallery, London/Photo John Webb © Aldus Books
211(L)	Robert McFarlane © Marshall Cavendish Ltd.
211(R)	Camera Press
213-214	Bill Carter © Aldus Books
216	TPL Magazines Ltd.
217	The Tate Gallery, London/Photo John Webb © Aldus Books
218	Bill Carter © Aldus Books
220-221	International Planned Parenthood Federation
222(T)	Reproduced by permission of the Trustees of the British Museum
222(B)	International Planned Parenthood Federation
223	Patricia Ludlow © Aldus Books
224(L)	International Planned Parenthood Federation
224(C)	Aldus Archives
225	Zefa
226(L)	Library of Congress, Washington/Robert Harding Associates
226(R), 227, 228-229(L)	International Planned Parenthood Federation
229(R)	Trewin Copplestone Publishing Ltd.
230	International Planned Parenthood Federation
231	S. J. Allen/*Daily Telegraph* Colour Library
232	Bruce Robertson © Aldus Books
233(T)	International Planned Parenthood Federation
233(B)	Photo Mike Busselle © Aldus Books
234(L)	Mel Calman
235	Bill Carter © Aldus Books
236	Transworld
237	Alan Holingbery © Aldus Books
238(T)	Bill Carter © Aldus Books
240	Transworld
241	*Parents Magazine*, Paris
242(T)	Aldus Archives
242(B)	International Planned Parenthood Federation
243	Landrum B. Shettles/Popperfoto
244(T)	Photo Mike Busselle © Aldus Books
244(B)	International Planned Parenthood Federation
245(T)	Asoc. Chilena de Protección de la Familia, Santiago
245(B)	Keystone
246-249	Bill Carter © Aldus Books
250-253	Patricia Ludlow © Aldus Books
254-256	Bill Carter © Aldus Books
258-259	Patricia Ludlow © Aldus Books
260-261	Bill Carter © Aldus Books
262	By Gracious Permission of Her Majesty Queen Elizabeth II
263(L)	Giraudon
264	John Garrett © Marshall Cavendish Ltd.
265	Photo Mike Busselle © Aldus Books
267	Wayne Miller/Magnum
269(T)	Rijksmuseum, Amsterdam
269(B)	Bill Carter © Aldus Books
270(L)	Schiff from Three Lions
271	*Man and Woman* © Marshall Cavendish Ltd.
273	Trewin Copplestone Publishing Ltd.
274	Keystone
276	Zdenek Burian courtesy Artia, Prague
277	National Gallery, London
278	Three Lions
279(L)	Michael Holford Library photo
279(R)	Aldus Archives
280	Scala
281	Camera Press
282(T)	Bibliothèque Nationale, Paris
282(B)	The Parker Gallery, London
283(T)	Photo Mike Busselle © Aldus Books
283(B)	Burt Uzzle/Magnum
285	Bill Carter © Aldus Books
286-287	Giraudon
288	Keystone
289	S.F. Distributors, London
290	Patricia Ludlow © Aldus Books